W9-BUM-710

Biblical Hebrew
Step-by-Step

Volume 1

Second Edition

Menahem Mansoor

BAKER BOOK HOUSE
Grand Rapids, Michigan

This work is dedicated to one of my best teachers—
Professor Jacob Weingreen of Trinity College, a sage,
scholar and friend.

First Edition, April 1978
Second Edition, August 1980

ISBN: 0-8010-6041-9

Eleventh printing, October 1991

Printed in the United States of America

PICTURE CREDITS

Helene Bieberkraut, 42; Consulate General of Israel, 56, 61; Esther Gerling, 47
(top left and right), 64, 79; Israel Office of Information, 8, 16, 141; Levant Photo
Service, 126, 136; The Oriental Institute, University of Chicago, 133, 217; Palestine Archaeological Museum, 198; J. D. Seger, 20; Turner, 151; University
Museum, Philadelphia, 185, 203; Trustees of the Wellcome Trust, 32.

This text may be used in independent study for four credits through the University
of Wisconsin-Extension, Madison, Wisconsin.

ACKNOWLEDGMENTS

I wish to express my sincere appreciation particularly to Mr. Arthur Sekki, a graduate student and project assistant in the Department of Hebrew and Semitic Studies, who worked with me to revise this text.

I also wish to express my deep gratitude to the Wisconsin Society for Jewish Learning for its initial grant to cover the expenses incurred in the preparation of this work. The continuous support of the Society for instructional materials has always been a source of encouragement and inspiration to me.

Menahem Mansoor
Madison, Wisconsin

61938

CONTENTS

INTRODUCTION

WHY STUDY HEBREW?

There are many reasons why people embark on the study of Hebrew, and a course in Hebrew must be designed with these reasons in mind. Some study Hebrew to read and understand the language for its own sake. Others use the language simply as a tool for the study of Hebrew literature. A few students are interested in learning Hebrew to teach it or use it professionally. Theological students are concerned with gaining a knowledge of the Hebrew language to enable them to read and understand the Old Testament in its original tongue; philologists are greatly interested in the forms of the language.

This text has been prepared for seminary, college, and high school students who have little or no knowledge of the Hebrew language. It can also be used by adult study groups, whose specific needs have been considered in the book's preparation. The approach and structure of the text, including vocabularies, notes, grammar, study hints, exercises, and written assignments should prove especially helpful to students who wish to study on their own.

The text was originally designed for use in the First Semester Hebrew—Biblical course offered at the University of Wisconsin; it has been the textbook for this course for twenty years. The method of instruction is the same method successfully used by the author to teach adults and university students in England, Ireland, and the United States. To keep the information up to date and to include material in response to continuing student needs, the text has been revised several times.

THE GOAL OF THIS TEXT

The goal of this Biblical Hebrew text is to enable the student (1) to gain a working knowledge of Hebrew grammar; (2) to become acquainted with essential vocabulary most frequently used in biblical texts; (3) to understand simple excerpts from the Bible; and (4) to become familiar with the use of Hebrew words through emphasis on the roots of verbs and nouns. About four hundred vocabulary words are used in this text.

STRUCTURE OF THE TEXT

The first five lessons are devoted to the reading and writing of Hebrew. The reading should not prove too difficult if the student remembers that Hebrew is a phonetic language and that each letter represents a distinct sound.

Once the student has covered the first five lessons, he should be able to read Hebrew with a fair degree of accuracy. In general, students who follow this method of study, including those with no previous knowledge of Hebrew, are able to read Hebrew texts after studying the language for only two weeks. After studying about a dozen lessons, the student should be able to construct his own sentences in Hebrew (within the limits of the vocabulary).

After the five introductory lessons, each of the remaining lessons follows the same general pattern:

1. vocabulary
2. grammar and notes, including examples
3. biblical word lists of the words most frequently used in the Bible
4. study hints to help the student work out the lessons
5. exercises to develop writing and translating skills, which are essential to a real understanding of Hebrew.

It is important to learn the roots of Hebrew verbs, since the knowledge of one root in Hebrew may mean knowledge of several related words. Similar English concepts and words are often derived from different verbal roots, yet they may correspond in meaning to Hebrew words that are derived from one single root. In Hebrew, for example, *to bear* (a child), *to beget, boy, girl, generation*, and *kindred* are all derived from one root, YLD, *to bear*. The corresponding English words, of course, are derived from a number of roots.

Since from its earliest beginnings Hebrew was a language with an alphabet composed only of consonants, it is easy to read Hebrew of any period, whether Biblical, Rabbinical, or Modern. The difference between the Hebrew of the Book of Genesis, for instance, and the Hebrew of a modern writer is far less than the difference between Shakespeare's English and the English of George Bernard Shaw.

As you study the text, make a practice of reviewing past lessons. Some exercise sections contain review exercises; study them carefully. As you enlarge your vocabulary, you may find it helpful to make your own system of flash cards. Or, you may want to jot down each new word and continuously review your vocabulary.

METHOD OF LEARNING

1. Read each lesson section by section. Never begin a new lesson until you are sure that you know the contents of the previous one.
2. Thoroughly master the vocabulary at the beginning of each lesson. Test your understanding of the vocabulary again before you do the exercises.
3. Study the material in the grammar and notes section and then carefully read the study hints.
4. When you feel that you understand the entire lesson, begin the exercises.
5. To benefit most from the text, *do all of the exercises*, either orally or in writing.

If you wish to pursue Hebrew grammar further, the author recommends Jacob Weingreen's *Practical Hebrew Grammar* (Oxford University Press).

KEY TO BIBLICAL HEBREW STEP BY STEP—A special key covering all written exercises in this book is available.

Lesson One

A BRIEF SURVEY OF THE SEMITIC LANGUAGES

Hebrew belongs to a great family of closely allied languages known as the Semitic languages, spread throughout western Asia (including Arabia) and northern Africa. The word *Semitic* is derived from *Shem*, the name of one of Noah's sons. (See Genesis 6:10.) It is a convenient, rather than a scientific, term adopted by scholars. Other Semitic languages have been discovered during the last one hundred years, such as Akkadian (a common name for Assyrian and Babylonian) and Ugaritic (akin to Hebrew and very important for biblical research).

A basic knowledge of Semitic languages is very important for the mastery of, and research in, Hebrew. Many peculiarities and grammatical forms in one Semitic language can often be explained only by analogy with the other Semitic languages, of which there are five main branches: Hebrew, Arabic, Aramaic, Akkadian and Ethiopic. (See Table 1, the chart of the Semitic languages.) Of the ancient Semitic languages, only Hebrew and Arabic are spoken today.

The principal peculiarities the Semitic languages have in common are
1. guttural or laryngeal letters, with special sounds;
2. three root-letters for almost all verbs and nouns;
3. meaning dependent on form or pattern of words;
4. pronominal suffixes to nouns, verbs, and prepositions; and some common basic consonantal vocabulary, for example: *ab—father, yd—hand, byt—house, ktb—write.*

Table 1

CHART OF THE SEMITIC LANGUAGES
(Main Distribution)

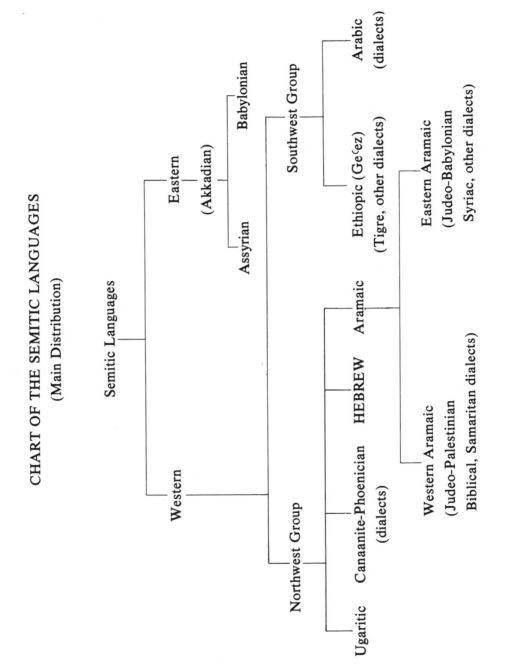

The Shrine of the Scrolls: The white cupola and the black basalt wall represent the War of the Sons of Light against the Sons of Darkness, described in one of the Dead Sea Scrolls that are to be preserved in the shrine.

The following paragraphs describe the origin and features of some of the Semitic languages listed in Table 1.

Hebrew—the original language of the Semitic settlers in the land of ancient Canaan (Palestine). Hebrew is closely related to (1) Canaanite, glosses of which exist on cuneiform tablets found in Tell el-Amarna in Upper Egypt, and dated around 1400 B.C.; (2) Moabite, of the famous King Mesha inscription, ninth century B.C.; (3) Phoenician, known from inscriptions of the ninth century B.C.; and (4) Ugaritic, a language closely related to Biblical Hebrew and written in an ancient cuneiform but alphabetic script. The discovery was accidentally made by an Arab farmer in Ras Shamra, a north Syrian coastal city known in ancient times as Ugarit. The hundreds of tablets so far deciphered have added much to knowledge of Canaanite culture and religion and to biblical studies and have revealed striking parallels with other ancient religious poetry and observances.

During the biblical period the language spoken by the Israelites was called in the Bible the "language of Canaan." (See Isaiah 19:18.) It is very similar to the languages of the other Canaanite-speaking nations mentioned above. Hebrew was a living language, used for speech and writing by the Israelites, until the Babylonian exile in 586 B.C. Aramaic, the political and cultural language of the

Near East, gradually replaced Hebrew from about the sixth century B.C., and probably by the first century A.D. Hebrew was no longer the dominant language. It is very likely that Hebrew may have been spoken by several communities and many individuals for several centuries longer.

Hebrew was used throughout the centuries as a vehicle for the important theological and philosophical writings, as well as for the secular and scientific works in the fields of poetry, astronomy, and medicine. And finally, early in the present century, considerable efforts, stemming from the Zionist colonization of Palestine and led and inspired by Eliezer ben-Yehudah (1858-1922), were made to revive the language. It is the only known revival of a dead language in the history of nations. Today in Israel all subjects, from history to physics and medicine, are taught in Hebrew. Hebrew is the language not only of kindergartens, schools, colleges, and universities, but also of the press, radio, and television.

There are four main phases of the Hebrew language:
1. Biblical Hebrew, known as Classical Hebrew.
2. Rabbinical, or Late, Hebrew, in which the Mishna (ca. second century A.D.) and the Hebrew portions in the Talmud and the Midrash were written.
3. Medieval, or Rabbinic, Hebrew, the Hebrew of the great theological, philosophical, and poetical works composed during the Middle Ages, mainly in Spain and North Africa. It is also the language of the translations from Arabic and the works written under the influence of the Arabic language. During the Middle Ages it served as a *lingua franca* for Jews throughout the world.
4. Modern Hebrew, the development of which has begun in the present century.

The vocabulary has changed from one period to another. The basic vocabulary, however, is that of the Bible, but it is very probable that the Bible does not contain all the vocabulary in actual use in biblical times, as indicated by archaeological texts uncovered since the beginning of this century.

Akkadian—the common name given to Babylonian and Assyrian languages. Akkadian was the original name used by the Mesopotamians for their own language. Akkad was the chief city of the first Semitic empire in Mesopotamia (ca. 2300 B.C.). It is also mentioned in Genesis 10:10. Before 4000 B.C. Mesopotamia was already inhabited by the Sumerians, a non-Semitic people who had attained a high degree of civilization. The Babylonians and the Assyrians adopted the cuneiform writing of the Sumerians for their own Semitic speech. Akkadian was superseded by Aramaic from about the first century B.C.

Aramaic—a group of dialects, first known from inscriptions of the late tenth or early ninth century B.C. In a phenomenal wave of expansion, Aramaic spread over Palestine and Syria and large tracts of Asia and Egypt, replacing many languages, including Hebrew and Akkadian. For about one thousand years it served as the official and written language of the Near East. At the time of Jesus the language of Palestine was generally Aramaic; Hebrew had become the property of the learned. The actual words of Jesus, for instance those quoted in Mark 5:41 and 7:34, were in Aramaic. It has also influenced the writing systems of several languages; Hebrew, in fact, adopted the Aramaic script. (See Lesson 4.)

By the time of the destruction of the Temple (A.D. 70) and the dispersal of the Jews, Aramaic had entirely replaced Hebrew in Palestine and neighboring lands. A large part of the Talmud, the gigantic postbiblical writings of the Rabbis, is written in Aramaic, and by the sixth century A.D. there existed an Aramaic version of the Bible, known as the *Targum*. Arabic began to supersede Aramaic and Syriac (an Eastern Aramaic dialect with a very rich theological literature left by the early Christian Fathers) about the middle of the seventh century A.D. and virtually replaced them by the ninth and tenth centuries. But some Syriac dialects are still spoken today in isolated patches in Syria and Iraq.

Ethiopic—known also as *Ge^cez*, spoken in Ethiopia in a very early period. It was first known to us from fourth century A.D. inscriptions. Christian missionaries brought the Bible to the Abyssinians and wrote many theological works in Ethiopic. A new language, Amharic, belonging to the Semitic family but greatly modified by non-Semitic influences, became the language of the court from the thirteenth century A.D. Ge^cez remained the language of the church and literature and is still represented by a number of dialects spoken in Ethiopia. However, the main present-day language of this group is Amharic, spoken by some five million people in Ethiopia.

Arabic—the language of Arabia. South Arabic preceded the Classical Arabic of today. It is preserved in inscriptions ranging from about 800 B.C. to the sixth century A.D. and is believed to be still spoken in several dialects, along the southern coast of Arabia. Classical Arabic is the language used as a literary medium by Arab writers from the time of the pre-Islamic poets to the present. The earliest record of it is a fourth century A.D. inscription. Classical Arabic owes its expansion, since the seventh century A.D., to the conquests of the Arabs and the spread of Islam. The most important work is the Qur'ān (Koran), which is accepted by Moslems not only as a divine revelation but also as a perfect model of grammar and composition, just as the Hebrew Bible is by the Jews.

The chief dialects are those of Egypt, Iraq, Syria, Palestine, and North Africa, to which the Maltese dialect is essentially allied. The latter is in the peculiar position of being the only Arabic dialect ordinarily written in Roman characters. Arabic is spoken today by some 80 million people, and in addition has served for centuries as the sacred, literary, and official language of Islam.

A Note on the Yiddish Language. Yiddish is a Jewish language, written in the Hebrew alphabet and spoken by Ashkenazi Jews as early as the Middle Ages, yet it is not a Semitic language. Basically, it is derived from a medieval German dialect of the Rhine region. According to the *Standard Jewish Encyclopedia*, German has supplied about 85 per cent of the vocabulary—many of the words having new applications—and the basic grammatical structure. Hebrew words predominate in the religious and intellectual writings and in speech. Yiddish has had a very rich literature, with the first important works published in the sixteenth century. Some of the famous classical writers in Yiddish during the nineteenth and twentieth centuries are Mendele Mokher Sephorim (Abramovitch), Isaac L. Peretz, and Sholem Aleikhem. It is estimated that at the outbreak of World War II, Yiddish speakers numbered between 10 and 12 million. The Jewish tragedy of 1939-1945 in Eastern Europe and Germany, together with Soviet repression, has annihilated the main centers of Yiddish literature. As a spoken language it is gradually losing ground, especially among the new generations in the United States, Europe, and Israel.

STUDY HINTS

1. The purpose of this lesson is to provide you with an idea of the history and development of the Semitic languages, especially of the Hebrew language. Hebrew is treated as part of a large family of closely allied languages known as the Semitic languages.

2. The most important points of this lesson are as follows: (1) the origin of the term *Semitic*, (2) the main peculiarities common to all Semitic languages, and (3) some history of the Hebrew language and its literature.

3. You are not expected to spend too much time on the other sections of this lesson. You should, however, know what languages belong to the Semitic group and what their peculiarities are. (Turkish and Persian do *not* belong to the Semitic group of languages.) The exercises in this lesson should give you some idea of what is expected from you. It is important that you read appropriate articles on Hebrew and the various Semitic languages discussed here. You can find these articles in one of the standard encyclopedias.

EXERCISES

A. Explain the origin of the term *Semitic*.

B. List the five main groups of the Semitic languages and give a brief description of each group.

C. What are the main peculiarities the Semitic languages have in common?

D. List eight of the Semitic languages or dialects.

E. Discuss the four phases of the Hebrew language.

F. Write two to four lines on each of the following:

1. Ugaritic
2. Phoenician
3. Cuneiform writing
4. Syriac
5. South Arabic

Lesson Two

THE HEBREW ALPHABET

There are 22 consonants in the Hebrew alphabet.

	Printed Form	*Name of Letter*	*Translit- eration*	*Numerical Value*
1.	א	áh-leph	)	1
2.	*בּ	beth	b	2
	ב	veth	v	
3.	*גּ	gée-mel	g	3
4.	*דּ	dáh-leth	d	4
5.	ה	heh	h	5
6.	ו	vahv, wahw	v, w	6
7.	ז	záh-yin	z	7
8.	ח	ḥeth	ḥ	8
9.	ט	teht	ṭ	9
10.	י	yodh	y	10
11.	*כּ	kahf	k	20
	כ	khahf	kh	
12.	ל	láh-med	l	30
13.	מ	mem	m	40

---

*See Note 5

13

	Printed Form	Name of Letter	Transliteration	Numerical Value
14.	נ	nun	n	50
15.	ס	sáh-mekh	s	60
16.	ע	áh-yin	ʿ	70
17.	*פ	peh	p	80
	פ	feh	f	
18.	צ	tsáh-dee	ṣ	90
19.	ק	kofh	q	100
20.	ר	rehsh	r	200
21.	שׂ	seen	ś	300
	שׁ	sheen	š, sh	300
22.	*ת	taw	t	400

NOTES

1. Each sign of the alphabet is also the initial letter of its corresponding Hebrew name; thus the fourth sign ד, d, is also the initial of its own Hebrew name *dáh-leth*.

2. There are no capital letters in Hebrew.

3. The printed forms are sometimes known as Square script. Students interested in Biblical Hebrew should use the simplified Square script in Lesson 4, Table 4.

4. Each letter of the alphabet, whether printed or written, stands alone. Unlike English or Arabic writing, no letters of the Hebrew alphabet are ever joined together.

5. Six consonants, ב, ג, ד, כ, פ, ת, conveniently pronounced *BeGaD KeFaT*, may be used with or without a dot. This dot is called a *dagesh*. When these letters occur at the beginning of a word, they take a dagesh. There is hardly any difference retained today in the pronunciation of ג or ד with or without a

---

*See Note 5

dot. For the sake of clearer pronunciation, however, the other four letters, בּ, כּ, פּ, תּ, with a dot, assume a hardened sound: *b, k, p, t,* respectively; whereas ב, כ, פ, ת without a dot are soft: *v, kh* (like *ch* in the Scottish word *loch*), *f, th* (as in *think*), respectively. In Modern Hebrew and in some universities and seminaries, both ת and תּ are pronounced like *t.*

6. Five letters when used at the end of words assume a special final form. They are sometimes known as final letters. Note that the lower horizontal lines of four of these consonants, כ, נ, פ, צ, terminate in a continuous downstroke: ך, ן, ף, ץ.

Regular Form	Final Form
כ	ך
מ	ם
נ	ן
פ	ף
צ	ץ

Note: In ancient Hebrew-Phoenician script, final forms did not exist.

7. Hebrew is read and written from right to left.

8. Each letter in Hebrew has a numerical value as indicated in the right column of the list at the beginning of this lesson. This usage is not biblical. The earliest traces of it are found on Maccabean coins (about the second century B.C.). Numerical values are given here for reference only.

STUDY HINTS

1. Remember there are only 22 letters in the Hebrew alphabet. Strictly speaking, there are no special letters to represent the vowels, although as we shall see later two consonants are sometimes used as vowels, which helps to facilitate reading.

2. Learn the alphabet carefully, together with the names of each letter, in the proper order. Master the transcription thoroughly. For practical purposes there is no difference in the pronunciation of ג or גּ *g,* or ד or דּ *d.* In Modern Hebrew there is also no difference in pronunciation of the last letter ת or תּ *t.*

3. The notes in this lesson are very important. Observe in particular Notes 5 and 6.

4. The final forms described in Note 6 are used, of course, only when placed at the end of words. There are only five such letters ץ, ף, ן, ם, ך.

EXERCISES

A. Identify the following letters by name and transliterate into the Roman (English) alphabet. (Remember to read Hebrew from right to left but transliterate from left to right.)

ח, ע, ל, י, ו, ﬨ, ט, ק, ב, שׁ, ג,

צ, ר, ה, א, ע, שׁ, ד, כ, נ, ם,

פ, כ, מ, ף, ס, ז, פ, ץ, ר, ך

Parchment of "The War of the Sons of Light against the Sons of Darkness," one of the Dead Sea Scrolls found at Qumran.

B. Give the names of the letters contained in the following words and their corresponding English sounds:

ראובן, שמעון, זכריה, יצחק, דוד, ישעיה

ברוך, טוביה, פנחס, מנחם יונה, יחזקאל

C. Transliterate the following words:

ויהי ערב ויהי בקר יום הששי

בראשית ברא אלהים את השמים ואת הארץ

ואלה שמות בני ישראל הבאים מצרימה

D. Answer the following questions:
1. How many letters has the Hebrew alphabet?
2. Are there any capital letters in Hebrew?
3. May letters of the alphabet be joined together in writing?
4. Which letters take a dagesh at the beginning of a word?
5. Which are the final letters?

Lesson Three

PHONOLOGY

Note the phonetic values of certain consonants:

א   is a glottal stop, as in the initial sound of *apple*. It is silent when it appears at the end of the word; it may sometimes be silent in the middle of a word. When א appears at the beginning of a word, it can be pronounced only with a vowel; its phonetical value is apparent when it assumes a vowel. It is transcribed as ʾ.

בּ   with a dot is *b*; ב without a dot is pronounced like *v*.

ג   or גּ (with or without a dot) is pronounced like *g* in *go*.

דּ   or ד (with or without a dot) is *d*.

ה   is *h* as in *him*.

ו   in Modern Hebrew is pronounced like *v*. In Biblical Hebrew it is sometimes pronounced like *w* in *water*.

ח   has a pharyngeal (guttural) sound which does not exist in English. It is transliterated as *ḥ*, with a dot underneath, to distinguish it from ה *h*. Owing to the difficulty experienced by Europeans in its pronunciation, it is usually pronounced, especially in Modern Hebrew, like *kh* (the same fricative sound of *ch* in the Scottish word *loch*). It is a sound produced by friction between the back of the tongue and the soft palate. (See the letter כ below.)

ט   is an emphatic *t*, produced by placing the tongue firmly against the palate. It is transliterated as *ṭ*. There is hardly any difference today between the pronunciation of ט and ת, especially in Modern Hebrew in which both are pronounced like *t*.

כ   with a dot is *k*; without a dot it is *kh*, like *ch* in the Scottish word *loch*.

ע   has a pharyngeal (guttural) sound; it is produced at the back of the throat and transcribed as ʿ. It is very difficult for Europeans to pronounce it without much practice because it does not exist in any of the European languages. It is usually pronounced in Modern Hebrew as a glottal stop, like א above.

פ   with a dot is *p*; without a dot it is *f*.

צ   is an emphatic *s*-sound produced further back in the mouth with the tongue touching the palate; it is something like the combined sound produced by *ts*, as in *fits*; it is transliterated as ṣ.

ק   is originally a *k*-sound, produced at the back of the throat; it is transliterated as *q*. In Modern Hebrew, however, it is pronounced like כ *k* above.

שׂ   with a dot over the *left-hand* corner is *s*. It is usually transliterated as ś. The letter שׁ with a dot over the *right-hand* corner is pronounced like *sh*. It is transliterated as š. שׂ and שׁ were originally one letter. In unpointed or unvocalized texts they are still represented by שׁ without a dot. The Samaritans to the present day pronounce both letters like š. (The English sound *ch* as in *church* does not exist in Biblical Hebrew.)

ת   with or without a dot is *t*. (In some theological seminaries and Ashkenazi Jewish communities outside Israel ת without a dot is pronounced like *th* in *think*.)

Distinguish carefully between consonants of similar form:

ב (b) and כ (k)		ו (v) and ן (final n)	
כ (v) and כ (kh)		ז (z) and ן (final n)	
ג (g) and נ (n)		ם (final m) and ס (s)	
ד (d) and ר (r)		ע (ʿ) and צ (ṣ)	
ד (d) and ך (final kh)		ע (ʿ) and ץ (final ṣ)	
ה (h) and ח (ḥ)		צ (ṣ) and א (ʾ)	
ו (v) and ז (z)		ת (t) and ח (ḥ)	
ט (ṭ) and מ (m)		שׂ (ś) and שׁ (š)	
י (y) and ו (w)			

Distinguish carefully between the following transcriptions:

(ʾ) for א and (ʿ) for ע

(h) for ה and (ḥ) for ח

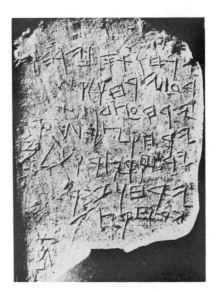

The Gezer Calendar, the earliest known inscription in Old Hebrew, ca. 925 B.C. Discovered in excavations of the Biblical city of Gezer.

(ṭ) for ט and (t) for ת

(k) for כ and (q) for ק

(s) for ס and (ś) for שׂ and (š) for שׁ

STUDY HINTS

1. Only by constant practice will you be able to pronounce the letters correctly. Pronounce each letter loudly at least five times. Try to find someone who knows Modern Hebrew and pronounce the letters aloud to him or her. Perhaps it would be advisable to engage a tutor for two or three hours only to go over the first four lessons with you.

2. The letters difficult to pronounce are usually ה, כ, ע, צ. Listen to the tape for help with the difficult sounds.

3. Note the difference between שׂ and שׁ (*ś* and *sh* respectively).

4. Study carefully the section on consonants of similar form of this lesson.

5. For further practice, take any excerpt in Hebrew from any page of this textbook or of the Bible and transliterate it into English equivalents.

Table 2

THE HEBREW CONSONANTS

	Plain Consonants		Emphatic and Emphatic-like Consonants		Sonants
	Voiced	Unvoiced	Voiced	Unvoiced	
Labial	*b* בּ *v* ב, ו	*p* פּ *f* פ			*m* מ
Dental	*d* ד *z* ז	*th*[1], *t* תּ *s* ס *s* שׂ		*ṭ* ט *ṣ* צ	 *n* נ
Lateral					*l* ל
Trill					*r* ר
Palatal	*g* גּ	שׁ *k* כּ		*q* ק	
Glide					*y* י
Velar				*kh*[2] ח, כ	
Laryngeal (Guttural)			ʿ[3] ע	*ḥ*[3] ח	
Laryngeal Glottal (Guttural)		ע[2] א ʾ *h* ה			

---

[1] *th* as in *think*

[2] by non-Oriental speakers

[3] by Oriental speakers—original sounds

EXERCISES

A. Distinguish between the following letters by adding the appropriate transliterations:

ה and ח   ת and ח

ד and ר   ם and מ

ר and ך   ע and צ

ע and ץ   ם and ס

ג and נ   ו and ז

B. Write the Hebrew for the following transliterated letters:

d	s
m	q
t	ś
k	g
b	r
v	ṭ
ʿ	h
ʾ	y
ḥ	š
p	l

C. Transliterate the following into English equivalents:

מה טבו אהליך יעקב

משכנותיך ישראל

אשרי האיש אשר לא הלך בעצת רשעים

והארץ היתה תהו ובהו

וחשך על פני תהום

ויאמר אלהים יהי אור

וירא אלהים כי טוב

Lesson Four

ORIGINS OF THE HEBREW ALPHABET

Early Writing Systems

In ancient days, Hebrew was written in the common Semitic alphabet used alike by the Moabites, Hebrews, Aramaeans, and Phoenicians. It is known as the Phoenician, Canaanite, or Paleo-Hebrew script. (See Table 3 in this lesson.) Inscriptions discovered in the Sinai peninsula on potsherds and other objects indicate that as early as the sixteenth century B.C. certain alphabetic writing was in circulation. This writing is generally believed to be the beginning of the Canaanite writing system. The Old Hebrew alphabet was probably derived from this Canaanite-Phoenician script.

In 1929, a large number of cuneiform inscriptions, dating from the fifteenth century B.C. and written in alphabetic script, were discovered in the north Syrian town of Ugarit, known today as Ras Shamra. (See Lesson 1.) The language of these inscriptions is now called Ugaritic. It is clear from some of these tablets that the present order of the Hebrew alphabet was known at Ugarit as early as the fifteenth century B.C. It is probably the oldest known alphabet in recorded history.

The earliest examples of ancient Hebrew occur, for instance, on the famous Moabite stone of King Mesha (ninth century B.C.), on the inscription discovered in the Pool of Siloam (about the eighth century B.C.), and on the Lachish inscriptions. All of these names are mentioned in the Bible. The transition from the Phoenician script to the Square script was first effected in the Aramaic language and then in Hebrew, about the fifth and fourth centuries B.C. This change occurred, no doubt, because of the growing influence of the Aramaic language immediately before the Christian Era. This script eventually became known as the Aramaic, Ashuri, or Square script. Ashuri is the Hebrew name for Assyrian. From this, the Square script we use today in print was developed. (See Table 4 in this lesson.) Jewish tradition ascribes this change to Ezra, but the scientific view is that it represents a gradual process. For a time, both forms were used, as is evidenced not only by the Maccabean coins of the second century B.C., but also by the Dead Sea Scrolls, believed to be of the second and first centuries B.C. Here we find some scrolls of the Pentateuch in Phoenician script, some in early Aramaic, or Square, script, and a few others in both scripts. Later, the ancient form was completely abandoned. The ancient script has been preserved until the present day by the Samaritans in Palestine.

The Greek Alphabet

It is generally agreed that the Greeks adopted, with some modifications and additions, this old Phoenician alphabet along with its Semitic names and order of the letters from the Phoenician traders who frequented their isles from about the ninth century B.C. It is obvious that the Greek *alpha, beta, gamma, delta,* etc. are Semitic and correspond to the Hebrew *ah-leph, beht, gee-mel, dah-let,* etc.

Table 3
SIMILARITIES BETWEEN THE GREEK AND PHOENICIAN SCRIPTS

Hebrew	Phoenician	Greek
א	∢	A
ד	△	Δ
ה	𐤄	E
ט	⊗	Θ
כ	𐤊	K
ל	𐤋	Λ
מ	𐤌	M
נ	𐤍	N
שׁ	w	Σ
ת	×	T

Table 4

THE HEBREW ALPHABET THROUGH THE CENTURIES

English Equivalent	Phoenician	Printed Square	Simplified Square*†	Rabbinic (Rashi)	Cursive*
ʾ		א			
b, v		ב			
g		ג			
d		ד			
h		ה			
v		ו			
z		ז			
ḥ		ח			
ṭ		ט			
y		י			
k, kh		כ, ך			
l		ל			
m		מ, ם			
n		נ, ן			
s		ס			
ʿ		ע			
p, f		פ, ף			
ṣ		צ, ץ			
q		ק			
r		ר			
ś, š		ש			
t		ת			

---

*Begin writing each letter as the arrow indicates.

†When writing Hebrew in Square script, use the letters in the Simplified Square column.

Moreover, there is a clear relationship between the Greek and the Phoenician scripts. (See Table 3; the corresponding Hebrew letters are given for reference.)

The Different Scripts Used by Jews

About the thirteenth century A.D., Rabbinic script, used mainly for religious treatises and commentaries and known as Rashi script, was developed. (See Table 4.) It is so called because this type was used for Rashi's commentaries on the Bible and the Talmud. (Rashi is a Hebrew abbreviation for Rabbi Shlomo Yitzhaqi, A.D. 1040-1105, a great Talmudic scholar and commentator.)

Finally, script known as German, or Cursive, was developed, probably about the end of the eighteenth century. This script was used in correspondence and in secular and informal documents that were not generally printed. The Cursive

The Manual of Discipline, *displayed at the "Shrine of the Book," Israel National Museum in Jerusalem.*

script is now generally used in handwriting and can be written more rapidly than the Square script.

In some universities and seminaries outside Israel, where the main interest is in Biblical Hebrew, only the Square script is used.

The different alphabets used by Jews since biblical times are given in the preceding Table 4. Study these alphabets carefully.

STUDY HINTS

1. It is important to know something about the development of the Hebrew script. This is a very brief survey. Try to read the article under "Alphabet" in a reference book or encyclopedia. If you are interested in biblical archaeology, read also the articles under "Mesha," "Lachish," and "Siloam." You can easily learn the Phoenician script.

2. *Observe that the Hebrew script we use today is not, strictly speaking, a Hebrew alphabet.* It is an Aramaic script first adopted in Aramaic and subsequently in Hebrew (about the third or second century B.C.). This is what is known today as Square script. (See the third column in Table 4.)

3. In writing your assignment for this lesson, use the simplified Square Hebrew script (fourth column). You are not expected to write in Rashi, printed Square, Cursive, or Phoenician script. However, if you wish, you may use the Cursive script.

EXERCISES

A. Transcribe the following into English letters:

אב, עם, בת, אם, צבא, חבר,

זך, פה, שמים, ילד, גר, כנען,

חלום, טוב, כסא, שלום, קול, עץ

B. Write each letter of the alphabet, including the finals, at least three times in simplified Square script. (See Table 4.)

C. Write the following in simplified Square script:

בקר, ערב, בטח, אף, שנה

שלום, מלך, עץ, גדול, זאת.

D. Copy Exercise A above in simplified Square script.

E. Write the following in simplified Square script:

יצחק, יעקב, שלום, אסתר, שלמה

F. Describe the different scripts of the Hebrew alphabet.

Lesson Five

VOWELS

Traditionally, Hebrew has 10 vowels divided into short and long vowels as follows:

Name and Sign		Equivalent English Sound	Description
Short Vowels			
1. Pataḥ	X̱	*a* in *card*	a short horizontal dash below the consonant
2. Seghol	X̤	*e* in *pen*	three dots forming an equilateral triangle below the consonant
3. Ḥiriq Qaṭan	X̣	*i* in *sit*	one dot below the consonant
4. Qubbuṣ	X̤	*u* in *pull*	three dots placed diagonally below the consonant
5. Qamats Qaṭan	X̣	*o* in *hop*	a sign resembling a small т below the consonant
Long Vowels			
6. Qamats	X̣	*ā* in *card**	a sign resembling a small т below the consonant
7. Ṣereh	X̤	*ē* in *prey*	two horizontal dots below the consonant

*The diacritical sign over the English vowels indicates the corresponding Hebrew long vowel.

29

Name and Sign		Equivalent English Sound	Description
Long Vowels			
7. (Ṣereh)	ʾX	*ē* in *prey*	two horizontal dots below the consonant, followed by the letter '
8. Ḥiriq Gadol	ʾX	*ī* in *marine**	one dot below the consonant, followed by '
9. Ḥolam	ʾX	*ō* in *lore*	a dot above the letter ו
Ḥolam, without the letter ו	X	*ō* in *lore*	a dot over left-hand corner of the consonant
10. Shuruq	ʾX	*ū* in *flute*	a dot in the middle of the letter ו

NOTES

1. The above transliterations of the vowels approximate the true phonetic sound of the Hebrew. Only by practice is one able to pronounce Hebrew correctly.

2. Most vowels are placed *under* the consonants. Two, namely, ו *ū* and ו *ō* are placed after the consonants. The dot of the vowel *ō* (9, above) is placed over the left-hand corner of the letter.

3. The difference between *o* (5, above) and *ā* (6, above) will be explained later. The short vowel *o* (5, above) is seldom used. It appears most often in the word כָּל *all*.

4. The sound of *a* (1, above) is almost the same as that of *ā* (6, above). On the whole, the difference between the long and the short sounds is one of quantity rather than quality. It is, however, important to know which is which because this is information relevant to many rules of grammar.

5. The Hebrew syllable is formed by a consonant and a vowel, like לְ *lā*, לְ *lu*, יִ

---

*The diacritical sign over the English vowels indicates the corresponding Hebrew long vowel.

yū, מוֹ *mō*, and שֶׁ *še*. Note that the vowel follows the consonant. Thus לְ *lā* is ל and ָ. A syllable which ends in one of the above vowels is regarded as an *open*, or *simple*, *syllable*.

6. A syllable may also be formed by a vowelled consonant followed by a vowelless consonant, like גַּל *gal*, שָׁם *šām*, דּוֹד *dōd*, and בֵּן *bēn*. Such a syllable is regarded as a *closed syllable*. The syllable will be explained more fully at a later stage.

   A consonant with a strong dagesh (see 15b, below) turns the preceding syllable into a closed one. Thus סִפּוּר is equivalent to *sip-pūr*, סִפּ–פּוּר consisting of two closed syllables. מִלָּה is equivalent to *mil-lā*, מִלְ–לָה consisting of a closed syllable and an open one. In both words, the syllable preceding the strong dagesh is a closed one.

7. In most words the accent is on the last syllable, or less frequently, on the second to the last. In some words the accent is indicated, for convenience, by the sign (<) placed above the syllable. To help you, this sign is used up to Lesson 19. You should *not* use it when writing Hebrew. It is important to note that when writing unvocalized Hebrew, you should not add *any* dots. On the other hand, the letters ו and י used with the long vowels should not be omitted. *Examples*: הַשִּׁיר–הַשִּׁיר, שָׁלוֹם–שָׁלוֹם, דּוֹד–דּוֹד.

8. The Hebrew Bible was originally written without vowels. The Hebrew of the Dead Sea Scrolls, dated between the second century B.C. and the first century A.D., has no vowels. When Hebrew had ceased to be a spoken language, several systems of vowel signs were invented by Jewish grammarians to help the public read Hebrew accurately. Our present system was probably adopted during the ninth or tenth century A.D. and is known as the Tiberian—developed by Jewish scholars of Tiberias in Palestine. Since the Hebrew text of the Bible was regarded as sacred, the Rabbis did not effect any changes in the consonantal text of the Bible but added the vowel signs above, below, and inside the consonants.

9. Modern Hebrew books and newspapers are usually printed without vowels. In fact, all writing in Hebrew is usually printed without vowels, with the exception of grammars, Hebrew texts for beginners, dictionaries, and printed Bibles (where the vowel signs are convenient and desirable).

Lachish Letter 4. Correspondence in Hebrew on broken pieces of pottery between Lachish and its military outpost during the time of the Babylonian invasion of Judah, ca. 588 B.C.

10. There are, generally speaking, two main pronunciations: the Ashkenazi, or German, originated by Central and Eastern European Jews and carried to all countries to which those Jews have emigrated (Western Europe, America, etc.); and the Sephardi, or Spanish, used by Jews of Spanish or Portuguese stock in Europe and America and also by Jews from Oriental countries.

11. In all universities and throughout Israel, the Sephardi pronunciation has been adopted, since it is generally believed that this is the pronunciation nearest to the original. In this work we, too, have adopted the Sephardi.

12. In contrast to English, a Hebrew vowel does not assume different pronunciations. Once you have mastered the correct sound of these vowels, you are assured of correct reading. Knowledge of Hebrew reading can be easily mastered by any beginner in less than six lessons.

13. *The Shva* (also *Shwa*)

   The shva is not, strictly speaking, a vowel. It is a sign composed of two dots in a straight vertical line (֡) placed under a letter to indicate the absence of a vowel. Thus, פְּרִי is pronounced *prī*; גַּל, *gal*. The shva which is placed at the beginning of a word or a syllable assumes a semi-vowel, a sort of short seghol X̱. The shva sign is usually omitted when it occurs at the end of a word. Only the final letter ךְ and sometimes תּ (with dagesh) take a shva at the end of a word, e.g. בָּרוּךְ, לֵךְ, יָשַׁבְתָּ, אַתְּ. There are, generally speaking, two kinds of shvas:

   a. *Vocal Shva*

   The shva occurs: 1. at the beginning of the word, שְׁלֹמֹה, בְּנִי, or 2. at the beginning of a syllable following a closed syllable, such as מְ in יִשְׁ–מְרוּ, or 3. following a long vowel, like תְ in כָּ–תְבוּ assumes a semi-vowel and is vocal, i.e., pronounced. Thus:

בְּנִי	pronounced	*b^eni*
שְׁלֹמֹה		*sh^elo-mo*
יִשְׁמְרוּ		*yish-m^eru*
כָּ–תְבוּ		*ka-t^evu*

   b. *Silent or Quiescent Shva*

   A silent shva indicates that the consonant is vowelless. It occurs in closed syllables and at the end of words. Thus:

סִפְרִי	*sif-ri* (here the *f* is vowelless)
יִכְתֹּב	*yikh-tov* (here *kh* and *v* are vowelless)

14. *The Compound Shva or Hataph*

Four letters in the Hebrew alphabet, ע, ח, ה, א, known as *gutturals* or *laryngeals*, have special peculiarities. We have already observed that their pronunciations present some difficulty. For this very reason, one of the main peculiarities is that they cannot take a shva at the beginning of a word or a syllable; instead, they assume one of the following compound signs below the guttural: אֳ (pronounced *o*), אֲ (pronounced *a*), or אֱ (pronounced *e* as in *pen*).

Examples:

אֳנִיָּה	pronounced	*oniyya*
עֲבוֹדָה		*avoda*
אֱלֹהִים		*elohim*

These are known as *ḥataph qamats*, *ḥataph pataḥ*, and *ḥataph seghol*, respectively. They are, in effect, helping vowels to enable the reader to pronounce them.

When guttural letters ע, ח, and ה occur at the end of the word, because of their peculiar pronunciation, a pataḥ (known as *furtive pataḥ*) is placed under the guttural to facilitate its pronunciation. It usually follows an accented consonant with a long vowel. Note the following:

יוֹדֵעַ	pronounced	*yo-de-a* or *yo-de-ya*
רוּחַ		*ru-ah* or *ru-wah*
גָּבוֹהַּ		*ga-vo-ah* or *ga-vo-wah*

In due course you should experience no difficulties in reading these forms correctly.

15. *The Dagesh*

The dagesh is a dot placed inside the letters. All the letters with the exception of the letter ר and the gutturals ע, ח, ה, א may take the dagesh. There are two kinds of dageshes.

a. *Weak, Gentle or Lene* דָּגֵשׁ קַל

The dagesh is inserted in the consonants ת, פ, כ, ד, ג, ב when the latter are placed at the beginning of the word—בַּיִת, דָּבָר, גַּן, כַּד, פֶּה—

or at the beginning of a syllable if preceded by another closed syllable—
יִשְׁ-פֹּט; מַל-כֵּנוּ; יִכְ-תֹּב. (See Note 6 above.)

b. *Strong, or Forte* דָּגֵשׁ חָזָק

The dagesh is inserted in a letter to compensate for a missing letter, or to indicate the doubling of a consonant. כָּרַתָּ really stands for כָּרַתְתָּ, אַתָּה for אַנְתָּה, יִסַּע for יִנְסַע, נִקַּח for נִלְקַח, מִשָּׁם for מִן־שָׁם, נִפֵּל for נִנְפֵּל. The above is not a complete treatment of the dagesh. In due course, you will learn more about it.

Note: You are expected to be familiar with these signs and rules. Proceed to the next lesson, however, even if you have not yet grasped all the information given here. You are strongly advised to refer to this lesson constantly.

STUDY HINTS

1. Study carefully the different vowels, their names, and their equivalent English sounds. As stated in the Notes of this lesson, the transcriptions into English sounds do not, on the whole, accurately express the true phonetic sound of the Hebrew. This is the nearest and the best we can do in the circumstances. The cassette is of great help here.

2. Study carefully the information in Notes 9 through 15.

3. Note 14 is very important. By knowing the peculiarities of the gutturals, you will understand many grammatical rules more easily and avoid many errors.

4. It is essential that you understand the role of the dagesh in Hebrew pronunciation. We have already noted in Lesson 2 that the letters ב, כ, and פ, for instance, assume the hard sound when a dagesh appears in them. (See Lesson 2, Note 5.)

5. The assignment for this lesson is mainly reading. You must be able to read correctly and fluently. Most future assignments include a Rapid Reading Exercise. You are expected to read these passages fluently and correctly. Read and reread them until you can read them with ease. Experience shows that by using this method you should be able to read Hebrew correctly by the end of two weeks and fluently by the end of six weeks.

6. Read Exercises A through G (below) aloud, over and over again. Ask some-one who knows Hebrew to listen to your reading. The Written Assignments will help you master both the consonant and vowel systems.

7. Remember that Hebrew writing is almost phonetic; therefore, the shortest and most efficient way to teach reading and writing is the old-fashioned way, the so-called synthetic method of teaching reading by combining the letters with their vowels.

Although it is generally accepted that the teaching of reading should precede that of writing, experience has shown that in teaching Biblical Hebrew to adults it is most vital to introduce reading and writing simultaneously. Reading is one of the most effective means of acquiring a knowledge of the language; it is an indispensable aspect of teaching any language and especially Hebrew. Therefore, carefully cultivate the art of reading from the very beginning of your studies.

According to Dr. Aharon Rosen of the Hebrew University of Jerusalem, who has taught Hebrew to thousands of adult foreign students, you should try to improve your reading in the following ways: (a) by correct pronunciation of every word and (b) by accentuated reading.

When pronouncing words do not slur syllables or run words together. Use the tape or have someone help you.

When the accent is indicated, read accordingly. Most words are accented on the last syllable. We shall often indicate the accented syllable with the sign (<) placed over the letter. In every word there is one syllable on which the main stress falls; you have to discover which syllable that is, and when you have found it, you can pronounce it with exaggerated emphasis. This is an important matter. If you place the stress on the wrong syllable you may change the entire meaning of the word. For instance חֵרֵשׁ *herésh* (with the accent on the last syllable) means *deaf* whereas חֶרֶשׁ *héresh* (with the accent on the first syllable) means *quiet*. From the beginning, therefore, read correctly.

EXERCISES

Read Exercises A through G aloud five times. Check your readings with the cassette.

A.   Illustrations of open syllables:

1. דָ, בְּ, לְ, מָ, נְ, תַ, נַ, דְ, תֶ,
פָּ, לְ, כְּ, שֶׁ, סַ, לוֹ, יוּ, שָׂ, לְ

2. נִי, יְ, נוֹ, טַ, רְ, פּוּ, פָ, מִי, מֶ,
רְ, עָ, נְ, חִי, בוּ, חַ, קָ, אוֹ, זִי

3. פָּ, פֶּ, צָ, נְ, טֶ, קוּ, בַּ, וְ, תַ,
עָ, הוֹ, גַ, שָׂ, דְ, תַ, סָ, אָ

B.   Illustrations of closed syllables:

4. כַּף, עֵץ, פֶּן, אִם, אַף, רָץ, דִי, גַּל, עַל, אֶל
שִׁיר, קוֹל, עִיר, סוּס, דּוּד, אִישׁ, טוֹב, אוֹר

C.   Words consisting of two syllables, open and closed:

5. יָשַׁב, לָמַד, לָקַח, יָדַע, עָמַד
מֶלֶךְ, גֶּשֶׁם, עֶרֶב, פֶּרַח, צֶמַח
שָׁלוֹם, יֶלֶד, בָּרוּךְ, אָדוֹן, מָלוֹן

D.   Words with the last syllable having the sound of *ie* as in the word *tie*:

6. מָתַי, אֲדוֹנָי, עֵינַי, דַי, שִׁירַי
חַי, דּוֹדִי, דּוֹדוֹתַי, שַׁי, אוּלַי

E.   Sets of words containing letters that look alike but are pronounced differently:

7.   ב b   ;   כ k
בַּיִת, הַבַּיִת, בֵּן, כָּבוֹד, כַּד
כֶּלֶב, הַכֶּלֶב, כֵּן, בְּכוֹר, בַּד

8.   ג g   ;   נ n
גֵּר, גַּם, גַּנִּי, גַּג, עָנָּה
נֵר, נֵס, אֲנִי, נָתַן

9.   ב v   ;   כ kh
טוֹב, לֵב, עֲרָבָה, טוֹבָה, עוֹבֵר
הָלְכָה, כָּכָה, בְּרָכָה, מִיכָה, מוֹכֵר

10.   ד d   ;   ר r
דּוֹר, דֹּב, דָּוִד, דֶּרֶךְ, דָּבָר
רֹאשׁ, רַב, עָשִׁיר, רֶכֶב, בֶּרֶךְ

11. ה h ; ח kh

הֵם, הָיָה, הַיּוֹם, הָאָב, אַהֲבָה

אָח, חָיָה, חַיִּים, הַחֵם, אַחִים

12. ו v ; ז z

דָּוִד, הַיֶּלֶד, וָו, וְהַסּוּס, וְלַד

זָנָב, זַיִת, הַזֶּה, וְזֹאת, זוּז

13. ט t ; מ m

טֶרֶם, עֵט, בֶּטַח, לְאַט, מִטָּה

בָּמָה, מֶלַח, מֶלֶךְ, מַטֶּה, מַיִם

14. ס s ; ם final m

סוֹד, סוּס, נָסָה, מַס, כִּסֵּא

יוֹם, מַיִם, קוּם, מְסִים, סַמִּים

15. שׂ ś ; שׁ sh

שָׂשׂוֹן, שָׂמֵחַ, שָׂם, נָשָׂא, יִשְׂרָאֵל

שִׁשָּׁה, שְׁלֹשָׁה, שָׁם, שֹׁרֶשׁ, שָׁאוּל

16. ע ʿ ; צ ṣ

עַם, עָשָׂה, יָדַע, עָבַד, עֵצִים

צוֹם, צָבָא, צֵלַע, עֵצָה, צָעִיר

F. Sets of words containing letters that have different forms but have the same pronunciation:

17. ב, ו v

אָב, אָבִיב, לֵב, גֶּבֶר, אָבִיו

קַו, וָו, גֵּו, קַוֵּה, תִּקְוָה

18. *א ʿ ע ʿ

אָח, אִם, אָמַר, מָצָא, אֶאֱמֹר

עַם, עִם, עָמַד, שָׁמַע, אֶעֱשֶׂה

19. *ח, כ kh

צָחַק, שָׁלַח, חַיִּים, אָח, קְחוּ

זָכַר, מֶלֶךְ, חֲכָמִים, כַּךְ, לְכוּ

*For non-Oriental readers.

20.   ת, ט   t

תַּלְמִיד, אֱמֶת, לָתֵת, כָּתַב, תּוֹרָה

טַבַּעַת, מְעַט, מִטָּה, קָטָן, טוֹבָה

21.   ק, כּ   k

כַּד, כָּבוֹד, מַכָּה, חַכָּה, כַּר

קַל, קָדוֹשׁ, בְּקֶרֶב, חֻקָּה, רַק

22.   שׂ, ס   s

סַל, נֵס, נָסַע, סוּסִים, סוֹפֵר

שַׂר, שָׂם, נָשָׂא, שָׂשׂוֹן, יִשְׂרָאֵל

G.   General drill in reading:

23.   רְאֵה, בְּנִי, אֱגוֹז, אֲנִיָּה, אֱמֶת, פְּרָחִים, אֲנִי

חֲלוֹם, שְׁלֹמֹה, עֲבוֹדָה, חֲבֵרִים, יַעֲשֶׂה, חֲמִשָּׁה, אֲדוֹנִי

24.   יִצְחָק, סְפָרֵנוּ, יִקְרָא, מַלְכֵּנוּ

יַרְדֵּן, יַלְדָּה, מַרְאֶה, בִּנְיָמִין

מַלְכְּכֶם, תִּכְתְּבוּ, יִצְחָק, מַמְלַכְתִּי, דַּרְכְּךָ

25.   **יוֹדֵעַ, תַּפּוּחַ, שָׂמֵחַ, רוּחַ, לוּחַ, מִזְבֵּחַ

שִׂיחַ, מָשִׁיחַ, גָּבוֹהַּ, יָדוּעַ, מָלוּחַ, רֵעַ

26.   מִלְחֶמֶת, מַחֲשֶׁבֶת, מֶמְשֶׁלֶת, מִשְׁפַּחַת, מְלֶאכֶת

מַהְפֵּכָה, מִשְׁקֶלֶת, מִשְׁמֶרֶת, מִשְׁמַעַת

H.   Rapid Reading: Read the following over and over again until you can read it
correctly and fluently. (The first line is the first verse of the Hebrew Bible.)

בְּרֵאשִׁית בָּרָא אֱלֹהִים אֵת הַשָּׁמַיִם וְאֵת הָאָרֶץ

וַיְהִי־עֶרֶב וַיְהִי־בֹקֶר יוֹם רִאשׁוֹן.

If you are familiar with this verse, substitute Exercise G, 26, above.

**See Study Hint 7 relating to the accent.

Lesson Six
GENDER; CONJUNCTION *AND*; DEFINITE ARTICLE *THE*

VOCABULARY

aunt	דּוֹדָה	uncle, beloved one	דּוֹד
prophetess	נְבִיאָה	prophet	נָבִיא
mare	סוּסָה	horse	סוּס
woman	אִשָּׁה	man	אִישׁ
mother	אֵם	father	אָב
daughter	בַּת	son	בֵּן
law, torah	תּוֹרָה	day	יוֹם
candlestick, lampstand	מְנוֹרָה	morning	בֹּקֶר
animal	בְּהֵמָה	evening	עֶרֶב
Rachel, ewe	רָחֵל	night (m.)	לַיְלָה לֵיל
door	דֶּלֶת	book	סֵפֶר
and	וְ–	song	שִׁיר
the	הַ–	field	שָׂדֶה
house (m.)	בַּיִת	voice	קוֹל

GRAMMAR AND NOTES

1. *Gender*

    The Hebrew language has only two genders: masculine and feminine. There is no neuter in Hebrew.

40

Note: This is the same, for instance, in French: *la ville* (f.), *the town*; *le livre* (m.), *the book*.

Obviously, words indicating males are masculine: אָב *father,* דּוֹד *uncle,* סוּס *horse;* whereas words indicating females are feminine: אֵם *mother,* רָחֵל *Rachel or ewe,* סוּסָה *mare.*

There is no special form to indicate the masculine nouns, but the feminine nouns are easily recognized by the ending ה– or ה– (with the vowel ָ in front of the ה): תּוֹרָה *law,* מְנוֹרָה *candlestick* or *lampstand,* סוּסָה *mare,* דֶּלֶת *door.*

The absence of ה– or ה– at the end of a word usually, but not always, indicates a masculine gender. *Examples:* קוֹל *voice,* יוֹם *day,* עֶרֶב *evening.* All of these are masculine.

Notes:

a. שָׂדֶה *field,* ends in ה–, but has no ָ in front of the ה; it is masculine.

b. לַיְלָה *night,* is an exception to the rule. Although ending with ה–, it is masculine. Actually, לַיְלָה is a lengthened form of לַיִל *night,* and the latter is masculine.

c. בַּיִת *house,* although ending in ת–, is masculine because here the ת is part of the root of the word and not a sign of the feminine gender.

2. *The Conjunction "And"* (–וְ)

And is usually expressed in Hebrew by –וְ prefixed to the following word; it does not stand alone: אִישׁ *a man,* וְאִישׁ *and a man,* יוֹם וְלַיְלָה *a day and a night.*

If the first letter has a dagesh, the dot is omitted when –וְ is added, e.g., כֹּהֵן *a priest,* וְכֹהֵן *and a priest,* דֶּלֶת *a door,* וְדֶלֶת *and a door.*

Hebrew has no word for the indefinite articles *a* and *an:* אִישׁ *a man,* עֶרֶב *an evening.*

3. *The Definite Article "The"* (–הַ)

In order to express *the,* we prefix –הַ to the noun. This –הַ is followed by a dagesh, known as strong dagesh, and is placed in the first letter of the word; for example, לַיְלָה *night,* הַלַּיְלָה *the night,* קוֹל *voice,* הַקּוֹל *the voice.*

If the word begins with a dagesh, no extra dot is necessary when –הַ is added: בַּת *daughter,* הַבַּת *the daughter,* תּוֹרָה *law,* הַתּוֹרָה *the law.*

STUDY HINTS

1. The vocabulary at the beginning of this lesson is composed of important basic words. Read the words in groups of five, first from Hebrew into English and then from English into Hebrew. Test yourself by writing the words first in English and then translating them into Hebrew. Be sure to insert the vowels. Observe the accent sign (<) given. If there is no sign, the accent is on the last syllable. Check your work by comparing it with the Vocabulary.

2. Note that in Hebrew there are two genders only. There is no neuter.

3. The rule about the feminine is very important. There are very few exceptions to this rule. At present, keep in mind the two exceptions given in this lesson. They are frequently used words and hence should be noted: לַיְלָה *night* and בַּיִת *house*; both are masculine.

4. You have probably noticed by now that –הַ *the* and –וְ *and* cannot stand alone. They must be used as prefixes.

5. Exercise E is very important. Read it repeatedly until you are able to read it fluently. Listen carefully to the cassette.

The Genesis Apocryphon, one of the original Dead Sea Scrolls, before unrolling.

EXERCISES

A. Read the following words, give their meaning, and identify their gender. (Use m. for masculine and f. for feminine.)

6. לַיְלָה   1. סֵפֶר

7. עֶרֶב   2. מְנוֹרָה

8. דֶּלֶת   3. קוֹל

9. בַּיִת   4. תּוֹרָה

10. שָׂדֶה   5. יוֹם

B. Translate the following into English:

7. הַבְּהֵמָה, וְהַסּוּסָה   1. יוֹם, וְיוֹם, הַיּוֹם

8. הַיּוֹם וְהַלַּיְלָה   2. יוֹם וְלַיְלָה, הַלַּיְלָה

9. הַנָּבִיא וְהַקּוֹל   3. אִישׁ וְאִשָּׁה

10. הַבַּיִת וְהַשָּׂדֶה   4. הַדֶּלֶת וְהַבַּיִת

11. הַבֵּן וְהַסֵּפֶר   5. הַבֵּן וְהַבַּת

12. הַסֵּפֶר וְהַתּוֹרָה   6. בֹּקֶר וְעֶרֶב

C. Translate the following into Hebrew:

1. the voice, and a voice
2. a horse, and a horse, and the horse
3. and the field, and a field
4. a door, the door, and the door
5. night and day
6. and the prophetess
7. the house, and the house
8. and a field, and the animal
9. and the law, and a law
10. the prophet, and a book

D. Give the feminine of the following:

4. נָבִיא   1. סוּס

5. אִישׁ   2. אָב

6. דּוֹד   3. בֵּן

E. Rapid Reading: Read the following over and over again until you can read it correctly and fluently (Gen. 6:9).

אֵלֶּה תּוֹלְדוֹת נֹחַ
נֹחַ (הָיָה) אִישׁ צַדִּיק
תָּמִים הָיָה בְּדֹרוֹתָיו

Note: The accent is indicated by the sign < placed over the word.

Lesson Seven

ADJECTIVES

VOCABULARY

A. *Adjectives*

Feminine		*Masculine*
טוֹבָה	good	טוֹב
רָעָה	bad	רַע
יָפָה	nice, beautiful	יָפֶה
גְּדוֹלָה	big, large, great	גָּדוֹל
קְטַנָּה	small, little	קָטָן
זְקֵנָה	old (persons, beings)	זָקֵן
יְשָׁנָה	old (things)	יָשָׁן
צְעִירָה	young	צָעִיר
שְׁחוֹרָה	black	שָׁחוֹר
לְבָנָה	white	לָבָן
קְדוֹשָׁה	holy	קָדוֹשׁ

B. *Nouns*

year	שָׁנָה	house (m.)	בַּיִת
girl	יַלְדָּה	boy	יֶלֶד
family	מִשְׁפָּחָה	tree	עֵץ
blessing	בְּרָכָה	name	שֵׁם
law	תּוֹרָה	light	אוֹר

44

C. *Prepositions* (unattached to words)

from	מִן	to	אֶל
with (beings)	עִם	upon, over	עַל
without	בְּלִי	under, instead of	תַּחַת

GRAMMAR AND NOTES

Study the following phrases carefully:

a good man	אִישׁ טוֹב
a good woman	אִשָּׁה טוֹבָה
a good name	שֵׁם טוֹב
a good year	שָׁנָה טוֹבָה

In English, the adjective remains unchanged, whether we use it with a masculine or feminine noun, in singular or plural. Thus we say a good son, a good daughter, good sons, good daughters.

In Hebrew, as in French, every adjective changes in agreement with its noun. Thus we say עֵץ יָפֶה *a beautiful tree*, but בְּרָכָה גְּדוֹלָה *a great blessing*.

Notice that the adjective always comes after the noun, e.g., שֵׁם טוֹב *a good name*. From Lesson 6 we know that feminine nouns usually end with הָ; accordingly, in order to form the feminine of adjectives, we add הָ to the masculine form, e.g., טוֹב (m.) טוֹבָה (f.) *good*; יָפֶה (m.) יָפָה (f.) *beautiful*. Note that the feminine of יָפֶה is יָפָה (not יְפֵהָה).

The definite article –הַ followed by a strong dagesh is joined to *both* the noun and the adjective. In other words, if the noun is definite, the adjective must also be made definite by adding the definite article ה. Thus in Hebrew, הַסֵּפֶר הַקָּדוֹשׁ *the holy book* is the same as *the book, the holy (one)*; similarly, הַשָּׁנָה הַטּוֹבָה *the good year* is the same as *the year, the good (one)*.

Observe the feminine of the following adjectives:

	Feminine	*Masculine*
holy, sacred	קְדוֹשָׁה	קָדוֹשׁ
big, great, large	גְּדוֹלָה	גָּדוֹל
white	לְבָנָה	לָבָן

	Feminine	*Masculine*
black	שְׁחוֹרָה	שָׁחוֹר
young	צְעִירָה	צָעִיר

The feminine forms of these adjectives display an important rule in Hebrew grammar: If a masculine noun or adjective of two syllables begins with the long vowel qamats (ָ) as in גָּדוֹל, לָבָן, etc., the qamats (ָ) is changed into a shva (ְ) when the feminine is formed.

STUDY HINTS

1. Read aloud Group A of the Vocabulary at the beginning of this lesson. First read the masculine and then the feminine nouns. Learn Groups B and C of the Vocabulary, following the instructions in Study Hint 1 in Lesson 6.
2. When dealing with the adjectives for the first time, bear in mind the following:
   a. Adjectives always follow the noun they qualify.
   b. Adjectives change in gender and number to agree with the noun.
   c. If the noun is definite, the adjective must also be definite.
3. Note carefully that the feminine of יָפֶה and קָטָן is יָפָה and קְטַנָּה respectively.
4. The rule about the feminine is very important. You will often come across this rule in one form or another. So make sure you understand it now.
5. Translate Exercise C orally. In 3, note that לַיְלָה is masculine, although ending in הָ . Translate the odd-numbered items in Exercises D and E orally. Remember that בַּיִת is masculine.
6. Exercise G, Rapid Reading (See instructions in Study Hint 5, Lesson 5.)

EXERCISES

A. Write the feminine of the following words:

4. לָבָן

5. זָקֵן

6. אִישׁ

1. טוֹב

2. גָּדוֹל

3. יָפֶה

9. דּוֹד   7. יֶלֶד

10. סוּס   8. קָדוֹשׁ

B. Give the feminine of the following:

1. אִישׁ צָעִיר

2. הַיֶּלֶד הַקָּטָן

3. הַדּוֹד הַזָּקֵן

4. הַסּוּס הַלָּבָן

5. הַיֶּלֶד הַטּוֹב

Samaritans with ancient Pentateuch on Mount Gerizim.

A modern seven-branched menorah (candlestick) erected in Jerusalem.

Judean Wilderness. On Jericho Road, halfway between Jerusalem and Jericho.

C. Translate the following into English:

1. מִשְׁפָּחָה גְדוֹלָה

2. אִשָּׁה צְעִירָה וְיָפָה

3. לַיְלָה טוֹב

4. בְּלִי הַבַּת הַצְּעִירָה

5. מִן־הַבַּיִת אֶל־הַשָּׂדֶה

6. אֶל־הַבַּיִת הַקָּטֹן

7. עַל הַסּוּס הַלָּבָן

8. בְּלִי הַמִּשְׁפָּחָה

9. תַּחַת עֵץ

10. עִם הַיֶּלֶד וְעִם הַיַּלְדָּה

D. Rewrite the following nouns and add an appropriate adjective. Translate the result into English: (*Example: a big horse* סוּס גָּדוֹל – סוּס)

1. בֵּן

2. הַבַּת

3. הַבַּיִת

4. בַּיִת

5. שָׂדֶה

6. הַתּוֹרָה

7. לַיְלָה

8. הַמִּשְׁפָּחָה

9. הַסֵּפֶר

10. אִישׁ

E. Translate the following into Hebrew:

1. from a house
2. good evening
3. without the book
4. the little door
5. under the house

6. on the horse
7. with the son
8. a holy book
9. a great blessing
10. the great day

F. Translate the following into Hebrew:

1. with a great man
2. to a big house*
3. from the big house*
4. and a beautiful day
5. without the white book

6. from an old uncle
7. on the black horse
8. under a little tree
9. without a bad name
10. with the beautiful daughter

G. Rapid Reading: Read the following over and over again until you can read it correctly and fluently (Lev. 19:18, Gen. 27:22).

וְאָהַבְתָּ לְרֵעֲךָ כָּמוֹךָ

הַקֹּל קוֹל יַעֲקֹב

וְהַיָּדַיִם יְדֵי עֵשָׂו

---

*Note that *a house*, although ending in ת, is masculine.

Lesson Eight

QUIZ ON LESSONS 1—7

Before proceeding with Lesson 9, do the following quiz without referring to Lessons 1-7. Remember to include the vowels when composing Hebrew. When you have completed the test, check your answers with Lessons 1-7 and correct your mistakes in red ink.

A. Check the correct answer(s) in the following statements:

 1. The Hebrew alphabet consists of
   (a) 28 letters.   (c) 22 letters.
   (b) 26 letters.   (d) 24 letters.
 2. Hebrew is a Semitic language. The following also belong to the Semitic group of languages:
   (a) Persian.   (c) Sanskrit.
   (b) Arabic.   (d) Aramaic.
 3. The Hebrew alphabet consists of
   (a) vowels or consonants.   (c) vowels only.
   (b) vowels and consonants.   (d) consonants only.

B. Answer True or False to the following:

   _____1. In most Hebrew words the accent is on the last syllable.
   _____2. Sometimes Hebrew words may be divided at the end of a line.
   _____3. The original Hebrew Bible had no vowels.
   _____4. Hebrew letters have numerical values.
   _____5. All feminine nouns in the singular end in ה‍ or ת.

_____6. Adjectives may be placed either before or after the noun they qualify.

_____7. Adjectives *never* take the definite article.

_____8. The roots of most Hebrew verbs consist of three letters.

C. Check the correct answers:

1. Which of the following vowels are long?

   (a) וֹ   (c) ֱ

   (b) ֲ   (d) ִ

2. The number of vowels in Hebrew is

   (a) 8.   (c) 10.

   (b) 9.   (d) 12.

3. Which of the following nouns are masculine?

   (a) שָׂדֶה   (c) דֶּלֶת

   (b) לַיְלָה   (d) בַּיִת

4. Which of the following letters are gutturals?

   (a) א   (c) כ

   (b) ח   (d) ע

5. Which of the following definite articles are correctly pointed?

   (a) הַמֶּלֶךְ   (c) הַדֶּלֶת

   (b) הַשִּׁיר   (d) הַלַּיְלָה

D. Pick out and explain the odd item in the following:

   Example: תּוֹרָה, שִׁיר, דֶּלֶת, אִשָּׁה

   In this group, the third word, שִׁיר, is the odd item because it is masculine, whereas the remaining words are feminine. (Some of the groups suggest two or three possibilities.)

   1. פ, מ, ב, ג

      Odd: _____because _____

      _____

   2. ל, מ, פ, כ

      Odd: _____because _____

      _____

Mosaic floor showing the seven-branched candelabrum, palm branch, incense shovel, and ram's horn at the Hamet-Tiberias synagogue, third to fourth century.

3. מ, ק, ב, ע

    Odd: _____because _____

---

4. (ָ) ,(ֶ) ,(וֹ) ,(ֹ)

    Odd: _____because _____

---

5. (ֵ) ,(ֱ) ,(וֹ) ,(ֶ)

    Odd: _____because _____

---

6. Arabic, Aramaic, Akkadian, Persian

    Odd: _____because _____

E. Write the Hebrew for the following words and indicate their gender by writing
(f.) for feminine and (m.) for masculine to the right of the word.

    For example: Rachel רָחֵל   (f.)

    1. law _____   evening _____

       woman _____   voice _____

       night _____   field _____

2. daughter _____   door _____

    name_____   light _____

    house _____   tree _____

F. Translate the following into Hebrew:

a beautiful day   _____

the good horse   _____

to the old king   _____

and the young son   _____

from the big house   _____

with a small horse under the tree   _____

a great light from the house   _____

Lesson Nine
NOUNS WITH ADJECTIVES; PLURALS; DEFINITE ARTICLE

VOCABULARY

A. *Masculine Nouns and Adjectives*

Plural		Singular
דּוֹדִים	uncle	דּוֹד
סוּסִים	horse	סוּס
שִׁירִים	song	שִׁיר
גּוֹיִם	nation	גּוֹי
כּוֹכָבִים	star	כּוֹכָב
טוֹבִים	good	טוֹב
רָעִים	bad	רַע
יָפִים	beautiful	יָפֶה
גְּדוֹלִים	big, great, large	גָּדוֹל
קְטַנִּים	small, little	קָטָן
זְקֵנִים	old (beings)	זָקֵן

B. *Feminine Nouns and Adjectives*

Plural		Singular
דּוֹדוֹת	aunt	דּוֹדָה
סוּסוֹת	mare	סוּסָה
מְנוֹרוֹת	lampstand	מְנוֹרָה
בְּרָכוֹת	blessing	בְּרָכָה
מִצְווֹת	commandment	מִצְוָה

53

Plural		*Singular*
פָּרוֹת	cow	פָּרָה
בְּהֵמוֹת	animal	בְּהֵמָה
מַמְלָכוֹת	kingdom	מַמְלָכָה
טוֹבוֹת	good	טוֹבָה
רָעוֹת	bad	רָעָה
יָפוֹת	beautiful	יָפָה
גְּדוֹלוֹת	big, great, large	גְּדוֹלָה
קְטַנּוֹת	small, little	קְטַנָּה
צְעִירוֹת	young	צְעִירָה

C. *Nouns With Adjectives*

Masculine

black horses	סוּסִים שְׁחוֹרִים
small trees	עֵצִים קְטַנִּים
the good songs	הַשִּׁירִים הַטּוֹבִים
the large stars	הַכּוֹכָבִים הַגְּדוֹלִים

Feminine

black mares	סוּסוֹת שְׁחוֹרוֹת
good commandments	מִצְווֹת טוֹבוֹת
the beautiful lampstands	הַמְּנוֹרוֹת הַיָּפוֹת
the white cows	הַפָּרוֹת הַלְּבָנוֹת

GRAMMAR AND NOTES

1. *Nouns With Adjectives*

   From studying the above list you have probably observed that

   a. masculine nouns and adjectives generally form their plurals by adding ים-
      to the singular (Group A);

   b. feminine nouns and adjectives generally form their plurals by dropping the
      ה- and adding וֹת- to the singular (Group B); and

   c. as stated in Lesson 7, the adjective always follows the noun and always
      agrees with the noun it qualifies (Group C), for example:

   a large horse   סוּס גָּדוֹל

a large mare	סוּסָה גְדוֹלָה
large horses	סוּסִים גְּדוֹלִים
large mares	סוּסוֹת גְּדוֹלוֹת

Note: If the noun is defined, i.e., is used with the definite article –הַ the adjective must also be defined.

The irregular plural forms of the following nouns are frequently used and must be learned well:

Plural		*Singular*
	Masculine	
אֲנָשִׁים	man	אִישׁ
דְּבָרִים	word, thing	דָּבָר
עַמִּים	people	עַם
רָאשִׁים	head	רֹאשׁ
יָמִים	day	יוֹם
בָּתִּים	house	בַּיִת
בָּנִים	son	בֵּן
אָבוֹת	father	אָב
לֵילוֹת	night	לַיְלָה
	Feminine	
נָשִׁים	woman	אִשָּׁה
בָּנוֹת	daughter	בַּת
שָׁנִים	year	שָׁנָה

2. *Dual Number*

There is another kind of plural, known as the *dual number*, for the double members of the body (eyes, hands, feet, and ears) and for other objects found in pairs. We shall study this form in Lesson 22.

3. *Definite Article Before the Letters* א, ע, *and* ר

In Lesson 6 we learned that the definite article is prefixed to the noun and followed by a strong dagesh: סֵפֶר *book,* הַסֵּפֶר *the book*. The guttural letters and the letter ר do not take a dagesh. When the definite article is added to a word beginning with any of the letters א, ע, or ר, we use –הָ (with qamats). We use the long vowel (ָ) instead of the short vowel (ַ) to "compensate" for the loss of the dagesh, for example:

הָאוֹר/אוֹר, הָאִישׁ/אִישׁ, הָעֶרֶב/עֶרֶב, הָרֶגֶל/רֶגֶל

Note: This rule does not apply to a word beginning with עָ (i.e., the letter ע with the vowel qamats). We shall deal again with the definite article in future lessons (see Lesson 28).

STUDY HINTS

1. The important points to remember in this lesson are the following:

   a. Masculine nouns and adjectives generally form their plural by adding ־ִים to their singular.

   b. The plural of feminine nouns and adjectives generally ends in ־וֹת.

   c. The adjective always follows the noun and agrees with it in gender and number.

   Learn the examples given in Vocabulary Sections A, B, and C.

Aerial view of Jerusalem.

2. Note the use of the definite article before words beginning with א, ר or ע. The definite article is הָ (not הַ).

3. Grammar and Notes 3 should raise no difficulty. You have only to bear in mind what you have already studied about the peculiarities of the gutturals and the letter ר. (See Lesson 5, Notes 14 and 15.)

4. Note carefully any peculiarities in the formation of the plural noun or adjective (e.g., עַמִּים/עַם, אֲנָשִׁים/אִישׁ).

EXERCISES

A. Write the plural of the following words, with vowels:

Regular Plural Forms

5. הַבְּרָכָה הַגְּדוֹלָה	1. סוּס גָּדוֹל
6. הַסּוּס הַלָּבָן	2. שִׁיר טוֹב
7. מְנוֹרָה שְׁחוֹרָה	3. הַדּוֹדָה הַטּוֹבָה
8. הַנְּבִיאָה הָרָעָה	4. נָבִיא צָעִיר

Irregular Plural Forms

6. בֵּן קָטָן	1. אִישׁ זָקֵן
7. בַּת טוֹבָה	2. הָאִשָּׁה הַיָּפָה
8. הַלַּיְלָה הָרַע	3. עַם גָּדוֹל
9. הַשָּׁנָה הַטּוֹבָה	4. הַיּוֹם הָרַע
10. הָאָב הַגָּדוֹל	5. הַבַּיִת הַלָּבָן

B. Translate the following into English:

6. הָעַמִּים הַגְּדוֹלִים	1. נָשִׁים זְקֵנוֹת
7. בָּתִּים לְבָנִים	2. הָאָבוֹת הַגְּדוֹלִים
8. הַיָּמִים הַטּוֹבִים	3. בָּנוֹת קְטַנּוֹת
9. שָׁנִים טוֹבוֹת	4. הַבָּנִים הַצְּעִירִים
10. אֲנָשִׁים זְקֵנִים	5. הַלֵּילוֹת הָרָעִים

Write the Hebrew for the following:

1. the white horses
2. great blessings

3. the little kingdoms
4. good families

5. the beautiful trees
6. the evil sons
7. small daughters

8. white houses
9. good women
10. the holy days

D. Write the plural of the following words with the definite article:
(*Example*: הָעַמִּים, עַם)

11. בַּיִת	6. סוּסָה	1. לַיְלָה
12. יוֹם	7. שָׁנָה	2. אִישׁ
13. כּוֹכָב	8. אָב	3. בַּת
14. דָּבָר	9. אִשָּׁה	4. נָבִיא
15. רֹאשׁ	10. מַמְלָכָה	5. עֵץ

E. Rapid Reading (Gen. 2:4):

אֵלֶּה תוֹלְדוֹת הַשָּׁמַיִם וְהָאָרֶץ בְּהִבָּרְאָם
בְּיוֹם עֲשׂוֹת אֱלֹהִים אֶרֶץ וְשָׁמָיִם.

F. Transliteration of Rapid Reading (Exercise E).
Line 1: ēl-leh tô-ledôt hash-shā-ma-yim
veha-ʾā-reṣ behib-bā-reʾām
Line 2: be-yôm ʿaśôt elō-him e-reṣ veshā-mā-yim.

Lesson Ten
SEGHOLATE NOUNS; PERSONAL PRONOUNS; PRESENT TENSE OF *TO BE*

VOCABULARY

A. *Segholate Nouns*
   Masculine

Group A

Plural		Singular
עֲרָבִים	evening	עֶרֶב
יְלָדִים	boy	יֶלֶד
גְּבָרִים	man	גֶּבֶר
מְלָכִים	king	מֶלֶךְ
כְּרָמִים	vineyard	כֶּרֶם
סְפָרִים	book	סֵפֶר
בְּגָדִים	garment	בֶּגֶד
גְּשָׁמִים	rain	גֶּשֶׁם
כְּלָבִים	dog	כֶּלֶב

Group B

נְעָרִים	youth, boy, child	נַעַר
נְחָלִים	wadi, river	נַחַל
שְׁעָרִים	gate	שַׁעַר
פְּרָחִים	bud, flower	פֶּרַח
זְבָחִים	sacrifice	זֶבַח

59

Feminine

Plural			Singular
נְפָשׁוֹת	soul, life		נֶפֶשׁ
אֲרָצוֹת	land		אֶרֶץ
דְּלָתוֹת	door		דֶּלֶת

B. *Personal Pronouns*

Plural			Singular	
we	אֲנַחְנוּ	I		אֲנִי, אָנֹכִי
you (m.)	אַתֶּם	thou, you (m.)		אַתָּה
you (f.)	אַתֶּן	thou, you (f.)		אַתְּ
they (m.)	הֵם	he, it* (m.)		הוּא
they (f.)	הֵן	she, it* (f.)		הִיא

GRAMMAR AND NOTES

1. *Segholate Nouns*

   In a large number of two-syllable masculine and feminine Hebrew nouns, the first syllable is accented and the second has the vowel seghol ( ). Grammarians usually call such nouns *segholates* (Group A of the vocabulary). However, when the second or third letter of the segholate noun is a guttural, the second syllable is pointed with pataḥ ( ) instead of seghol ( ) (Group B).

   Note: This is another peculiarity of the gutturals; they usually take pataḥ ( ) rather than any other vowel. (What are the other peculiarities of the guttural? See Lesson 9.)

   The segholate masculine nouns form their plural according to the following pattern: XXXיִם

boys	יֶלֶד – יְלָדִים	kings	מֶלֶךְ – מְלָכִים
books	סֵפֶר – סְפָרִים	boys	נַעַר – נְעָרִים
flowers	פֶּרַח – פְּרָחִים	gates	שַׁעַר – שְׁעָרִים

---

*The pronoun *it* is translated הוּא or הִיא according to whether it stands for a masculine or feminine noun.

2. *Present Tense of the Verb "To Be"*

Hebrew has no special words for the English verbs *am, are,* or *is*. They are understood from the context. Thus, the present tense of *to be* is not expressed in Hebrew. When you translate into English, you must add the appropriate English verb.

Moses is a man	מֹשֶׁה אִישׁ
I am the mother	אֲנִי הָאֵם
you are the father	אַתָּה הָאָב
we are old	אֲנַחְנוּ זְקֵנִים
thou art the man	אַתָּה הָאִישׁ
the king is old	הַמֶּלֶךְ זָקֵן
But: the old king	הַמֶּלֶךְ הַזָּקֵן

3. *Biblical Word List*

Beginning with this lesson you will find a special list of the most frequently used biblical words in most lessons. The words given here are only those which occur in the Hebrew Bible from 100 to 5000 times. After mastering

View of the Mount of Olives from the Temple Mount area.

about 150 to 200 words, you should be able to read and understand easy narrative passages from the Bible without much difficulty.

Study the Biblical Word List with the following suggestions in mind:

- Read each word aloud five times and note its meaning.
- Cover the English column and see if you know the meaning of the Hebrew words.
- Cover the Hebrew column and test yourself by giving the Hebrew orally.
- Finally, cover the Hebrew column and write the Hebrew corresponding to the English word, with vowels.

Biblical Word List One (nouns occurring 500 to 5000 times)

father	אָב
man, Adam	אָדָם
brother	אָח
man	אִישׁ

STUDY HINTS

1. Read the Vocabulary aloud several times. You can hardly fail to observe that the nouns in Group A and Group B have the same pattern. They belong to a large number of words known as *segholates*. (See Grammar and Notes 1.) Note that the pattern of all plurals is XXX‑ים. Thus, the plural of the word דֶּגֶל (banner, flag), being a segholate, is דְּגָלִים. There are very few exceptions to this rule. Study carefully the feminine plural of the segholates.

2. The accent of all the segholate nouns in the singular is on the first syllable. It is very important to remember this when reading aloud.

3. Another important peculiarity of the gutturals is explained in Section 1; namely, the gutturals take the vowel pataḥ rather than any other vowel. (What are the two other peculiarities of the gutturals? See Lesson 5, Notes 14 and 15.)

4. Memorize the personal pronouns and learn to write them correctly.

5. The present tense of *to be* is not expressed in Hebrew. Thus, אַתָּה הָאִישׁ *you are the man*, הָאִישׁ זָקֵן *the man is old*. However, *the old man* is written הָאִישׁ הַזָּקֵן.

6. The list of frequently used biblical words is extremely useful. After learning 150 to 200 of these words, you should be able to read the narrative sections of the Hebrew Bible without much difficulty. When studying the Biblical Word List, follow the instructions in this lesson.

EXERCISES

A. Write the plural of the following:

6. כֶּלֶב		1. סֵפֶר	
7. יֶלֶד		2. נַחַל	
8. נַעַר		3. שַׁעַר	
9. בֶּגֶד		4. פֶּרַח	
10. כֶּרֶם		5. מְנוֹרָה	

B. Write the personal pronouns from memory, without vowels.

C. Translate the following into English:

11. גֶּשֶׁם טוֹב		1. אֲנִי הָאִישׁ	
12. הַכֶּלֶב הַקָּטָן		2. הַבֶּגֶד הַיָּפֶה	
13. נַחַל גָּדוֹל		3. הַבֶּגֶד יָפֶה	
14. הַכֶּרֶם הַיָּפֶה		4. הָעֵץ קָטָן	
15. נַעַר צָעִיר		5. הַסּוּסָה הַטּוֹבָה	
16. הַשַּׁעַר הַגָּדוֹל		6. הַדֶּלֶת קְטַנָּה	
17. הַדֶּלֶת הַלְּבָנָה		7. אֶרֶץ טוֹבָה	
18. סוּס שָׁחוֹר		8. הַנֶּפֶשׁ הָרָעָה	
19. הַמֶּלֶךְ הַצָּעִיר		9. זֶבַח גָּדוֹל	
20. הַסֵּפֶר טוֹב		10. הַשַּׁעַר הַגָּדוֹל	

D. Write the Hebrew in Exercise C in the plural.

E. Translate the following into Hebrew, without vowels:

1. a good book
2. the good book

3. the book is good

4. the books are good

5. the good books

6. the black garment is on the white book

7. the horse is under the tree

8. the boy is without the books

9. a great day, the day is great, the great day

10. a good year, the good year, good morning

F. Translate the following into English:

6. אִשָּׁה טוֹבָה   1. הַשַּׁעַר הַגָּדוֹל

7. הָאִשָּׁה נְבִיאָה   2. הַשְּׁעָרִים הַגְּדוֹלִים

8. הַנָּשִׁים הַטּוֹבוֹת   3. הַשְּׁעָרִים גְּדוֹלִים

9. הַנָּשִׁים הַיָּפוֹת   4. הַסְּפָרִים הַקְּדוֹשִׁים

10. שָׁנָה טוֹבָה   5. הַסְּפָרִים קְדוֹשִׁים

G. Rapid Reading (Gen. 5:1):

זֶה סֵפֶר תּוֹלְדוֹת אָדָם

בְּיוֹם בְּרֹא אֱלֹהִים אָדָם

בִּדְמוּת אֱלֹהִים עָשָׂה אֹתוֹ.

"Hassidim" in the streets of Jerusalem.

REVIEW OF LESSONS 1-10

IMPORTANT POINTS TO REMEMBER

1. Main peculiarities of the Semitic language. (Lesson 1)
   a. Guttural letters
   b. Three root-letters for most verbs
   c. Meaning dependent on form or pattern of words
   d. Pronominal suffixes to nouns, verbs, and prepositions
   e. Common basic vocabulary

2. The following are among the Semitic languages:
   Hebrew, Arabic, Ugaritic, Aramaic, Samaritan, Syriac, Phoenician, and Ethiopic. (Lesson 1)

3. The Hebrew alphabet consists of 22 letters, all consonants. Each letter has a numerical value. (Lesson 2)

4. Five letters have final forms: ץ, ף, ן, ם, ך (Lesson 2)

5. Six letters take a dagesh at the beginning of the word or a syllable: ב, ג, ד כ, פ, ת conveniently pronounced *BeGaD KeFaT*. (Lesson 2)

6. Hebrew is read and written from right to left. (Lesson 2)

7. Hebrew has several scripts. Those used today are the Square and the Cursive. (Lesson 4)

8. Hebrew has four guttural letters: ע, ח, ה, א (Lesson 5)

9. Hebrew has five long vowels: (ָ), (ֵ), (ִי), (וֹ), (וּ).

10. Hebrew has five short vowels: (ַ), (ֶ), (ִ), (ָ), (ֻ).

11. Shva (ֽ) is used to denote the absence of a vowel. (Lesson 5)

12. There are two different pronunciations: Sephardi, or Spanish, and Ashkenazi, or German. (Lesson 5)

13. The gutturals never begin a word with a shva; instead they take a ḥataph. (Lesson 5)

14. The gutturals and the letter ר do not take a dagesh. (Lesson 5)

15. There are two kinds of dageshes: *lene* or weak (for the letters ת, פ, כ, ד, ג, ב only), and *forte* or strong. (Lesson 5)

16. The definite article is ה, followed by a strong dagesh, e.g., יוֹם, הַיּוֹם. (Lesson 6)

17. Before the gutturals א, ע, and the letter ר, הָ is used instead of הַ. This rule does not apply to a word beginning with עָ, e.g., הָאָרֶץ, הָראשׁ, הָעִיר. (Lesson 9)

18. A word ending in הָ- or ת- is feminine. Exceptions are לַיְלָה (m.) and בַּיִת (m.). (Lesson 6)

19. To form the feminine of an adjective, add הָ- to the masculine form, e.g., גָּדוֹל, גְּדוֹלָה. (Lesson 7)

20. An adjective changes in agreement with the noun it qualifies, e.g., אִישׁ זָקֵן, אִשָּׁה זְקֵנָה. (Lesson 7)

21. An adjective follows the noun it qualifies. (Lesson 7)

22. The definite article is added to the adjective if the noun is definite, e.g., הָאִישׁ הַזָּקֵן. (Lesson 7)

23. The masculine plural of nouns and adjectives ends in ים-, e.g., סוּס, סוּסִים (noun), גָּדוֹל, גְּדוֹלִים (adj.). (Lesson 9)

24. The feminine plural of nouns and adjectives ends in וֹת-, e.g., תּוֹרָה, תּוֹרוֹת (noun), גְּדוֹלָה, גְּדוֹלוֹת (adj.). (Lesson 9)

25. The personal pronouns are as follows: (Lesson 10)

אֲנִי, אַתָּה, אַתְּ, הוּא, הִיא

אֲנַחְנוּ, אַתֶּם, אַתֶּן, הֵם, הֵן

26. Segholate nouns are of two syllables; the first is accented and the second has a seghol (ֶ). If the second or third letter of the segholate noun is a guttural, the second syllable will have a (ַ). (Lesson 10) e.g.,

כֶּרֶם, מֶלֶךְ, יֶלֶד, נַעַר, פֶּרַח, זֶבַח

27. The plural of segholate masculine nouns follows the pattern of XֳXֶXׅים.
    (Lesson 10)

boy	יֶלֶד – יְלָדִים	boy, youth	נַעַר – נְעָרִים
book	סֵפֶר – סְפָרִים	river, wadi	נַחַל – נְחָלִים
vineyard	כֶּרֶם – כְּרָמִים	flower	פֶּרַח – פְּרָחִים

28. The present tense of *to be* is not expressed in Hebrew. The words *are, am,*
    and *is* are understood from the context. (Lesson 10)

מֹשֶׁה אִישׁ Moses is a man.

הוּא הַנָּבִיא הַגָּדוֹל He is the great prophet.

אַתָּה הַמֶּלֶךְ You are the king.

29. Note the difference between the following: (Lesson 10)

אִישׁ זָקֵן an old man

Masada, a natural fortress on the shores of the Dead Sea. Intended as a last place of refuge, a function it fulfilled in 40 B.C. and again in A.D. 73.

the old man   הָאִישׁ הַזָּקֵן

the man is old   הָאִישׁ זָקֵן

30. Biblical Word List One. (Lesson 10) אָב, אָדָם, אָח, אִישׁ

STUDY HINTS

1. The purpose of this review lesson is to make sure that you understand the material in Lessons 1-10. When you study the Important Points to Remember at the beginning of this lesson, always refer to the lessons given in parentheses. As you do Exercise A, you will be able to judge for yourself whether you have really benefited from this course. If you have faithfully followed the instructions given in previous assignments, you should be able to do at least 80 per cent of Exercise A correctly.

2. You must know all of the Vocabulary in Lessons 1-10, from Hebrew to English and from English to Hebrew. Be certain you are able to write the Hebrew words with the vowel points carefully inserted.

EXERCISES

A. Write groups of three examples each (do not use the words in this lesson) to illustrate the rules given in this lesson under

    1. Point 16 (*Example:* סוּס, הַסּוּס)
    2. Point 17
    3. Point 20
    4. Point 19
    5. Point 23 (*Example:* סוּס, סוּסִים)
    6. Point 21
    7. Point 24
    8. Point 26
    9. Point 27
   10. Point 29

B. Review all the vocabulary in Lessons 1-10.

Lesson Twelve

VERBS

VOCABULARY

In common with other Semitic languages, the roots of *almost all* Hebrew verbs consist of three letters, conveniently pronounced as follows:

to eat	אָכַל	to finish	גָּמַר
to learn	לָמַד	to give	נָתַן
to write	כָּתַב	to guard, keep	שָׁמַר
to say	אָמַר	to walk, go	הָלַךְ
to give birth	יָלַד	to shut	סָגַר
to sit	יָשַׁב	to stand	עָמַד

Note: The root has three consonants without any reference to vowels.

GRAMMAR AND NOTES

1. *Qal*

   The simple form of the verb is known as *Qal* קַל meaning *light* or *easy,* i.e., *simple.* In this course we shall study the Qal form only. The verbs given in the Vocabulary above are all of the Qal pattern.

2. *Tenses*

   Strictly speaking, Biblical (i.e., Classical) Hebrew has no tense similar to those used in English, French, or German. The action is regarded as either *complete* or *incomplete.* Hence most scholars prefer to call a completed

69

action *perfect* and an incompleted action *imperfect*. The perfect tense, in Hebrew, expresses a completed action. Thus, לָמַ֫דְתִּי means *I studied, I have studied, I had studied, I had been studying* or *I did study*. The imperfect tense expresses an incomplete action: אֶסְגֹּר *I shall shut, I shall be shutting*. For the time being, translate the imperfect as a simple future.

3. *Active Participles of Qal Verbs*

   Let us first consider the following active participles before we study one of the chief ways of expressing present action.

eating	אוֹכֵל	finishing	גּוֹמֵר
learning	לוֹמֵד	giving	נוֹתֵן
writing	כּוֹתֵב	going, walking	הוֹלֵךְ
saying	אוֹמֵר	shutting	סוֹגֵר
sitting	יוֹשֵׁב	standing	עוֹמֵד

These Hebrew words are active participles, corresponding to the English present participles ending in *-ing*. The participles are usually formed by inserting the vowel (וֹ) after the first letter of the root and pointing the second letter of the root with (ֵ). The accent is on the last syllable. *Example:* כּוֹתֵב, לוֹמֵד, יוֹשֵׁב. The participles may be written without (וֹ): הֹלֵךְ or הוֹלֵךְ *going*, נֹתֵן or נוֹתֵן *giving*.

   The participles agree with the nouns and pronouns associated with them. They may precede or follow the subject.

The man is walking.	הָאִישׁ הוֹלֵךְ or הוֹלֵךְ הָאִישׁ
The son is writing.	הַבֵּן כּוֹתֵב or כּוֹתֵב הַבֵּן
The boys are learning.	הַיְלָדִים לוֹמְדִים* or לוֹמְדִים הַיְלָדִים*
The women are eating.	הַנָּשִׁים אוֹכְלוֹת or אוֹכְלוֹת הַנָּשִׁים

   The following are the principal parts of the active participles of the Qal verb:

---

*When the definite article is attached to a word beginning with יְ (the letter י with shva), the dagesh is usually omitted.

	Plural			Singular	
	Feminine	*Masculine*	*Feminine*		*Masculine*
	לוֹמְדוֹת	לוֹמְדִים	לוֹמֶדֶת לוֹמְדָה †		לוֹמֵד
	כּוֹתְבוֹת	כּוֹתְבִים	כּוֹתֶבֶת כּוֹתְבָה †		כּוֹתֵב

4. *Biblical Word List Two* (verbs occurring 500 to 5000 times)

to eat	אָכַל	to speak	דִּבֶּר
to say	אָמַר	to be	הָיָה
to come	בּוֹא		

STUDY HINTS

1. The term *Classical Hebrew* refers mainly to Biblical Hebrew as distinct from post-Biblical (i.e., Modern) Hebrew. (In Classical Hebrew the tenses are designated as either perfect or imperfect, whereas in Modern Hebrew they are called past or future.)

2. This is one of the most important lessons so far. It is of utmost importance that you learn the root of each Hebrew verb you study. Master thoroughly the three letters of the root of each verb. All other verbs and nouns associated by meaning with this verb will also contain this root. Note, for example, the root ילד, which in the Qal means *to bear* or *to bring forth*: יֶלֶד *boy,* יַלְדָּה *girl,* תּוֹלְדוֹת *generations,* מוֹלֶדֶת *kindred,* יַלְדוּת *childhood, youth.*

3. The use of the Hebrew tenses is relatively easy to learn. You have probably observed, for instance, that *I had eaten, I ate, I did eat,* or *I have eaten* are all expressed in Hebrew as אָכַלְתִּי. Thus, many different types of past action are expressed by the Hebrew perfect tense. This reductionism is largely true of the Hebrew imperfect tense in expressing various types of future (and sometimes also present) action.

4. In English we have only one pattern of present active participles ending in *-ing*. In Hebrew these participles agree with the nouns and pronouns associated with them. At the present stage of your work, study each participle

---

† This form is not frequently used.

together with its four principal parts as given in this lesson. Remember that the feminine singular form may end in ‎ת- or ‎ה-, either of which is an indication of the feminine gender.

5. Follow the instructions given in Lesson 10 for the Biblical Word List.

EXERCISES

A. Write the Hebrew of the following verbs, without vowels:

1. to finish
2. to eat
3. to write
4. to say
5. to sit

6. to go
7. to learn
8. to shut
9. to give
10. to stand

B. Give the principal parts of the active participles of the following verbs: (*Example:* ‎לוֹמֵר—לָמַר, לוֹמֶרֶת, לוֹמְרִים, לוֹמְרוֹת)

1. נָתַן   3. אָמַר   5. גָּמַר   7. הָלַךְ

2. עָמַר   4. יָשַׁב   6. כָּתַב   8. סָגַר

C. Read aloud and translate the following into English:

1. הָאִישׁ יוֹשֵׁב תַּחַת הָעֵץ עִם הַכֶּלֶב.
2. הַבַּת לוֹמֶרֶת מִן־הַסֵּפֶר.
3. הוֹלֶכֶת הָאִשָּׁה מִן־הַבַּיִת אֶל־הַשָּׂדֶה.
4. יוֹשְׁבִים הַנְּבִיאִים עַל־הָעֵץ.
5. הַמִּשְׁפָּחָה הוֹלֶכֶת מִן־הַשַּׁעַר אֶל־הַבַּיִת.

D. With which of the roots in the Vocabulary of this lesson are the following words closely associated?

1. food
2. saying
3. a letter (in correspondence)
4. to teach
5. standing

6. boy
7. to feed
8. settle
9. lock
10. gift

E. Rapid Reading (Ex. 3:1, Ex. 20:8, Gen. 1:31):

וּמֹשֶׁה הָיָה רֹעֶה אֶת־צֹאן יִתְרוֹ

חֹתְנוֹ כֹּהֵן מִדְיָן

זָכוֹר אֶת־יוֹם־הַשַּׁבָּת לְקַדְּשׁוֹ

וַיְהִי־עֶרֶב וַיְהִי־בֹקֶר יוֹם הַשִּׁשִּׁי

Lesson Thirteen

THE PRESENT TENSE; MORE ABOUT GENDER

VOCABULARY

Qal Simple Verbs

Singular

I go, I am going, I do go	m.	אֲנִי הוֹלֵךְ
I go, I am going, I do go	f.	אֲנִי הוֹלֶכֶת
you (thou) go, you are going, you do go	m.	אַתָּה הוֹלֵךְ
you (thou) go, you are going, you do go	f.	אַתְּ הוֹלֶכֶת
he (it) goes, he is going, he does go	m.	הוּא הוֹלֵךְ
she (it) goes, she is going, she does go	f.	הִיא הוֹלֶכֶת

Plural

we go, we are going, we do go	m.	אֲנַחְנוּ הוֹלְכִים
we go, we are going, we do go	f.	אֲנַחְנוּ הוֹלְכוֹת
you go, you are going, you do go	m.	אַתֶּם הוֹלְכִים
you go, you are going, you do go	f.	אַתֶּן הוֹלְכוֹת
they go, they are going, they do go	m.	הֵם הוֹלְכִים
they go, they are going, they do go	f.	הֵן הוֹלְכוֹת

GRAMMAR AND NOTES

1. *Present Tense*

Memorize the above conjugation of the present tense. (Strictly speaking,

74

there is no present tense in Biblical Hebrew, but the idea of present action can be conveyed in various ways.) From the above you can see that the idea of present action is expressed by using the personal pronouns with the appropriate participle; for example, הִיא הוֹלֶכֶת we (m.) eat, אֲנַחְנוּ אוֹכְלִים she goes, אַתֶּן עוֹמְדוֹת you (f. pl.) stand.

Recite the present tense of the following verbs:

to give	נָתַן	to learn	לָמַד
to guard, keep	שָׁמַר	to say	אָמַר

2. More About Gender

In Lesson 6 we noted that most nouns ending in ה֖ or ת– are feminine. Also, nouns indicating females are feminine, even though they do not end in ה֖ or ת–; for example, אֵם *mother*, רָחֵל *ewe, Rachel*. Study carefully the following classes of nouns.

a. Nouns denoting organs of the body that come in pairs are usually feminine:

hand	יָד	eye	עַיִן
foot	רֶגֶל	ear	אֹזֶן

b. The following parts of the body are also feminine:

finger	אֶצְבַּע	rib	צֵלָע
tooth	שֵׁן	bone	עֶצֶם

c. Most of the members of the body that do not come in pairs are masculine:

mouth	פֶּה	nose	אַף
head	רֹאשׁ	back	גַּב

Exceptions: לָשׁוֹן *tongue* and בֶּטֶן *belly* are feminine, whereas שַׁד *breast* is masculine.

3. Biblical Word List Three. (Verbs occurring 500 to 5000 times)

to give birth	יָלַד
to go out	יָצָא
to go	הָלַךְ
to know	יָדַע
to sit	יָשַׁב

STUDY HINTS

1. Memorize the present tense of הָלַךְ *to go.* Write it from memory and check your work with the Vocabulary in this lesson. For the meaning of the term Qal, see Lesson 12.

2. Recite in the plural the present tense of the *Qal* verbs in the Vocabulary.

3. After learning the material on gender thoroughly, give at sight the gender of the following:

לָשׁוֹן	יָד	אַף
אֶצְבַּע	עַיִן	רֹאשׁ
פֶּה	גַּב	רֶגֶל
אֹזֶן	צֵלָע	שֵׁן

Can you give the English for these parts of the body? If not, review the material. In future lessons, do not hesitate to refer to this material on the parts of the body.

4. Remember to study the Biblical Word Lists in accordance with the instructions in Lesson 10.

5. Strictly speaking, there is no special form for the present tense in Hebrew. In Biblical Hebrew the present tense does not exist as such. In Modern Hebrew, however, the present tense is formed by using the personal pronouns with the appropriate participles.

EXERCISES

A. Write the present tense, in full, of יָשַׁב *to sit* and אָמַר *to say,* with vowels.

B. After studying the following list, carefully identify the gender, state the reason for using that gender, and translate the list into English.

7. בַּיִת		1. מְנוֹרָה	
8. פֶּה		2. בֶּטֶן	
9. רֶגֶל		3. יָד	
10. שֵׁן		4. יוֹם	
11. לָשׁוֹן		5. לַיְלָה	
12. רֹאשׁ		6. אֵם	

C. In each of the following cases give the correct form of the adjective:

1. אִישׁ (צָעִיר, צְעִירָה)
2. מְנוֹרָה (יָפֶה, יָפָה)
3. יָד (גָּדוֹל, גְּדוֹלָה)
4. פֶּה (קָטָן, קְטַנָּה)
5. לָשׁוֹן (רַע, רָעָה)
6. לַיְלָה (טוֹב, טוֹבָה)
7. בַּיִת (לָבָן, לְבָנָה)
8. רֶגֶל (קָטָן, קְטַנָּה)

The Qumran caves, site of the Dead Sea Scroll findings.

D. Give the appropriate form in the present tense of each of the following verbs:

6. הֵן (אכל)		1. אֲנִי (גמר) (m. & f.)	
7. אֲנַחְנוּ (הלך) (m. & f.)		2. אַתֶּם (למד)	
8. הִיא (כתב)		3. הֵם (עמד)	
9. אַתֵּן (סגר)		4. הוּא (הלך)	
10. אַתָּה (נתן)		5. אַתְּ (ישב)	

E. Read aloud and translate the following into English:

1. אֲנַחְנוּ אוֹכְלִים מִן־הַיָּד אֶל־הַפֶּה.

2. הוֹלְכוֹת הַיְלָדוֹת אֶל־הַשָּׂדֶה.

3. רָחֵל לוֹמֶדֶת מִן־הַסֵּפֶר.

4. אוֹכֵל אֲנִי עִם הָאִישׁ הַזָּקֵן.

5. אוֹכֵל הַבֵּן הַקָּטָן עִם הָאֵם וְעִם הָאָב.

6. הָאֵם עוֹמֶדֶת וְהָאָב יוֹשֵׁב.

F. Translate the following into Hebrew, without vowels:

1. The man says, "I am the king."
2. The black dog is standing under the tree.
3. The uncles are learning and the aunts are writing the songs.
4. "You are good boys," says the prophet.
5. Sarah (שָׂרָה) is a good woman. She gives flowers to the girls.

G. Give an adjective in Hebrew with vowel points which agrees with each of the following nouns and translate: (*Example:* הָרֶגֶל, הָרֶגֶל הַגְּדוֹלָה the big foot)

7. לֵילוֹת	1. אֲנָשִׁים
8. הַשֵּׁם	2. נָשִׁים
9. הָאֵם	3. הַבָּנוֹת
10. הַיָּד	4. הַבַּיִת
11. שָׂדֶה	5. אֶרֶץ
12. הַפֶּה	6. דֶּלֶת

Lesson Fourteen

MORE ABOUT VERBS

VOCABULARY

Nouns			*Verbs*	
mountain	(הָרִים)	הַר	to remember	זָכַר
land, earth	(אֲדָמוֹת)	אֲדָמָה	to ride	רָכַב
tent	(אֹהָלִים)	אֹהֶל	to go out	יָצָא
messenger, angel	(מַלְאָכִים)	מַלְאָךְ	to sit	יָשַׁב
eternity, world	(עוֹלָמִים)	עוֹלָם	to know	יָדַע
apple (m.)	(תַּפּוּחִים)	תַּפּוּחַ	to see	רָאָה
tablet (m.)	(לוּחוֹת)	לוּחַ	to steal	גָּנַב
city (f.)*	(עָרִים)	עִיר		

GRAMMAR AND NOTES

1. *The Basic Verbal Pattern*

   The Hebrew verbs are simpler than, for instance, the French or German verbs. As stated in Lesson 12, almost all Hebrew verbs have roots consisting of three letters, without any reference to the vowels; for example, למד *to learn,* כתב *to write,* נתן *to give.* These verbs usually have only one basic meaning.

   When we conjugate a verb, we add certain letters at the beginning (prefixes), in the middle (infixes), or at the end of the root (suffixes). These prefixes, infixes, or suffixes that are added to the root are the same for all

---

*Note that *city* עִיר is feminine.

79

verbs; for example, למד *to learn,* לָמַדְתִּי *I have learned,* ישב *to sit,* יָשַׁבְתִּי *I sat,* ידע *to know,* יָדַעְתִּי *I knew.* There are no exceptions.

Similarly, we form the first person singular of the imperfect tense by prefixing –א, for example, גמר *to finish;* אֶגְמֹר *I shall finish;* כתב *to write,* אֶכְתֹּב *I shall write.*

The Medieval Hebrew term for *verb* is פֹּעַל (biblical meaning, *action, deed*). Since the root of Hebrew verbs consists of three letters, Jewish grammarians in the Middle Ages called the first root-letter of any verb פ' הַפֹּעַל. (The פ is the first letter of the word פֹּעַל; similarly, the second root-letter is ע' הַפֹּעַל, and the third is ל' הַפֹּעַל.)

Observe the following verbs:

a. אמר   to say
b. ישב   to sit
c. בוא   to come
d. ראה   to see

In a, א, the first letter of the root, is called פ' הַפֹּעַל. In b, י is also פ' הַפֹּעַל. In c, ו is ע' הַפֹּעַל, and א is ל' הַפֹּעַל. In d, ה is called ל' הַפֹּעַל.

At this stage we are concerned with the *regular* or *strong* verbs. These are verbs which preserve their three root-letters throughout the different verbal inflections: שמר *to keep, guard,* שָׁמַרְתִּי *I guarded,* אֶשְׁמֹר *I shall guard,* אֲנִי שׁוֹמֵר *I am guarding.* The root-letters שמר are preserved in all forms. But from the verb קום *to get up, to rise,* we form קַמְתִּי *I got up* (the letter ו is omitted). Such verbs which do not preserve the root-letters throughout are known as *weak* verbs. Generally a verb containing י, ו, ה, א, or an initial נ, is a weak verb. We shall deal fully with these verbs in future lessons.

The verbs ילד, ישב, and ידע have the letter י as the first letter (פ' הַפֹּעַל) of their respective roots. Such verbs are פ"י (*pe-yud*) verbs. This means that the first letter of the root or the פ of the פֹּעַל (verb) is *yud.* Similarly, the verbs קנה, בנה, and ראה are known as ל"ה (*lamed-he*) verbs because the third letter of their roots is ה. The verbs קום and שוב are called ע"ו (*ayin-waw*) verbs. The verbs נפל and נתן are called פ"נ (*peh-nun*) verbs, and so forth. Remember, only י, ו, ה, א, and initial נ are considered for this purpose.

2. *The Perfect (Past) Tense*

In Lesson 13 we studied the present tense and the Qal simple verbs. The perfect tense is formed by adding certain suffixes to the root letters. These suffixes are the same for the perfect tense of all Hebrew verbs.

The suffixes are used to indicate person, gender, and number. It is not necessary, therefore, to use the personal pronouns in the perfect (or in the imperfect, for that matter). *Example:* אָמַ֫רְתִּי *I said*. Here the suffix תִּי– contains the personal pronoun אֲנִי *I*.

Notes:

a. The personal pronouns may be used for special emphasis: יָדַ֫עְתָּ *you* (m., sg.) *knew*, but אַתָּה יָדַ֫עְתָּ *it is you who knew*. הָאִשָּׁה . . . הִיא נָתְנָה לִי מִן־הָעֵץ "The woman . . . it was she who gave me from the tree" (referring to Eve, in Genesis 3:12).

b. The Hebrew perfect expresses several of the past tenses used in English or French.

   Example: אָמַ֫רְתִּי *I said*, or *I have said, I had said, I did say*.

c. Learn the perfect tense of the strong verb שָׁמַר *to guard, keep,* as given below.

Singular

I have kept, I kept, I had kept, etc.	m. or f.	שָׁמַ֫רְתִּי	(אֲנִי)
you have kept, etc.	m.	שָׁמַ֫רְתָּ	(אַתָּה)
you have kept, etc.	f.	שָׁמַרְתְּ	(אַתְּ)
he (it) has kept, etc.	m.	שָׁמַר	(הוּא)
she (it) has kept, etc.	f.	שָׁמְרָה	(הִיא)

Plural

we have kept, etc.	m. or f.	שָׁמַ֫רְנוּ	(אֲנַ֫חְנוּ)
you have kept, etc.	m.	שָׁמַרְתֶּם	(אַתֶּם)
you have kept, etc.	f.	שָׁמַרְתֶּן	(אַתֶּן)
they have kept, etc.	m.	שָׁמְרוּ	(הֵם)
they have kept, etc.	f.	שָׁמְרוּ	(הֵן)

(1) Note that the qamats in the first syllable becomes shva in the second person plural (m. and f.). This is due to the shifting of the accent from the second to the third syllable:

שְׁמַרְתֶּן but שְׁמַרְתֶּם and שָׁמַרְנוּ

(2) The root in itself does not constitute a word. It is therefore generally convenient to pronounce it with the vowels of the third person singular, masculine, of the perfect tense—this usually being the simplest of all verbal forms.

3. *Biblical Word List Four* (nouns occurring 500 to 5000 times)

land, earth (f.)	אֶרֶץ
one	אֶחָד
Lord*	יְהֹוָה (אֲדוֹנָי)*
God (do not confuse אֵל *God* with אֶל *to*)	אֱלֹהִים, אֵל

STUDY HINTS

1. When learning the perfect tense you must be able to distinguish between the root of the verb and the suffixes. Observe that in this conjugation, the root of the verb consists of three letters only, e.g. שׁמר. The other letters constitute the suffixes. These suffixes are the same for all the perfect tenses of the Hebrew verb. There are no exceptions. It is therefore necessary to learn the suffixes carefully and be able to recognize them. Once you know them, you will always be able to use them with any verb.

2. Bear in mind that the Hebrew perfect tense expresses several past tenses in other languages. אָכַלְנוּ may mean *we ate, we have eaten, we had eaten, we did eat* or *we have been eating*.

3. Note the shva in the second person plural, m. and f. שָׁמַרְתִּי *I guarded,* שָׁמַרְתָּ

---

*When writing the Hebrew for *Lord*, use the form יְהֹ. The word for Jehovah or Yahweh in Hebrew is יְהֹוָה but it is read אֲדֹנָי (*adonay*), meaning "my Lord." The four Hebrew letters יהוה are often referred to as the *tetragrammaton*, and observing Jews will not use the real name for "Lord" due to reverence.

you guarded, but שְׁמַרְתֶּם (m.) and שְׁמַרְתֶּן (f.) *you guarded* (pl.).

4. In Biblical Word List Four note that 'ה stands for יְהוָה or אֲדֹנָי *the Lord*. This usage is postbiblical, originating from the third commandment "Thou shalt not bear the name of the Lord, thy God, in vain."

5. Note carefully the plural forms of the nouns in the Vocabulary. For example, the plural of הַר is הָרִים and the plural of לוּחַ is לוּחוֹת (not הָרִים and לוּחִים as one might expect). Both are masculine nouns.

6. Note that both עִיר *city* and אֶרֶץ *land, country* are feminine.

EXERCISES

A. Recite the perfect tense of the following verbs:

יָשַׁב	to sit	גָּמַר	to finish
לָמַד	to learn	כָּתַב	to write
רָכַב	to ride		

B. Write the perfect and present tense of the following verbs:

סָגַר	to shut	זָכַר	to remember

C. Translate the following into English:

11. לָמְדָה	6. סָגַרְתָּ	1. יָשְׁבָה
12. שְׁמַרְתְּ	7. הָלְכָה	2. כָּתַב
13. יְשַׁבְתֶּן	8. עָמַדְנוּ	3. לָמַדְנוּ
14. לָמְדוּ	9. אָמַר	4. סָגַרְתִּי
15. גָּמַרְתִּי	10. כְּתַבְתֶּם	5. גָּנְבוּ

D. Write the perfect tense of the following verbs, as indicated:

6. הִיא (הלך)		1. אֲנִי (ישב)	
7. אַתְּ (עמד)		2. אֲנַחְנוּ (כתב)	
8. אַתֶּם (ידע)		3. הֵם (למד)	
9. הֵן (הלך)		4. אַתָּה (סגר)	
10. אֲנַחְנוּ (אמר)		5. אַתֵּן (זכר)	

E. Read aloud and translate the following into English:

‏1. שָׁמַר הַכֶּלֶב עַל־הַבַּיִת וְעַל־הַיֶּלֶד.

‏2. הָלַכְתִּי אֶל־הַשָּׂדֶה בְּלִי הַסְּפָרִים.

‏3. יָשְׁבָה הַיַּלְדָה תַּחַת הָעֵץ וְלָמְדָה.

‫4. אֲנַחְנוּ אָכַלְנוּ מִן־הָעֵץ.‬

‫5. כָּתְבוּ הַגְּבָרִים דְּבָרִים עַל־הַלּוּחַ.‬

‫6. אָמַר הָאִישׁ שָׁלוֹם וְיָצָא מִן־הַבַּיִת.‬

‫7. זָכַר הַנָּבִיא בְּרָכָה מִן־הַסֵּפֶר.‬

F. Write the following in Hebrew, without vowels:

1. without

2. to eat

3. to know

4. blessing

5. to remember

G. Write the following in English:

‫1. אֶצְבַּע‬

‫2. אֹהֶל‬

‫3. אֲדָמָה‬

‫4. לוּחַ‬

‫5. לָשׁוֹן‬

Lesson Fifteen

DEMONSTRATIVE PRONOUNS AND ADJECTIVES

VOCABULARY

to hear	שָׁמַע	this (m.)	זֶה
to take	לָקַח	this (f.)	זֹאת
to do, make	עָשָׂה	these (m. or f.)	אֵלֶּה
to send	שָׁלַח	law	תּוֹרָה
to forget	שָׁכַח	work	מְלָאכָה
to forgive	סָלַח	people	עַם
to read, call	קָרָא	gift	מִנְחָה

GRAMMAR AND NOTES

1. *The Demonstrative Pronouns "This" and "These"*

    Read the following carefully:

this is a man	זֶה אִישׁ
this is the man	זֶה הָאִישׁ
this is a woman	זֹאת אִשָּׁה
this is a lamp	זֹאת מְנוֹרָה
these are books	אֵלֶּה סְפָרִים
these are the books	אֵלֶּה הַסְּפָרִים
these are the words (or things)	אֵלֶּה הַדְּבָרִים
these are the commandments	אֵלֶּה הַמִּצְוֹות

85

Hence, it is clear that

זֶה *this* is used for masculine nouns.

זֹאת *this* is used for feminine nouns.

אֵלֶּה *these* is used for masculine and feminine nouns.

2. *The Demonstrative Adjectives*

Compare the following:

1.	this is a boy	זֶה יֶלֶד
	this boy	הַיֶּלֶד הַזֶּה
	this little boy	הַיֶּלֶד הַקָּטָן הַזֶּה
2.	this is the blessing	זֹאת הַבְּרָכָה
	this blessing	הַבְּרָכָה הַזֹּאת
	this great blessing	הַבְּרָכָה הַגְּדוֹלָה הַזֹּאת
3.	these are the horses	אֵלֶּה הַסּוּסִים
	these horses	הַסּוּסִים הָאֵלֶּה
	these beautiful horses	הַסּוּסִים הַיָּפִים הָאֵלֶּה
4.	these are the commandments	אֵלֶּה הַמִּצְווֹת
	these commandments	הַמִּצְווֹת הָאֵלֶּה
	these good commandments	הַמִּצְווֹת הַטּוֹבוֹת הָאֵלֶּה

Thus, the demonstrative adjectives הַזֶּה, הַזֹּאת, and הָאֵלֶּה always follow the noun and are used with nouns having the definite article. When demonstrative adjectives are used, the word order is the reverse of that in English:

this book	הַסֵּפֶר הַזֶּה
this great book	הַסֵּפֶר הַגָּדוֹל הַזֶּה

as if we translate *the book, the great (one), the this (one)*.

Similarly,

this great blessing	הַבְּרָכָה הַגְּדוֹלָה הַזֹּאת
these small girls	הַיְלָדוֹת הַקְּטַנּוֹת הָאֵלֶּה

3. *General Review of Adjectives, Demonstrative Adjectives, and Demonstrative Pronouns.*

	a good man	אִישׁ טוֹב
	the good man	הָאִישׁ הַטּוֹב
	the man is good	הָאִישׁ טוֹב
Or:	good is the man	טוֹב הָאִישׁ

this is the man	זֶה הָאִישׁ
this man	הָאִישׁ הַזֶּה
this is a good man	זֶה אִישׁ טוֹב
this good man	הָאִישׁ הַטּוֹב הַזֶּה
this man is good	הָאִישׁ הַזֶּה טוֹב

4. *Biblical Word List Five* (nouns occurring 500 to 5000 times)

mountain	הַר
mountains	הָרִים
year	שָׁנָה
people	עַם
city	עִיר

STUDY HINTS

1. The vocabulary words in this lesson are frequently used and, hence, should be well mastered. Learn the correct vowels that go with these words. The feminine singular form of the demonstrative pronoun is זֹאת, with a silent א in the middle. Very few words in the Hebrew language contain unpronounced letters. Some examples of words containing unpronounced letters are ראֹשׁ *head*, צאֹן *sheep*, and שְׂמֹאל *left*.

2. There is a great difference between זֶה הַיֶּלֶד, which is a complete sentence and means *this is the boy*, and הַיֶּלֶד הַזֶּה which is not a sentence and simply means *this boy*. In the first example, זֶה is a pronoun, and in the second it is an adjective. If the phrase הַיֶּלֶד הַזֶּה is literally translated, it would be *the boy, the this (one)*; here הַזֶּה is an adjective; therefore it takes the article along with the noun it modifies.

   Note the order of the words when using demonstrative adjectives. The word order in Hebrew is the reverse of that in English. Thus, *this great book* in Hebrew is *the book, the great (one), the this (one)*,

   הַסֵּפֶר הַגָּדוֹל הַזֶּה

3. Study carefully the General Review of Adjectives, Demonstrative Adjectives and Demonstrative Pronouns. Take any similar constructions such as אִישׁ זָקֵן, מְנוֹרָה יָפָה, etc. for further practice.

   Example: הָאִישׁ הַזָּקֵן, אִישׁ זָקֵן

4. Study the Biblical Word List carefully. For instructions, see Lesson 10.

EXERCISES

A. Read aloud and translate the following into English:

1. הַסֵּפֶר הַזֶּה

2. הָאִשָּׁה הַזֹּאת

3. הָעִיר הַזֹּאת

4. הַיֶּלֶד הַזֶּה

5. הַסְּפָרִים הָאֵלֶּה

6. זֶה הַבַּיִת

7. הַסּוּסוֹת הָאֵלֶּה

8. זֹאת הָאִשָּׁה

9. הַסְּפָרִים הָאֵלֶּה

10. אֵלֶּה הַדְּבָרִים

B. Read aloud and translate the following into English:

1. הָאִישׁ טוֹב

2. הָאִישׁ הַטּוֹב

3. הָאִישׁ הַזֶּה

4. הָאִישׁ הַטּוֹב הַזֶּה

5. זֶה הָאִישׁ הַטּוֹב

6. הַבָּנִים הָאֵלֶּה טוֹבִים

7. הַיֶּלֶד הַצָּעִיר הַזֶּה

8. זֶה הַנָּבִיא הַזָּקֵן

9. אֵלֶּה הָאֲנָשִׁים הַטּוֹבִים

10. הַיְלָדִים הָאֵלֶּה קְטַנִּים

Archaeological excavations near the southern wall of the Temple Mount in Jerusalem.

C. Rewrite the Hebrew in Exercise B in the feminine gender.

D. Translate the following into Hebrew:

1. this king
2. the great king
3. this great king
4. This king is great.
5. This great king went to the city.
6. this law
7. this holy law
8. This law is holy.
9. This is the holy law.
10. This prophet read from this holy law.

E. (Review) Give the Hebrew for the following, with vowels:

1. we remembered
2. you (m. sg.) remembered
3. he went
4. she has eaten
5. she is eating
6. she has forgotten
7. you (f. pl.) forgive
8. I have sent
9. they have known
10. you (m. pl.) are hearing
11. we remember
12. I (f.) am eating
13. I have eaten
14. you (f. sg.) are going
15. we (m.) remember
16. she has gone out
17. they (f.) are standing
18. they (m.) are writing
19. they have gone
20. he took

F. Translate the following into English:

1. אֲנַחְנוּ רוֹכְבִים עַל־הַסּוּס הַזֶּה.

2. הָלַךְ הַכֶּלֶב מִן־הַבַּיִת אֶל־הַכֶּרֶם.

3. אֵלֶּה הַפָּרוֹת. הֵן יוֹצְאוֹת מִן־הַשָּׂדֶה הַזֶּה.

4. רָכְבָה הָאִשָּׁה הַזֹּאת עַל־הַסּוּס הַגָּדוֹל הַזֶּה.

5. נָתְנָה הָאִשָּׁה תַּפּוּחִים אֶל הַיְלָדוֹת הָאֵלֶּה.

Lesson Sixteen

PREPOSITIONS

VOCABULARY

A. *Unattached Prepositions*

with (somebody)	עִם	upon, on	עַל
after	אַחֲרֵי	from	מִן
by the side of, near	אֵצֶל	under, instead of	תַּחַת
between, among	בֵּין	without	בְּלִי
opposite	מוּל	until	עַד
before, in front of, ago (of time)	לִפְנֵי	like, as	כְּמוֹ

B. *Prefixed Prepositions*

from	־מֶ ,־מִ	in, with, at	־בְּ
for, to	־לְ	like, as	־כְּ

GRAMMAR AND NOTES

1. *Unattached Prepositions*

Memorize the prepositions in Group A above. These prepositions are used as separate words and are sometimes known as *simple prepositions*.

Examples:

like water	כְּמוֹ מַיִם	without water	בְּלִי מַיִם
near the house	אֵצֶל הַבַּיִת	between the trees	בֵּין הָעֵצִים

90

after the flood	אַחֲרֵי הַמַּבּוּל	until the morning	עַד הַבֹּקֶר
before the king	לִפְנֵי הַמֶּלֶךְ	to the river	אֶל־הַנַּחַל
with the daughter	עִם הַבַּת	under the house	תַּחַת הַבַּיִת

2. *Prefixed Prepositions*

The prepositions in Group B are used as prefixes only and cannot stand alone. They are, therefore, usually known as prefixed, or inseparable, prepositions.

a. There are only four inseparable prepositions:

-לְ *to, for* (shortened from אֶל *to*)

-בְּ *in, with* (possibly shortened from בַּיִת *house*, which carries the idea of being "inside" or "within")

-כְּ *like* (possibly from כֵּן *yes, so*, or from כְּמוֹ *like*)

-מִ *from* (shortened from מִן *from*)

Note that when -מִ is used, it is followed by a dagesh to compensate for the loss of the nun, e.g., מִמֶּלֶךְ *from a king*. This will be discussed in detail in Lesson 27.

b. The sign under the first three prepositions, בְּ, כְּ, and לְ is shva.

to a day	לְיוֹם	like a man	כְּאִישׁ
in a night	בְּלַיְלָה	in a year	בְּשָׁנָה
to Joseph	לְיוֹסֵף	like Moses	כְּמֹשֶׁה

If the word begins with a shva, then -בְּ, -כְּ, and -לְ become -בִּ, -כִּ, and -לִ, respectively, because words in Hebrew never begin with two shvas, for example:

for a blessing	לִבְרָכָה	(not לְבְרָכָה)
like Samuel	כִּשְׁמוּאֵל	(not כְּשְׁמוּאֵל)
in books	בִּסְפָרִים	(not בְּסְפָרִים)

c. If the first letter of the word has a dagesh (i.e., begins with one of the letters בגד כפת), the dagesh is omitted when -בְּ, -כְּ, or -לְ are used.

house	בַּיִת	to a house	לְבַיִת
door	דֶּלֶת	like a door	כְּדֶלֶת

d. Study the following:

the book	הַסֵּפֶר
in the book	בַּסֵּפֶר (ב+הַ+סֵּפֶר for)

the man	הָאִישׁ
to the man	(for לְ+הָ+אִישׁ) לָאִישׁ

From the above illustrations it is clear that when one of the prepositions
–בְּ, –כְּ, or –לְ is placed before a noun with a definite article, the –ה is
omitted and the preposition assumes the vowel of the definite article.
Thus:

the horse	הַסּוּס	to the horse	לַסּוּס
the father	הָאָב	like the father	כָּאָב
the evening	הָעֶרֶב	in the evening	בָּעֶרֶב

(In בָּעֶרֶב, for instance, the ב takes the vowel [ָ] of the definite article הָ
which is omitted.)

e.   Read the following carefully:

in a good book	בְּסֵפֶר טוֹב
in the good book	בַּסֵּפֶר הַטּוֹב
like a great blessing	כִּבְרָכָה גְדוֹלָה
like the great blessing	כַּבְּרָכָה הַגְּדוֹלָה

Thus, if the inseparable prefix contains the definite article (e.g., כַּבְּרָכָה
like the blessing), the adjective must also be made definite: e.g.,
כַּבְּרָכָה הַגְּדוֹלָה.

3.   *Biblical Word List Six* (nouns occurring 500 to 5000 times)

way (f.)	דֶּרֶךְ
heart	לֵב
voice	קוֹל
head	רֹאשׁ
seven	שִׁבְעָה

STUDY HINTS

1.   There is no need to point out the importance of the prepositions. Therefore,
learn thoroughly the Vocabulary at the beginning of this lesson. You should
already know at least six prepositions. (See Lesson 7.)

2.   The prepositions in Group A are used as separate words and hence they are
often referred to as "unattached." Those in Group B can never be used alone;
they must be used as prefixes.

Mount Tabor, one of the high places in lower Galilee.

3. The prefix –מִ *from*, given in Grammar and Notes 2a, is not used in the same
   way as the other three inseparable prepositions.

4. Grammar and Notes 2b is important. Since *no* word in Hebrew may begin
   with two shvas, the first of the two is changed to *hiriq*; for example, *with a
   blessing* is written בִּבְרָכָה (not בְּבְרָכָה).

5. Distinguish carefully between לְבַיִת *to a house* and לַבַּיִת *to the house*; כְּאִישׁ
   like a man and כָּאִישׁ *like the man*.

6. Grammar and Notes 2e must be carefully learned. *In the good book* should
   be translated into Hebrew as *in the book, the good (one)*. Notice that when
   the noun is defined, the adjective must also be defined.

7. We cannot emphasize enough the importance of studying the Biblical Word
   Lists thoroughly. Experience has shown that by the time you finish this
   course, you should be able to read easy biblical narrative selections.

8. Review the vocabulary in Lessons 1-16 and find out how much vocabulary you have mastered. If you know 80 per cent, or four out of five, you have achieved a good average.

EXERCISES

A. Give the English for the following:

11. מִן	6. מוּל	1. בְּלִי
12. אֵצֶל	7. אֶל	2. עַל
13. כְּ-	8. עַד	3. אַחֲרֵי
14. לְ-	9. בֵּין	4. לִפְנֵי
15. כְּמוֹ	10. *עִם	5. מֶ-
16. *בְּ-		

B. Translate the following into English:

15. בְּבַיִת	8. מִשָּׁנָה	1. כְּתַפּוּחַ
16. בַּבַּיִת	9. לְשָׁנָה	2. כַּתַּפּוּחַ
17. לִבְרָכָה	10. כְּאִישׁ	3. לְיוֹם
18. לַבְּרָכָה	11. כָּאִישׁ	4. לַיּוֹם
19. כִּמְנוֹרָה	12. מִבַּיִת	5. מִיּוֹם
20. כַּמְּנוֹרָה	13. לְשָׁנָה	6. בְּעִיר
	14. לְבַיִת	7. בָּעִיר

C. Translate the following into Hebrew:

1. a horse, the horse
2. for the horse
3. for a blessing
4. like a horse
5. like the big horse
6. to a woman, for the woman
7. for this good woman

8. a father, the father
9. like the father
10. like a father
11. like the good father
12. in the house, in the white house
13. to the good father
14. for a father

---

*עִם *with* when used with beings: עִם הַיֶּלֶד *with the boy*, עִם הַסּוּסִים *with the horses*; -בְּ *with* when used with inanimate things: בַּיָּד *with the hand* (יָד, by itself, is not a being).

D. Translate the following into English:

1. הָלְכוּ הָאֲנָשִׁים אֶל־הַכְּרָמִים הָאֵלֶּה.

2. יָצְאָה הַפָּרָה הַזֹּאת מִן־הַשַּׁעַר הַקָּטָן.

3. הָלַךְ הַסּוּס אַחֲרֵי הַכֶּלֶב הַשָּׁחוֹר.

4. עָמַד הַבֵּן הַקָּטָן לִפְנֵי הָאֲנָשִׁים כְּמֶלֶךְ גָּדוֹל.

5. הָלַךְ הַבֵּן עִם הָאִישׁ הַזָּקֵן אֶל־הַשָּׁעַר.

6. יְשַׁבְתֶּם תַּחַת הָעֵץ הַזֶּה.

7. הָלְכוּ הָאֲנָשִׁים הַזְּקֵנִים עַד הָהָר הַגָּדוֹל.

8. עָמְדוּ הַסּוּסִים מוּל הַבַּיִת הַזֶּה.

9. הָלְכוּ בֵּין הָעֵצִים הָאֵלֶּה וְזָכְרוּ יָמִים טוֹבִים.

10. יָשַׁב הַנָּבִיא הַזֶּה עַל־הָהָר הַזֶּה וְקָרָא בַּסֵּפֶר.

E. Translate the following into Hebrew, without vowels (use the unattached prepositions):

1. to this house
2. after the woman
3. from this great city*
4. before this year
5. among these white garments
6. until this day
7. without water
8. upon the horse
9. with the king
10. under the trees

F. Translate the following into English:

1. קָרָא בַּסֵּפֶר הַזֶּה.

2. נָתַן אֱלֹהִים אִשָּׁה לָאָדָם.

3. הָלַךְ אֶל־הַבַּיִת הַיָּפֶה הַזֶּה.

4. כָּתַבְתִּי אֶל־הַמֶּלֶךְ.

5. הָלַכְנוּ אֶל־הָעִיר הַזֹּאת.

6. לָמַדְתָּ בַּבַּיִת כְּמוֹ יֶלֶד טוֹב.

7. יָשַׁבְתָּ בַּשָּׂדֶה אֵצֶל הַנָּחַל.

8. הָלַךְ בַּלַּיְלָה אֶל־הָעִיר.

9. עָמְדוּ בַּגֶּשֶׁם מוּל הַשַּׁעַר.

10. יָצְאָה הַבַּת מִן־הַבַּיִת.

G. Write 10 sentences of at least four words each. Include in each sentence a verb, a noun, and an adjective and use one of the following prepositions:

לִפְנֵי, אֵצֶל, עַד, אַחֲרֵי, בֵּין, מוּל, עַל, מִן, תַּחַת, בְּלִי, עִם

Example:

הָלַךְ הָאִישׁ הַגָּדוֹל אֶל־הַשָּׂדֶה הַזֶּה.

_____

*Note that *city* עִיר is feminine.

H. Translate the following into English:

1. ‏הָלְכָה הָאִשָּׁה בָּעֶרֶב בֵּין הָעֵצִים.

2. ‏יָצָא הָאִישׁ עִם הַסּוּס מִן־הָעִיר הַזֹּאת.

3. ‏עָמְדוּ הָאֲנָשִׁים בַּגֶּשֶׁם מוּל הַשַּׁעַר הַזֶּה.

4. ‏אָמְרוּ הַזְּקֵנִים אֶל הָעָם: שָׁלַח ה׳ נָבִיא גָּדוֹל. אֶל־הָעִיר הָרָעָה הַזֹּאת.

Lesson Seventeen

RELATIVE PRONOUNS; HEBREW PARTICLE אֵת

VOCABULARY

to see	רָאָה	who, whom	אֲשֶׁר
who?	מִי	which, that	אֲשֶׁר
dream (m.)	חֲלוֹם (חֲלוֹמוֹת)	flood	מַבּוּל
heaven	שָׁמַיִם	people	עַם
blessed	בָּרוּךְ	here is, here are, behold	הִנֵּה
ark	תֵּבָה	God	אֵל, אֱלֹהִים
Moses	מֹשֶׁה	garden	גַּן
Jerusalem	יְרוּשָׁלַיִם	bread	לֶחֶם
Joseph	יוֹסֵף	rib (f.)	צֵלָע (צְלָעוֹת)
prayer	תְּפִלָּה	likeness, form	תְּמוּנָה

GRAMMAR AND NOTES

1. *The Relative Pronouns "Who," "Whom," "Which," "That"*

Study the following carefully:

The man *who* went to the house	הָאִישׁ אֲשֶׁר הָלַךְ אֶל־הַבַּיִת
The woman *who* ate from the tree	הָאִשָּׁה אֲשֶׁר אָכְלָה מִן־הָעֵץ
The prayers *which* (are) in the book	הַתְּפִלּוֹת אֲשֶׁר בַּסֵּפֶר
The song *which* (is) to David (i.e., David's song)	הַשִּׁיר אֲשֶׁר לְדָוִד
The horses *which* stood under the tree	הַסּוּסִים אֲשֶׁר עָמְדוּ תַּחַת הָעֵץ

97

The songs *which* you have heard   הַשִּׁירִים אֲשֶׁר שָׁמַעְתָּ

Who is the boy *whom* you took   מִי הַיֶּלֶד אֲשֶׁר לָקַחְתָּ אֶל־הַגָּן?

     to the garden?

From the above examples, you have probably observed that the relative pronoun אֲשֶׁר is invariable for persons and things, for all genders and numbers.

The relative pronoun may sometimes be omitted in English. This is not permitted in Hebrew. As in French, the relative pronoun must always be used, for example:

The book I took from the prophet   הַסֵּפֶר אֲשֶׁר לָקַחְתִּי מִן־הַנָּבִיא

A contracted form of אֲשֶׁר, used as a prefix, is –שְׁ (followed by a dagesh if the following letter is not a guttural or ר). It cannot stand as a separate word:

the house that he built   הַבַּיִת שֶׁבָּנָה

the man who ate   הָאִישׁ שֶׁאָכַל

the book which he took   הַסֵּפֶר שֶׁלָּקַח

The contracted form –שְׁ is not frequently employed in Biblical Hebrew. Although there are a few occurrences of it in Judges, it is most frequently found in later writings such as Ecclesiastes and The Song of Songs.

In due course we shall learn more about the use of אֲשֶׁר.

2. *The Hebrew Particle אֵת or אֶת־*

This is one of the most frequently used words in the Bible. Read the following sentences:

Adam ate an apple.   אָכַל אָדָם תַּפּוּחַ

Adam ate the apple.   אָכַל אָדָם אֶת־הַתַּפּוּחַ

Joseph saw a dream.   רָאָה יוֹסֵף חֲלוֹם

Joseph remembered the dream.   זָכַר יוֹסֵף אֶת־הַחֲלוֹם

In these sentences, the verb *ate* and *saw* are transitive, and therefore they can take a direct object. *Apple* is the direct object of *ate*, and *dream* is the direct object of *saw*. When the word אֵת is used, the direct object is used *with* the definite article.

I took the books.   לָקַחְתִּי אֶת־הַסְּפָרִים

God created the man.   בָּרָא אֱלֹהִים אֶת־הָאָדָם

Study the following carefully:

The man saw. (*man* is the subject)   רָאָה הָאִישׁ or הָאִישׁ רָאָה

He saw the man. (*man* is the direct object)   רָאָה אֶת־הָאִישׁ

The boy remembered. (*boy* is the subject)   זָכַר הַיֶּלֶד or הַיֶּלֶד זָכַר

He remembered the boy. (*boy* is the direct object)   זָכַר אֶת־הַיֶּלֶד

Who took the book? (*Who* is the subject)   ?מִי לָקַח אֶת־הַסֵּפֶר

David took the book.   דָּוִד לָקַח אֶת־הַסֵּפֶר

Whom did the father take? (*Whom* is the   ?אֶת־מִי לָקַח הָאָב
    direct object)

The father took the son.   לָקַח הָאָב אֶת־הַבֵּן

From the above examples it is clear that

a. אֶת־ governs the direct object when it is defined. (In the sentence next to the last, אֶת־מִי *whom* refers to a definite person.)

b. When translating a simple sentence into Hebrew, you may begin either with the subject or the verb. (Example: *the man took* is either לָקַח הָאִישׁ or הָאִישׁ לָקַח. In Classical Hebrew, however, the verb usually precedes the noun.)

Study the following sentences:

The man remembered Joseph.   זָכַר הָאִישׁ אֶת־יוֹסֵף

The king built Jerusalem.   בָּנָה הַמֶּלֶךְ אֶת־יְרוּשָׁלַיִם

The particle אֶת־ is generally used whenever the direct object of the verb is known or defined. In the first sentence above, *Joseph* is a proper noun and therefore represents a definite person. Similarly, *Jerusalem* in the second sentence represents a definite location. Hence אֶת־ is added when these sentences are used in Hebrew.

Notes:

a. There is no English word for the Hebrew אֶת־; it is merely an indication that the following word is a defined direct object of the verb. It cannot be translated into English.

b. In Classical (Biblical) Hebrew, אֵת is pointed with sereh (ֵ). When it is hyphenated, it is pointed with seghol אֶת־: אֶת־הָאִישׁ, but אֵת הָאִישׁ.

c. Proper nouns and names, with few exceptions, are not used with the definite article: יוֹסֵף *Joseph* (not הַיּוֹסֵף). Exceptions: הַיַּרְדֵּן the *Jordan River*, הָאָדָם *Adam*, also *mankind, man*.

d. If there is more than one direct object to the verb, אֶת־ is repeated before each of them.

Examples:

God created the heavens and the earth.   בָּרָא אֱלֹהִים אֵת הַשָּׁמַיִם וְאֵת הָאָרֶץ

The boy took the book and the garments.   הַיֶּלֶד לָקַח אֶת־הַסֵּפֶר וְאֶת־הַבְּגָדִים

e. אֶרֶץ *earth, land, ground, country*. This noun is feminine. With the definite article, it is always pointed הָאָרֶץ (not הָאֶרֶץ).

f. Note the following: עַם *people*, הָעָם *the people* (not הָעַם), הַר *mountain*, הָהָר *the mountain* (not הָהַר).

g. עַם *people* is usually used as a masculine noun in the singular. Thus,

this great people   הָעָם הַגָּדוֹל הַזֶּה

The people remembered the law.   זָכַר הָעָם אֶת־הַתּוֹרָה

h. עִיר *city*, like אֶרֶץ *land, country* is also feminine, e.g., הָעִיר הַיָּפָה הַזֹּאת *this beautiful city*.

3. *Biblical Word List Seven* (verbs occurring 500 to 5000 times)

to see	רָאָה
to remember	זָכַר
to create	בָּרָא
to build	בָּנָה
to take	לָקַח

STUDY HINTS

1. Learn the vocabulary. Remember that the words selected for the vocabulary are among those most frequently occurring in the language. They constitute, therefore, a basic vocabulary, and a basic vocabulary is a *must* in any language.

2. The relative pronoun in Hebrew, אֲשֶׁר or its abbreviated form –שֶׁ, is invariable; it is used for persons and things, for all genders and numbers. Such use of the relative pronoun is a great deal simpler than in English or French, for instance. In Hebrew, אֲשֶׁר stands for *who, whom, which* and *that*.

3. The abbreviated form –שֶׁ is rarely found in the Old Testament. It is mainly

postbiblical. In modern colloquial Hebrew it is very frequently used. When writing Classical Hebrew, use the unattached form אֲשֶׁר only.

4. It is important that you understand clearly Grammar and Notes 2 on the Hebrew word אֵת. If you do not understand it thoroughly, ask your instructor for assistance. When אֵת is used with a hyphen, it is pointed אֶת־.

5. Note that אֶרֶץ *land, country, ground,* or *earth*, and עִיר *city, town* are both feminine.

EXERCISES

A. Translate the following into English.

1. רָאָה הָאִישׁ סוּס גָּדוֹל בַּשָּׂדֶה.

2. רָאָה הָאִישׁ אֶת־הַסּוּס אֲשֶׁר עָמַד בַּגַּן אֵצֶל הָאִשָּׁה.

3. כָּתַב מֹשֶׁה אֶת־הַדְּבָרִים הָאֵלֶּה עַל־הַלּוּחַ.

4. כָּתְבוּ הַנְּבִיאִים אֶת־הַדָּבָר הַזֶּה עַל־הַלּוּחַ.

5. זָכַר הַמֶּלֶךְ אֶת־יוֹסֵף וְאֶת־הַחֲלוֹם.

6. רָאָה הָאִישׁ אֶת־יְרוּשָׁלַיִם לִפְנֵי שָׁנָה.*

7. לָקַח הַיֶּלֶד. לָקַח אֶת־הַיֶּלֶד. לָקַח הָאָב אֶת־הַיְלָדוֹת הָאֵלֶּה אֶל־הָעִיר.

8. זָכְרָה הָאִשָּׁה אֶת־הַשִּׁיר אֲשֶׁר לָמְדָה מִן־הַסֵּפֶר.

9. זָכְרָה הַיַּלְדָּה אֶת־הָאִשָּׁה אֲשֶׁר לָקְחָה אֶת־הַבְּגָדִים הַיָּפִים אֶל־הַבָּיִת.

10. אָכְלוּ הַיְלָדִים אֶת־הַתַּפּוּחִים וְאֶת־הַלֶּחֶם.

B. Translate the following into Hebrew, without vowels:

1. He read a book. He read the book.

2. The man saw. He saw the man.

3. Who remembered? Whom did he remember? Whom did the prophet remember?

4. I took a book from the man. We took the book from the woman.

5. He ate the apples. He saw apples on the tree in this garden.

6. He took the bread from the ground.

---

*לִפְנֵי שָׁנָה *before a year*, i.e., *a year ago*.

7. He was in this country a year ago.

8. The man saw the mountain from this field.

9. He saw the man on this mountain.

10. The people (sg.) built this beautiful land.

C. Translate the following into English:

1. בָּרָא אֱלֹהִים אֶת־הָאָדָם מִן־הָאֲדָמָה.

2. הִיא אָכְלָה מִן־הָעֵץ אֲשֶׁר בַּגָּן.

3. רָאָה הָאִישׁ אֶת־הָאוֹר.

4. הַמַּבּוּל הָיָה עַל־הָאָרֶץ.

5. נָתַן אֱלֹהִים אֶת־הָאִשָּׁה לְאָדָם.

6. זָכַר אֱלֹהִים אֶת־נֹחַ אֲשֶׁר הָיָה בַּתֵּבָה.

7. אָמַר הָאָדָם אֶל־הָאִשָּׁה: שָׁמַעְתִּי קוֹל בַּגָּן.

8. מִן־הָהָר רָאָה מֹשֶׁה אֶת־הָאָרֶץ אֲשֶׁר נָתַן אֱלֹהִים אֶל־הָעָם.

9. לָקְחָה הָאֵם תַּפּוּחִים מִן־הָעֵץ וְנָתְנָה לָאִישׁ אֲשֶׁר עָמַד מוּל הַשַּׁעַר.

10. בָּרָא אֱלֹהִים אִשָּׁה מִן־הַצֵּלָע אֲשֶׁר לָקַח מִן־הָאָדָם.

D. Translate the following into Hebrew, without vowels:

1. The man who went to the city remembered the house and the name.

2. The woman who wrote the book read the songs before the people.

3. We read the beautiful prayer which you (m. sg.) had written (translate "wrote").

4. The boy remembered the dream which he saw at night (translate "in the night").

5. Who is the man who went to the great city with the king?

E. (Review) Write at sight the present tense and the perfect tense of רָכַב *ride*.

F. (Review) Translate the following into Hebrew:

1. I remembered

2. we sat

3. he stood

4. they said

5. you (f. sg.) went

6. we (m.) are sitting

7. they have eaten

8. you (f. pl.) wrote

9. you (m. sg.) finished

10. she knew

G. Translate the following into English:

‎1. בְּרֵאשִׁית* בָּרָא אֱלֹהִים אֵת הַשָּׁמַיִם וְאֵת הָאָרֶץ.

‎2. בָּרָא אֱלֹהִים אֶת־הָאָדָם מִן־הָאֲדָמָה.

‎3. אַחֲרֵי הַדְּבָרִים הָאֵלֶּה הָלַךְ מֹשֶׁה אֶל־הָהָר עִם הַלּוּחוֹת.

‎4. לָקְחָה הָאִשָּׁה אֶת־הַתַּפּוּחַ מִן־הָעֵץ וְנָתְנָה לָאָדָם.

‎5. אָכַל הָאָדָם אֶת־הַתַּפּוּחַ עִם הָאִשָּׁה תַּחַת הָעֵץ אֲשֶׁר בַּגָּן.

---

*In the beginning, from ‎רֹאשׁ head.

Lesson Eighteen

REVIEW OF LESSONS 12-17

IMPORTANT POINTS TO REMEMBER

1. Simple form of the Hebrew verbs is known as *Qal*. (Lesson 12)
2. Participles follow the pattern of XXﯞX.

   יוֹשֵׁב *sitting*,   יָשַׁב *sit*

   Similarly, עוֹמֵד, סוֹגֵר, כּוֹתֵב, לוֹמֵד, אוֹכֵל (Lesson 12)
3. Participles agree with the nouns and pronouns associated with them. (Lesson 12)

   הֵן כּוֹתְבוֹת   הָאִשָּׁה הוֹלֶכֶת

   הַמּוֹרֶה יוֹשֵׁב   הַיְלָדִים אוֹכְלִים
4. The principal parts of the active participles of למד *to learn* are:

   לוֹמֵד, (לוֹמְדָה) לוֹמֶדֶת, לוֹמְדִים, לוֹמְדוֹת

   Similarly, כּוֹתֵב, כּוֹתֶבֶת, כּוֹתְבִים, כּוֹתְבוֹת. (Lesson 12)
5. Biblical Word List Two: דִּבֵּר, הָיָה, בּוֹא, אָמַר, אָכַל (Lesson 12)
6. Present tense of הָלַךְ *to go* (Lesson 13):

(m., sg.)	אֲנִי, אַתָּה, הוּא – הוֹלֵךְ
(m., pl.)	אֲנַחְנוּ, אַתֶּם, הֵם – הוֹלְכִים
(f., sg.)	אֲנִי, אַתְּ, הִיא – הוֹלֶכֶת
(f., pl.)	אֲנַחְנוּ, אַתֶּן, הֵן – הוֹלְכוֹת

7. The following classes of nouns are usually feminine (Lesson 13):

   a. Words ending in הָ– or ת–

   b. Words denoting female beings

c. Nouns denoting organs of the body that come in pairs

עַיִן, אֹזֶן, יָד, רֶגֶל

Notes:

(1) The following parts of the body—more than two—are also feminine:

שֵׁן, אֶצְבַּע, צֵלָע, עֶצֶם

(2) The following, which do not come in pairs, are masculine:

רֹאשׁ, גַּב, פֶּה, אַף

(3) Exceptions: לָשׁוֹן *tongue* and בֶּטֶן *belly* are feminine; שַׁד *breast* is masculine.

8. Biblical Word List Three: הָלַךְ, יָדַע, יָצָא, יָשַׁב, יָלַד (Lesson 13)

9. The Hebrew word for *verb* is פֹּעַל; the root of every Hebrew verb consists of three letters. We therefore call the first letter of the root פ' הַפֹּעַל, the second letter ע' הַפֹּעַל, and the third ל' הַפֹּעַל. (Lesson 14)

10. The first letter of the following group of verbs is י (yod): ילד, יצא, ידע, ירד, ישב. We therefore class them as פ"י (pronounced *pe-yud*) verbs. (Lesson 14)

11. The perfect tense of זָכַר *to remember* (Lesson 14)

זָכַרְתִּי, זָכַרְתָּ, זָכַרְתְּ, זָכַר, זָכְרָה

זָכַרְנוּ, זְכַרְתֶּם, זְכַרְתֶּן, זָכְרוּ, זָכְרוּ

12. Biblical Word List Four: אֲדוֹנָי, אֱלֹהִים, אֵל, אֶחָד, אֶרֶץ (Lesson 14).

13. The demonstrative pronouns (Lesson 15)

this, for masculine singular	זֶה
this, for feminine singular	זֹאת
these, for masculine or feminine plural	אֵלֶּה
This is a man.	זֶה אִישׁ
This is a woman.	זֹאת אִשָּׁה
These are boys.	אֵלֶּה יְלָדִים
These are girls.	אֵלֶּה יְלָדוֹת

14. The demonstrative adjectives are the same as the demonstrative pronouns, but the former have the definite article. They follow nouns having the definite article. (Lesson 15)

this man	הָאִישׁ הַזֶּה
this woman	הָאִשָּׁה הַזֹּאת
these boys	הַיְלָדִים הָאֵלֶּה

these girls   הַיְלָדוֹת הָאֵלֶּה

15. When demonstrative adjectives are used, the order of the words is the reverse of that in English. (Lesson 15)

this book is *the book, the this (one)*   הַסֵּפֶר הַזֶּה

this holy book is *the book, this (one)*   הַסֵּפֶר הַקָּדוֹשׁ הַזֶּה

16. Biblical Word List Five: הַר, הָרִים, שָׁנָה, עַם, עִיר (Lesson 15)

17. Simple prepositions (Lesson 16)

אֶל, עַל, מִן, תַּחַת, בְּלִי, עַד, כְּמוֹ, עִם

לִפְנֵי, אַחֲרֵי, אֵצֶל, בֵּין, מוּל

18. Inseparable prepositions (Lesson 16)

in, with, at	בְּ–
like, as	כְּ–
to, for	לְ–
from	מִ–

David's Tower in Jerusalem. Located near the Jaffa Gate entrance to the old walled city of Jerusalem, the tower is one of the dominant landmarks on the Jerusalem skyline. The heavy stone building dates back to the days of King Herod.

19. Note the difference in the following phrases: (Lesson 16)

בְּבַ֫יִת   in a house   בַּבַּ֫יִת   in the house

כְּבַ֫יִת   like a house   כַּבַּ֫יִת   like the house

לְבַ֫יִת   to a house   לַבַּ֫יִת   to the house

20. Biblical Word List Six: (Lesson 16) דֶּ֫רֶךְ, לֵב, קוֹל, רֹאשׁ, שִׁבְעָה.

21. The relative pronoun אֲשֶׁר stands for *who, whom, which,* and *that.* (Lesson 17)

22. A contracted form of אֲשֶׁר is ־שֶׁ followed by a dagesh and used as a prefix. (Lesson 17)

23. The word אֵת is placed before the direct object of the verb when the direct object is defined. (Lesson 17)

24. If there is more than one direct object, the word אֵת is placed before each one of them. (Lesson 17)

25. Note the difference in the following:

the man took   לָקַח הָאִישׁ

he took the man   לָקַח אֶת־הָאִישׁ

26. Biblical Word List Seven: (Lesson 17). בָּנָה, רָאָה, לָקַח, זָכַר, בָּרָא

27. Note that both אֶ֫רֶץ *land, country, ground* and עִיר *city, town* are feminine.

28. Note that אֶ֫רֶץ *land* etc. with the article is הָאָ֫רֶץ (not הָאֶ֫רֶץ).

STUDY HINTS

1. The purpose of this lesson is to help you review the material in Lessons 1 through 17 in preparation for the test in the next lesson. Carefully review all the points in this lesson making sure you understand each one. If you do not, restudy the lesson indicated in the parentheses under the point you do not understand.

2. Learn the Vocabulary of each lesson.

EXERCISES

A. Study the following verbs: קָרָא, רָאָה, אָמַר, יָשַׁב, נָפַל, יָצָא, קוּם, קָנָה בּוֹא.

    1. Which of the above are פ״י verbs?

2. Which are ע״ו verbs?

3. Which is a פ״נ verb?

4. Which is a ל״ה verb?

5. Which verb is both ע״ו and ל״א?

6. Which verb is both פ״י and ל״א?

B. Write the present tense of זָכַר *to remember.*

C. Write the perfect tense of זָכַר *to remember.*

D. Add an adjective to each of the following nouns:

6. מְנוֹרָה	1. אִישׁ
7. רֶגֶל	2. בַּיִת
8. שִׁירִים	3. שָׂדֶה
9. לַיְלָה	4. ראשׁ
10. דֶּלֶת	5. יָד

E. Use the following words in simple Hebrew sentences, without vowels. Each sentence should include a verb, a noun, and an appropriate adjective.

6. בְּלִי	1. אֲשֶׁר
7. בֵּין	2. עַם
8. לִפְנֵי	3. חָזֶה
9. זאת	4. אֶל
10. אֶת	5. עַל

F. Translate the following sentences into Hebrew, without vowels.

1. The lad who went to the field is on the horse.

2. The song is beautiful.

3. These are the words which are in this book.

4. Who is the man whom you sent to the city?

5. Whom did you take to the city?

Lesson Nineteen

REVIEW TEST

This one-hour test reviews the material covered in the previous lessons (approximately six weeks of work).

Part I: Grammar

1. Of the following letters, נ ,פ ,ב ,א ,ע ,צ ,ג ,ר ,מ
   a. which are gutturals? _____
   b. which have final forms? _____
   c. which do not admit dagesh *at all*? _____
   d. which take dagesh at the beginning of a word? _____

   _____

2. State whether the following statements are True or False.
   _____ a. Hebrew letters have a numerical value.
   _____ b. There are 26 letters in the Hebrew alphabet.
   _____ c. There are 10 vowels in Hebrew.
   _____ d. The division of a word at the end of a line is not permitted.
   _____ e. The original Hebrew Bible has few vowels.

3. Which four of the following languages belong to the Semitic group?
   _____ a. Persian   _____ e. Arabic
   _____ b. Samaritan   _____ f. Turkish
   _____ c. Phoenician   _____ g. Aramaic
   _____ d. Sanskrit

109

4. Of the following signs, ָ , ּ , ֻ , וֹ , ֵ , ֳ , ֶ , and וּ

   a. select three long vowels. _____

   b. select three short vowels. _____

   c. state which is not a vowel. _____

5. Rewrite each word with the definite article (vowels included):

_____	רֹאשׁ .d	_____	עֶרֶב .a
_____	לַיְלָה .e	_____	בַּיִת .b
_____	כֶּלֶב .f	_____	אִישׁ .c

6. Identify the gender, putting (m.) for masculine and (f.) for feminine. (Do *not* translate.)

_____	אוֹר .f	_____	תְּמוּנָה .a
_____	רֹאשׁ .g	_____	יָד .b
_____	אֶרֶץ .h	_____	לָשׁוֹן .c
_____	לַיְלָה .i	_____	בַּיִת .d
_____	שֵׁן .j	_____	דֶּלֶת .e

7. Write the feminine of the following:

   _____ יֶלֶד טוֹב .a

   _____ הַדּוֹד הַזָּקֵן .b

   _____ הַסּוּס אוֹכֵל .c

   _____ אַתָּה נָבִיא .d

   _____ אִישׁ גָּדוֹל .e

8. Write the plural of the following:

   _____ שִׁיר .a

   _____ סֵפֶר .b

   _____ מֶלֶךְ .c

   _____ פֶּרַח .d

   _____ נַחַל .e

   _____ אֶרֶץ .f

   _____ מִשְׁפָּחָה .g

   _____ אָב .h

   _____ אֲדָמָה .i

j. מַלְאָךְ   _____

k. בַּת   _____

l. תַּפּוּחַ   _____

m. אִישׁ   _____

n. אִשָּׁה   _____

9. Translate the following into English:

a. כָּתַבְתָּ   _____

b. כְּתַבְתֶּן   _____

c. כָּתְבָה   _____

d. כָּתַבְנוּ   _____

e. כָּתְבוּ   _____

Part II: Translation and Vocabulary

10. Translate the following into English:

a. אָמַר הָאָדָם אֶל־הָאִשָּׁה: הָאוֹר טוֹב.

_____

b. בָּרָא אֱלֹהִים אֶת־הָאָדָם מִן־הָאֲדָמָה.

_____

c. הַמַּבּוּל הָיָה עַל־הָאָרֶץ.

_____

d. בָּרָא אֱלֹהִים אִשָּׁה מִן־הַצֵּלָע אֲשֶׁר לָקַח מִן־הָאָדָם.

_____

11. Translate the following into Hebrew:

a. I ate bread.

a. _____

b. We ate bread.

b. _____

c. The little boy stood near the tree.

c. _____

d. The horse stood before the big house.

d. _____

e. This woman is going to the house which is in the field.

_____ e.

f. He saw the man who read these words.

_____ f.

g. This man saw the beautiful horse which stood under the tree.

_____ g.

h. She sat between the king and (between)* the small son.

_____ h.

i. They remembered the book which the prophet had read.

_____ i.

j. In the beginning God created the heavens and the earth.

_____ j.

12. Vocabulary Exercise: Translate only 10 words.

_____	זָכַר .g	_____	יָדַע .a
_____	בָּנָה .h	_____	לָקַח .b
_____	הָלַךְ .i	_____	אָכַל .c
_____	דִּבֶּר .j	_____	יָלַד .d
_____	אָמַר .k	_____	בָּרָא .e
_____	הָיָה .l	_____	יָשַׁב .f

13. Give the Hebrew of the following:

1. which _____   6. finger _____
2. without _____   7. gate _____
3. apple _____   8. river _____
4. dream _____   9. city _____
5. head _____   10. law _____

14. Translate the following into Hebrew, without vowels.

1. Who is this woman who is sitting near the door?

_____

2. Whom did you (m. sg.) send to the house?

_____

_____

*In Hebrew the preposition is always repeated.

3. Who is the woman who ate the bread?

_____

4. Who is the man who has eaten the apples?

_____

15. Write the equivalent of the following in Hebrew, with vowels.

    1. before the gate   _____

    2. after the prophet   _____

    3. near the city   _____

    4. among the trees   _____

    5. opposite the house   _____

    6. to the field   _____

    7. upon the earth   _____

    8. from the garden   _____

    9. under the trees   _____

    10. without the books   _____

    11. until the evening   _____

    12. like the father   _____

Lesson Twenty
VERBS WITH GUTTURAL ROOT-LETTERS; MORE ABOUT GENDER

VOCABULARY

to read, call	קָרָא	rare, precious	יָקָר
to pass over, transgress	עָבַר	pen, stylus	עֵט
to give	נָתַן	morning	בֹּקֶר (בְּקָרִים)
to send	שָׁלַח	sheep	צֹאן
to find	מָצָא	sword (f.)	חֶרֶב (חֲרָבוֹת)
to go up	עָלָה	sea	יָם (יַמִּים)
to answer, reply	עָנָה	scribe	סוֹפֵר
to drink	שָׁתָה	that, because (conj.)	כִּי
desert	מִדְבָּר	peace	שָׁלוֹם

GRAMMAR AND NOTES

1. *More About the Active Participle of Qal Verbs*

   In Lesson 12, we learned that the principal parts of the active participle of יָשַׁב *to sit,* for instance, are: יוֹשֵׁב, יוֹשֶׁבֶת, יוֹשְׁבִים, יוֹשְׁבוֹת.

   When the last letter of the root (ל' הַפֹּעַל) is a guttural (usually ע or ח), such as שָׁכַח, יָדַע, שָׁלַח or סָלַח, the participle is formed as follows:

knowing	יוֹדְעוֹת	יוֹדְעִים	יוֹדַעַת	יוֹדֵעַ
taking	לוֹקְחוֹת	לוֹקְחִים	לוֹקַחַת	לוֹקֵחַ
hearing	שׁוֹמְעוֹת	שׁוֹמְעִים	שׁוֹמַעַת	שׁוֹמֵעַ
sending	שׁוֹלְחוֹת	שׁוֹלְחִים	שׁוֹלַחַת	שׁוֹלֵחַ

The present tense of יָדַע *to know,* is therefore formed accordingly:

m. sg.	יוֹדֵעַ	....	הוּא	אַתָּה	אֲנִי
f. sg.	יוֹדַעַת (יוֹדְעָה)	....	הִיא	אַתְּ	אֲנִי
m. pl.	יוֹדְעִים	....	הֵם	אַתֶּם	אֲנַחְנוּ
f. pl.	יוֹדְעוֹת	....	הֵן	אַתֶּן	אֲנַחְנוּ

2. *Past tense*

When the לֹ' הַפֹּעַל is a guttural, ח *or* ע, only the second person feminine singular verb of the past tense is changed. The guttural takes pataḥ, instead of shva. All the other forms of the past are regular.

	You wrote (f.)	כָּתַבְתְּ
but:	You knew (f.)	יָדַעַתְּ
	You ate (f.)	אָכַלְתְּ
but:	You sent (f.)	שָׁלַחַתְּ

3. *More About Gender*

We have already observed (Lesson 13) that the following classes of nouns, although not ending in הָ or ת, are feminine:

a. Nouns denoting female beings.

b. Nouns denoting organs of the body that come in pairs.

We can now add another class: Names of countries, cities, and towns are also feminine (singular); these may have been regarded by the ancient Semites as the "mothers" of their inhabitants.

Examples:

Jerusalem	יְרוּשָׁלַיִם	Egypt	מִצְרַיִם
Canaan	כְּנַעַן	Persia	פָּרַס
Ashdod	אַשְׁדּוֹד	Aram	אֲרָם
Bethlehem	בֵּית־לֶחֶם	Assyria	אַשּׁוּר
Babylon	בָּבֶל	Gezer	גֶּזֶר
Jericho	יְרִיחוֹ	Bethel	בֵּית־אֵל

Names of people, rivers, and mountains are masculine; for example:

Israel (people)	יִשְׂרָאֵל	Lebanon	לְבָנוֹן
Carmel (Mt.)	כַּרְמֶל	Sinai	סִינַי
Jordan (River)	יַרְדֵּן	Tabor	תָּבוֹר
Nebo	נְבוֹ		

Note: יִשְׂרָאֵל   the people of Israel (masculine)

יִשְׂרָאֵל   the country of Israel (feminine)

Similarly,

מִצְרַיִם   the people of Egypt (masculine)

מִצְרַיִם   the country of Egypt (feminine)

Remember that the Hebrew words אֶרֶץ *land, earth, country* and עִיר *town, city* are feminine; both nouns are probably understood to be the "mothers of their inhabitants." This is a possible explanation for the fact that names denoting countries or cities are feminine.

3. *Biblical Word List Eight* (verbs occurring from 500 to 5000 times)

to rise, get up	קוּם
to go up	עָלָה
to give	נָתַן
to read, call	קָרָא
to do, make	עָשָׂה

STUDY HINTS

1. Master the Vocabulary thoroughly. Note that קָרָא *to read* also means *to call*; שָׁלוֹם means *peace,* but in Modern Hebrew it is also a common word of greeting and farewell.

2. The present participle of verbs whose roots contain a guttural letter as a third root-letter should not cause any difficulty if you remember that gutturals take the vowel pataḥ rather than any other vowel. (See Lesson 10 on the segholates.) Carefully learn the four principal parts: יָרַע, for instance, יוֹדֵעַ, יוֹדַעַת, יוֹדְעִים, יוֹדְעוֹת.

3. The material on gender is very important. In Lesson 13 we learned that paired members of the body such as יָד *hand,* רֶגֶל *foot,* עַיִן *eye,* etc. are feminine; now carefully learn the important rule that names of countries, cities, or towns are also feminine.

4. Names of mountains and rivers are masculine nouns. יַרְדֵּן *Jordan* (river) and כַּרְמֶל *Mt. Carmel,* for instance, are masculine. *Jordan* as a country (אֶרֶץ־יַרְדֵּן) is feminine.

5. Note that both words אֶרֶץ *land, country* and עִיר *city, town* are feminine.

6. Study carefully Biblical Word List Eight.

7. Read aloud Exercise D before translating it.

EXERCISES

A. Write the four principal parts of the active participles of the following verbs:
(*Example:* The principal parts of כתב are כּוֹתֵב, כּוֹתֶבֶת, כּוֹתְבִים, כּוֹתְבוֹת.)

to shut	סָגַר	to know	יָדַע
to hear	שָׁמַע	to send	שָׁלַח

B. Write in full the present tense of לָקַח *to take*.

C. Identify the gender of the following and translate into English:

11. סִינַי	6. דֶּלֶת	1. יְרוּשָׁלַיִם
12. מְדִינָה	7. עִיר	2. אֹזֶן
13. עַיִן	8. כְּנַעַן	3. פֶּה
14. רֹאשׁ	9. לַיְלָה	4. אַשּׁוּר
15. מִצְרַיִם	10. יַרְדֵּן	5. אֶרֶץ

D. Read and translate the following into English:

1. הַיּוֹם הַגָּדוֹל אֲשֶׁר עָשָׂה ח'

2. זֶה הָאִישׁ אֲשֶׁר לָקַח אֶת־הַסֵּפֶר מִן־הַבַּיִת.

3. הָלַךְ הַמֶּלֶךְ מִן־הָעִיר הַזֹּאת אֶל־הַשָּׂדֶה.

4. אָמַר אֱלֹהִים אֶל־הָאָדָם אֲשֶׁר בָּרָא מִן־הָאֲדָמָה: הָאוֹר טוֹב.

5. הָאִשָּׁה הַזֹּאת לָקְחָה תַּפּוּחַ מִן־הָעֵץ הַזֶּה.

6. אֵלֶּה הַדְּבָרִים אֲשֶׁר דִּבֶּר הַמֶּלֶךְ אֶל־הָעָם.

7. שָׁלַח הַמֶּלֶךְ אֶת־מֹשֶׁה וְאֶת־אַהֲרֹן אֶל־מִצְרַיִם.

8. קָרָא הָעָם אֶת־הַתְּפִלָּה אֲשֶׁר כָּתַב הַנָּבִיא.

9. אַחֲרֵי הַדְּבָרִים הָאֵלֶּה עָמַד מֹשֶׁה עַל־הַר גָּדוֹל
מִן־הָהָר הַזֶּה רָאָה מֹשֶׁה אֶת־הָאָרֶץ אֲשֶׁר נָתַן ח' לְיִשְׂרָאֵל.

10. אָמַר מֹשֶׁה: יָדַעְתִּי כִּי הָאָרֶץ הַזֹּאת הִיא אֶרֶץ גְּדוֹלָה וְטוֹבָה.

E. Make your own sentences for each of the following verbs (use the present or the perfect tense only):

עָמַד, יָשַׁב, אָכַל, שָׁמַע, זָכַר, יָדַע

Lesson Twenty-one
SENTENCES IN THE NEGATIVE;
DECLENSION OF NOUNS IN THE SINGULAR

VOCABULARY

who?	מִי?	there is	יֵשׁ
what?	מַה?	no, not	לֹא
how?	אֵיךְ?	also, too	גַּם
to whom? for whom? whose?	לְמִי?	where?	אֵיפֹה? אַיֵּה?
why?	לָמָּה? מַדּוּעַ?	where?	אָן?
when?	מָתַי?	how long?	עַד מָתַי?
little, few	מְעַט	how many? how great?	
only	רַק	how often?	כַּמָּה?
when, as	כַּאֲשֶׁר	word, thing	דָּבָר (דְּבָרִים)
another, other	אַחֵר	stone (f.)	אֶבֶן (אֲבָנִים)
if	אִם	darkness	חֹשֶׁךְ
no, not, there is (are) not	אֵין	to hear	שָׁמַע
		to obey	שָׁמַע בְּקוֹל

GRAMMAR AND NOTES

1. *Negatives "no," and "not"*

The negative אֵין is translated *no, not, there is not, there are not*, etc. (Any sentence in the present tense may be changed into negative simply by placing אֵין before it.)

The man is at home.	הָאִישׁ בַּבַּיִת
The man is not at home.	אֵין הָאִישׁ בַּבַּיִת
The scribe writes (is writing).	הַסּוֹפֵר כֹּתֵב
The scribe does not write.	אֵין הַסּוֹפֵר כּוֹתֵב

The negative לֹא *no, not* is used with the imperfect or the perfect; it is placed immediately *before* the verb.

Moses did not write on the tablet.	מֹשֶׁה לֹא כָּתַב עַל הַלּוּחַ
I have not eaten the apple.	לֹא אָכַלְתִּי אֶת־הַתַּפּוּחַ
We did not know this thing.	לֹא יָדַעְנוּ אֶת־הַדָּבָר הַזֶּה
The man did not go to the city.	הָאִישׁ לֹא הָלַךְ אֶל־הָעִיר
I shall not write the book.	(אֲנִי) לֹא אֶכְתֹּב אֶת־הַסֵּפֶר

We shall deal more with the negatives in future lessons.

2. *Declension of Regular Nouns—The Pronominal Suffixes*

In Semitic languages, the possessive adjectives (i.e., *my, your, his,* etc.) are not expressed by special words separately used but by special suffixes added to the noun. These are known as "pronominal suffixes." When we say we "decline" or "inflect" a noun, we refer to the attaching of these pronominal suffixes to the noun. These suffixes are *regular* and do *not* change.

The following are the pronominal suffixes to masculine nouns in the singular:

our	־נוּ	my	־י
your (m., pl.)	־כֶם	your (m., sg.), thy	־ךָ
your (f., pl.)	־כֶן	your (f., sg.), thy	־ךְ
their (m., pl.)	־ם	his, its (m.)	־וֹ
their (f., pl.)	־ן	her, its (f.)	־הָ

The declension of שִׁיר *a song* is therefore formed as follows:

our song	שִׁירֵנוּ	my song	שִׁירִי
your song	שִׁירְכֶם	your song	שִׁירְךָ
your song	שִׁירְכֶן	your song	שִׁירֵךְ
their song	שִׁירָם	his song	שִׁירוֹ
their song	שִׁירָן	her song	שִׁירָהּ

Notes:

a. The suffix ־הָ of the third person feminine singular *always* has a dot called *mappiq* מַפִּיק. This is not a dagesh, because ה, being a guttural, never takes dagesh. This mappiq distinguishes the pronominal suffix הָ (meaning *her*), from הָ, the sign of the feminine gender. Moreover, in reading, the former is pronounced whereas the latter is silent.

Examples:

prophetess	נְבִיאָה	her prophet	נְבִיאָהּ
aunt	דּוֹדָה	her uncle	דּוֹדָהּ
mare	סוּסָה	her horse	סוּסָהּ
song	שִׁירָה	her song	שִׁירָהּ

b. Many nouns, when declined, undergo some change in their inner structure (such as vocalization), but the suffixes remain the same. We will study such nouns in future lessons.

c. Note the following interrogative expressions:

where? whither?	אָן?	how long?	עַד אָן?
where? where from?	מֵאַיִן? מֵאָן?	how long?	עַד אָנָה?
how long?	עַד מָתַי?		

d. The pronominal suffixes to the plural nouns are different from those used for the masculine singular nouns. We shall study these in due course.*

e. Declined nouns are *never* used with the definite article. שִׁירִי *my song* (never הַשִׁירִי)

3. *Biblical Word List Nine* (nouns occurring from 500 to 5000 times)

voice	קוֹל
two (f.) שְׁתַּיִם (m.) שְׁנַיִם	
eye	עַיִן
city	עִיר

STUDY HINTS

1. The Vocabulary given in this lesson is very useful. There are two words for *why?* (לְמָה and מַדּוּעַ) and three words for *where?* (אָן, אַיֵּה, and אֵיפֹה), with slight differences in their usage. הַיּוֹם is *the day* or *today*.

_____

*For the declension of feminine nouns ending in הָ, see Lesson 27.

2. The negative אֵין is used with sentences containing the present tense, written or implied. הָאִישׁ אוֹכֵל *the man eats* or *is eating*; אֵין הָאִישׁ אוֹכֵל *the man does not eat* or *is not eating*. We shall learn more about the use of אֵין in future lessons. לֹא is used with the past or future tense. Study the examples given in this lesson.

3. The pronominal suffixes attached to the nouns are regular and invariable for nearly all of the nouns. Hence, once you learn them carefully, you can apply them to almost all nouns and most prepositions. (In Hebrew, prepositions can be inflected: עִם *with*, עִמִי *with me*, עִמְּךָ *with you*, etc.)

4. The dot, or mappiq, in the הּ in the third person feminine singular is not a dagesh, for ה being a guttural letter cannot admit a dagesh. It is equivalent to the English possessive adjective *her* for singular nouns.
    Example: שִׁירָהּ *her song*, but שִׁירָה *song*; סוּסָהּ *her horse*, but סוּסָה *mare*.

5. Memorize the full declension of שִׁיר as given in this lesson.

6. Note that דָּבָר means both *word* and *thing*.

EXERCISES

A. Rewrite the following sentences in the negative: (Use אֵין before the present tense and לֹא before the past tense.)

6. הָאִישׁ הָלַךְ אֶל־הָעִיר הַזֹּאת.	1. הָאִישׁ בַּבַּיִת.
7. הוּא כּוֹתֵב.	2. כָּתַבְנוּ אֶת־הַסֵּפֶר.
8. שָׁמַרְתָּ עַל הַבַּיִת וְעַל הַכֶּרֶם.	3. הֵם כּוֹתְבִים.
9. יְשַׁבְתֶּם תַּחַת הָעֵץ.	4. זָכַרְתִּי אֶת־הַדָּבָר הַזֶּה.
10. אֲנִי סוֹגֵר אֶת־הַדֶּלֶת.	5. הוּא לוֹמֵד מִן־הַסֵּפֶר.

B. Translate the following into Hebrew:
    1. I am eating.
    2. You (m. sg.) sat.
    3. We remembered.
    4. You (m. pl.) have written.
    5. the man says
    6. Rachel is learning.
    7. He has given.
    8. The apple is on the tree.
    9. You (f. sg.) stood.
    10. They closed the door.

C. Put the Hebrew sentences in Exercise B into the negative.
    1. I do not eat, etc.

D. Decline the following in full:

1. horse   סוּס
2. voice   קוֹל
3. city   עִיר

E. Translate the following into English:

11. סוּסְכֶן	6. אוֹרוֹ	1. שִׁירֵנוּ
12. עִירְכֶם	7. יָדְךָ	2. דּוֹדְכֶם
13. דּוֹדָהּ	8. קוֹלֵךְ	3. יָדִי
14. עִירְךָ	9. שִׁירָן	4. קוֹלָהּ
15. יָדֵנוּ	10. עִירִי	5. רֹאשְׁךָ

F. Translate the following into Hebrew:

1. my song
2. your (m. sg.) city
3. your (f. sg.) head
4. his voice
5. her hand
6. our horse
7. your (m. pl.) light
8. your (f. pl.) light
9. their (m. pl.) head
10. their (f. pl.) head
11. my hand
12. our song

G. Write from memory the first verse of the Hebrew Bible, without vowels.

H. Translate the following sentences into English:

1. אַחֲרֵי־הַדְּבָרִים הָאֵלֶּה קָרָא הַנָּבִיא לִפְנֵי הָעָם אֶת־הַדְּבָרִים אֲשֶׁר שָׁמַע עַל־הָהָר.

2. לָמָּה קוֹרֵא הָעָם הַזֶּה אֶל־הָעֵצִים וְאֶל־הָאֲבָנִים בַּשָּׂדֶה?

3. מִי בָּרָא אֶת־הַשָּׁמַיִם וְאֶת־הָאָרֶץ?

4. מִי עָשָׂה אֶת־הַטּוֹב וְאֶת־הָרָע?

5. אֵין אֱלֹהִים אֲחֵרִים; לֹא בַשָּׁמַיִם וְלֹא בָאָרֶץ.

6. אַיֵּה הָאֲנָשִׁים אֲשֶׁר נָתְנוּ לָעָם מַיִם וְלֶחֶם?

7. מַדּוּעַ לֹא שָׁמַעְנוּ בְּקוֹלָם?

I. Translate the following sentences into English (pay special attention to the interrogatives):

1. לָמָּה כָּתַב הָאִישׁ אֶת־הַסֵּפֶר וּמַדּוּעַ לָקַח אֶת־הָעֵט מִן־הַנָּבִיא?

2. ‏אַיֵּה בָא הַנַּעַר וּלְמִי נָתַן אֶת־הַסֵּפֶר?‏

3. ‏כַּמָּה מְלָכִים בַּבַּיִת הַזֶּה אָנָה הוֹלְכִים הֵם?‏

4. ‏*מָתַי הָלַךְ הָאִישׁ? הָלַךְ הָאִישׁ *כַּאֲשֶׁר רָאָה אֶת־הַמֶּלֶךְ.‏

5. ‏אֵיךְ עָלָה הַנָּבִיא עַל־הָהָר וּמִי נָתַן לַנָּבִיא אֶת־הַמִּצְוֹת?‏

J. Translate the following into Hebrew, with vowels, and be careful to use the proper interrogative expressions:

1. Who took the books from the house and to whom did the man give the horses?

2. How long will you not obey (present participle plus pronoun) the commandment?

3. Where did the prophet go and how many words did he speak to the people?

4. What did the king do to the prophet and why did he speak these words?

5. When did you go to this city and how did you pass this great sea?

6. When the man saw the prophet, what did he say?

---

*‏מָתַי‏ *when?* is used to express a question. ‏כַּאֲשֶׁר‏ *as, when* is used in non-interrogative statements. Examples: ‏מָתַי אָכַל?‏ When did he eat? ‏אָכַל כַּאֲשֶׁר הָלַךְ‏ ‏אֶל־הַבַּיִת.‏ He ate when he went to the house.

Lesson Twenty-two

DUAL NUMBER

VOCABULARY

	Dual-Plural	*Singular*
hand	יָדַיִם	יָד
foot	רַגְלַיִם	רֶגֶל
eye	עֵינַיִם	עַיִן
ear	אָזְנַיִם	אֹזֶן
tooth	שִׁנַּיִם	שֵׁן
wing	כְּנָפַיִם	כָּנָף
lip	שְׂפָתַיִם	שָׂפָה
breast (m.)	שָׁדַיִם	שַׁד
horn	קַרְנַיִם	קֶרֶן
sandal, shoe (f.)	נַעֲלַיִם	נַעַל

GRAMMAR AND NOTES

1. *Dual Number*

We have already learned that masculine nouns generally form the plural by adding ים- to their singular form (סוּס, סוּסִים *horse*) and feminine nouns generally form their plural by dropping the ending ה, of the singular and adding the suffix ות– (תּוֹרָה, תּוֹרוֹת *law*; מְנוֹרָה, מְנוֹרוֹת *lamp*).

In addition, there is another kind of plural in Hebrew, known as the dual

124

number, for the paired organs of the body such as hands, ears, eyes, etc., and for things that come in pairs, such as shoes, wings, etc. (See Lesson 9.) It is usually formed by attaching the suffix יִם‑ to the singular: יָד–יָדַיִם etc. (See the Vocabulary for this lesson.)

Notes:

a. The dual merely signifies the plural number and not necessarily the dual number *two.* Thus יָדַיִם means *hands,* not *two hands.*

b. The plural of שָׂפָה *lip* is שְׂפָתַיִם. The ה is changed into ת before the dual ending יִם‑ is used.

c. The words מַיִם (m.) *water* and שָׁמַיִם (m.) *sky* are dual in form but singular in meaning: שָׁמַיִם יָפִים *beautiful sky,* מַיִם טוֹבִים *good water.*

d. The dual form is not used with verbs, pronouns, or adjectives.

e. All paired members of the body, listed above, except שַׁד *breast* are feminine. (See Lesson 13.)

2. *Nouns with Plural Form Only*

The following nouns are found in the plural form only. They are plural in form but may be singular or plural in meaning.

God	אֱלֹהִים	face (m. or f.)	פָּנִים
mercy	רַחֲמִים	water	מַיִם
life	חַיִּים	sky, heaven	שָׁמַיִם

Notes:

a. All the above nouns are masculine, with the exception of פָּנִים *face,* which is of common gender.

b. When you translate these words into English, use the singular number. The adjective in Hebrew qualifying the above nouns is always in the plural.

beautiful face	פָּנִים יָפִים
great mercy	רַחֲמִים גְּדוֹלִים
good life	חַיִּים טוֹבִים

3. *Biblical Word List Ten* (verbs occurring from 500 to 5000 times)

to command	צִוָּה
to hear	שָׁמַע
to return	שׁוּב

to love   אָהַב

to pass   עָבַר

STUDY HINTS

1. In this lesson you again have a very useful list of common words. Read them and their corresponding plurals aloud several times.
2. Dual does not necessarily mean the number "two"; it indicates the plural form for the paired organs of the body or for things that come in pairs such as shoes, eyeglasses, etc.
3. The Notes are important, so make sure you understand them.

Bethlehem from Shepherd's Fields.

4. Learn the nouns that occur in the plural only. Observe that the adjectives modifying these nouns are also used in the plural, though the meaning may be in the singular.

EXERCISES

A. Write the plural of the following nouns:

9. אִישׁ	5. נַעַר	1. יָד
10. שָׂפָה	6. אֹזֶן	2. מְנוֹרָה
11. שֵׁן	7. קֶרֶן	3. סֵפֶר
12. נַעַל	8. עַיִן	4. רֶגֶל

B. Add *any* of the following adjectives to the above nouns (1) in the singular (with translation) and (2) in the plural:

Example: יָד גְּדוֹלָה *a big hand,* יָדַיִם גְּדוֹלוֹת

גָּדוֹל, קָטָן, רַע, לָבָן

צָעִיר, טוֹב, יָפֶה, שָׁחוֹר

C. Translate the following into Hebrew using the appropriate gender of the adjective:

1. a small lip
2. the good ear
3. this white tooth
4. this good shoe
5. the short horn
6. a short wing
7. this short foot
8. this eye
9. the beautiful wing
10. a big horn

D. Put the Hebrew phrases in Exercise C into the plural.

E. Read and translate the following into English:

1. הָלַךְ הָאִישׁ אֶל־הָעִיר בַּלַּיְלָה.

2. הָאִישׁ הַזָּקֵן יָצָא מִן־הָעִיר בָּעֶרֶב.

3. נָתַן אֱלֹהִים אוֹר בַּשָּׁמַיִם וּבָאָרֶץ.

4. קָרָא הַנָּבִיא אֶת־הַדְּבָרִים הָאֵלֶּה
מִן־הַסֵּפֶר אֲשֶׁר בְּיָדוֹ.

5. בַּיּוֹם אוֹר, בַּלַּיְלָה חֹשֶׁךְ.

F. Answer the following questions, based on Exercise E, in complete Hebrew
    sentences.

1. מִי הָלַךְ אֶל־הָעִיר?

2. מָתַי הָלַךְ הָאִישׁ אֶל־הָעִיר?

3. מָה נָתַן אֱלֹהִים בַּשָּׁמַיִם?

4. מָה קָרָא הַנָּבִיא?

5. מָתַי אוֹר? מָתַי חֹשֶׁךְ?

Lesson Twenty-three

IMPERFECT TENSE

VOCABULARY

	B			A	
to forgive	סָלַח		to write	כָּתַב	
to laugh	צָחַק		to shut	סָגַר	
to shout, cry	צָעַק		to finish	גָּמַר	
to forget	שָׁכַח		to reign	מָלַךְ	
to choose	בָּחַר		to break	שָׁבַר	
to ask	שָׁאַל		to sell	מָכַר	

GRAMMAR AND NOTES

1. *The Imperfect Tense*

Basically, the imperfect tense indicates an incompleted action and so can be used to refer to more than a simple action in the future. In some contexts, for example, it can be used to express continuous action in the present; at this point, however, we will deal with it simply as expressing a future action. It is usually formed by adding certain letters to the root as prefixes or as suffixes or both. The imperfect Qal of the regular verb שָׁמַר, for instance, is as follows:

Singular

| I shall keep | m. or f. | אֶשְׁמֹר |
| you (thou) will keep | m. | תִּשְׁמֹר |

129

you (thou) will keep	f.	תִּשְׁמְרִי
he will keep		יִשְׁמֹר
she will keep		תִּשְׁמֹר

Plural

we shall keep	m. or f.	נִשְׁמֹר
you will keep	m.	תִּשְׁמְרוּ
you will keep	f.	תִּשְׁמֹרְנָה
they will keep	m.	יִשְׁמְרוּ
they will keep	f.	תִּשְׁמֹרְנָה

Observe that the second person masculine singular and third person feminine singular are always identical in Hebrew: תִּשְׁמֹר *you will keep* (m. sg.) or also *she will keep* (f. sg.) according to context; תִּמְלֹךְ *you will reign* (m. sg.) and *she will reign* (f. sg.). Similarly, the second and third person feminine plural are also identical: תִּשְׁמֹרְנָה *you* or *they will keep* (f. pl.), תִּמְלֹכְנָה *you* or *they will reign* (f. pl.). The meaning can be decided only in the context of the sentence.

If the second letter of the root (ע' הַפֹּעַל) is one of the *BeGaD KeFaT* letters, it must take a dagesh when the imperfect is formed:

he broke	שָׁבַר	he will break	יִשְׁבֹּר
he remembered	זָכַר	we shall remember	נִזְכֹּר
he shut	סָגַר	you (f. sg.) will shut	תִּסְגְּרִי
he wrote	כָּתַב	I shall write	אֶכְתֹּב

Study the following:

I shall send	אֶשְׁלַח	I shall finish	אֶגְמֹר
he will laugh	יִצְחַק	he shall guard	יִשְׁמֹר
we shall hear	נִשְׁמַע	we shall write	נִכְתֹּב
he will ask	יִשְׁאַל	he shall steal	יִגְנֹב
you (m. sg.) will hear		you (m. sg.) will sell	
or she will hear	תִּשְׁמַע	or she will sell	תִּמְכֹּר

The second or third letter of the root of the verbs under Group B in the Vocabulary is a guttural (usually ע or ח). Since the gutturals take the vowel pataḥ rather than any other vowel (Lesson 10), the imperfect of these verbs is therefore formed with pataḥ, not holam. Thus אֶשְׁמַע (not אֶשְׁמֹע) *I shall hear,*

נִצְעַק *we shall cry*, יִשְׁכַּח *he shall forget.*

2. *Biblical Word List Eleven* (nouns occurring from 500 to 5000 times)

door (f.)	דֶּלֶת
heart	לֵב
voice	קוֹל

STUDY HINTS

1. Again, as in the case with the pronominal suffixes attached to the nouns (see Lesson 21), the prefixes and suffixes attached to the roots of verbs are also regular and invariable for all roots. Hence, at this stage it is important for you to learn the imperfect thoroughly.

2. Although the imperfect tense is used quite often in Biblical Hebrew to convey the idea of future action; the most basic idea underlining its use is one of *incompleted* action. Hence, it is inaccurate to refer to it simply as a future tense, since it can express, for example, continuous action in the present. For the time being, however, translate the imperfect as a simple future.

3. Note that תִּשְׁמֹר may mean either *you* (m. sg.) *will keep* or *she will keep* as decided by the context in which it is found. Similarly, תִּשְׁמֹרְנָה *you* (f. pl.) or *they* (f. pl.) *will guard.*

4. The imperfect of verbs with a guttural letter in ל׳ הַפֹּעַל or ע׳ הַפֹּעַל should present no difficulty for you if you bear in mind that the gutturals take the vowel pataḥ rather than any other vowel. (See Lesson 10.)

EXERCISES

A. Write the imperfect tense of the following:

צָחַק	to laugh	שָׁלַח	to send
שָׁכַח	to forget	שָׁמַע	to hear

B. Write in full, with English translation, the perfect, present, and imperfect tenses of גָּמַר *to finish.*

C. Translate the following into English:

11. יִגְנֹב	6. תִּכְתָּבְנָה	1. אֶשְׁבֹּר
12. יִסְגְּרוּ	7. תִּזְבֹּר	2. תִּמְכְּרוּ
13. תִּמְלֹךְ	8. תִּשְׁבְּרִי	3. תִּגְמְרִי
14. תִּגְמֹרְנָה	9. תִּשְׁבְּרוּ	4. תִּכְתֹּב
15. אֶמְכֹּר	10. נִסְגֹּר	5. יִמְלֹךְ

D. Translate the following into English:

11. נִשְׁכַּח	6. תִּשְׁאַלְנָה	1. אֶבְחַר
12. תִּשְׁמַע	7. יִשְׁלַח	2. יִצְעַק
13. תִּסְלְחִי	8. תִּשְׁכְּחִי	3. תִּסְלַחְנָה
14. אֶשְׁאַל	9. יִצְחַק	4. יִשְׁמְעוּ
15. תִּשְׁמְעוּ	10. תִּשְׁלְחִי	5. תִּצְעַק

E. Translate the following into English:

11. לָמַדְתִּי	6. יִשְׁכַּח	1. נִשְׁבֹּר
12. אַתֶּן שׁוֹמְעוֹת	7. שָׁבַרְנוּ	2. שָׁמְעוּ
13. סָלַחְתְּ	8. יִמְכֹּר	3. הֵם גּוֹמְרִים
14. יִכְתְּבוּ	9. גָּמְרָה	4. כְּתַבְתֶּם
15. מָכַר	10. הִיא סוֹגֶרֶת	5. אֶשְׁמַע

F. Translate the following into Hebrew, with vowels.
1. The prophet will send the people to the city.
2. I will shut the door.
3. She will write a book.
4. They (m.) will not forget the words which I will write on this tablet.
5. You (f. sg.) will remember these words.
6. You (m. pl.) will hear this law, and you will remember these great commandments.

Limestone horned altar from Megiddo.

Lesson Twenty-four

VOCABULARY REVIEW

STUDY HINTS

1. This lesson contains a general review of the words you have covered. The words in Exercise A are by no means the most difficult words you have hitherto learned. Do not be content with this exercise unless you know at least 90 per cent of the list. The answers to this exercise are in Lesson 25, Exercise N.

2. Exercise D should be of interest to you. You are about to solve your first Hebrew crossword puzzle. If you like this method of reviewing, please let your instructor know.

EXERCISES

A. Give at sight or write, the English of the following words:

25. גַּב	17. עַיִן	9. אָדָם	1. אָכַל
26. בּוֹא	18. אֹזֶן	10. בַּיִת	2. לָמַד
27. דִּבֶּר	19. יָד	11. נָתַן	3. יָשַׁב
28. חָיָה	20. רֶגֶל	12. גָּמַר	4. אָמַר
29. אַתָּה	21. פֶּה	13. הָלַךְ	5. כָּתַב
30. אַתְּ	22. לָשׁוֹן	14. סָגַר	6. אָב
31. אֲנַחְנוּ	23. רֹאשׁ	15. עָמַד	7. אִישׁ
32. הֵם	24. אַף	16. סֵפֶר	8. אָח

134

84. אִשָּׁה	67. שָׁחוֹר	50. יֶלֶד	33. אֲנִי
85. אֵם	68. מִשְׁפָּחָה	51. בֵּן	34. הוּא
86. צִוָּה	69. שָׁנָה	52. יָם	35. נַעַר
87. אֲשֶׁר	70. יַלְדָּה	53. חֹשֶׁךְ	36. נַחַל
88. מַבּוּל	71. אֶל	54. אֹהֶל	37. פֶּרַח
89. אֲדָמָה	72. עַל	55. גָּדוֹל	38. שֵׂעָר
90. לֹא	73. בְּלִי	56. זָקֵן	39. אֶבֶן
91. תַּפּוּחַ	74. שָׂרָה	57. יָפֶה	40. כֶּלֶב
92. שָׁמַיִם	75. אֶחָד	58. רַע	41. גֶּשֶׁם
93. חֲלוֹם	76. לַיְלָה	59. מְנוֹרָה	42. בֶּגֶד
94. בָּרָא	77. עֶרֶב	60. טוֹב	43. פָּרָה
95. בָּנָה	78. יוֹם	61. דּוֹרָה	44. בְּהֵמָה
96. לָקַח	79. קוֹל	62. בְּרָכָה	45. מֶלֶךְ
97. רָאָה	80. תַּחַת	63. יֵשׁ	46. שֵׁם
98. זָכָר	81. מִן	64. צָעִיר	47. לָבָן
99. אֵלֶּה	82. דֶּלֶת	65. קָטָן	48. שִׁיר
100. שָׁכַב	83. עַם	66. עֵץ	49. סוּס

How many of these words do you really know? For satisfactory progress, you should know 90 of the 100 words.

B. Write either the opposite *or* the feminine of the following words: (*Example:* The opposite of טוֹב is רַע and of דּוֹר is דּוֹרָה.)

11. הָלַךְ	1. אָב
12. אַתֶּם	2. אַתָּה
13. זֶה	3. יוֹם
14. זָכָר	4. עֶרֶב
15. אוֹר	5. צָעִיר
16. יֶלֶד	6. קָטָן
17. אֶל	7. לָבָן
18. יֵשׁ	8. עַם
19. אִישׁ	9. תַּחַת
20. לָקַח	10. הֵן

This mud-brick house with thatch roof in modern Jericho is typical of the valley structures in ancient Palestine.

C. Write the English of the following words:

1. עִיר	6. שָׁמַע	11. שָׁלַח	16. יָדַע
2. קוֹל	7. אָהַב	12. קָרָא	17. קוּם
3. עַיִן	8. שְׁנַיִם	13. שׁוּב	18. יָצָא
4. עָלָה	9. לֵב	14. שִׁבְעָה	19. עָשָׂה
5. נָתַן	10. דֶּרֶךְ	15. עַם	20. עָבַר

D. Solve the Hebrew Crossword Puzzle on the following page.

　Follow these important directions:

- Do not insert vowels.
- Do not use final letters.
- Write only one letter in each square.
- Fill in the words *without* referring to the Vocabulary or the dictionary.

DOWN

1. day
2. in the beginning, or the first word in the Hebrew Bible
3. who?
4. why?
6. in a voice
9. from a river
11. I shall stand
12. he commanded
15. sea

ACROSS (right to left)

2. in the king
5. and in the mountains
7. two letters whose numerical values are 40 and 100, respectively
8. they
10. and a wife
12. my rib
13. garden
14. when?
16. the hand
17. opposite

Lesson Twenty-five

REVIEW EXERCISES FOR LESSONS 1–24

STUDY HINTS

1. This lesson consists of review exercises to test your knowledge of the lessons you have so far covered.
2. These exercises constitute an important review for your twelve-weeks test. (See Lesson 30.)

EXERCISES

A. Which four of the following words are segholates; which four are feminine by form; and which four are feminine by meaning?

9. עַיִן	5. שָׂדֶה	1. עֶרֶב
10. בְּרָכָה	6. סֵפֶר	2. יְרוּשָׁלַיִם
11. צֶלַע	7. יָד	3. מִצְוָה
12. שָׂפָה	8. דֶּלֶת	4. נַחַל

B. Rewrite the following words in Hebrew, with vowels, adding the definite article:

6. רֹאשׁ		1. אִישׁ
7. עַיִן		2. עֶרֶב
8. קוֹל		3. סֵפֶר
9. רֶגֶל		4. בֵּן
10. שָׁם		5. עִיר

138

C. Add the prepositions בְּ, כְּ, and לְ to each of the following words (with translation): לַיְלָה, סֵפֶר, עֶרֶב, עִיר, מַיִם.

Examples:

a man	אִישׁ	in a man	בְּאִישׁ
the man	הָאִישׁ	in the man	בָּאִישׁ
to a man	לְאִישׁ	like a man	כְּאִישׁ
to the man	לָאִישׁ	like the man	כָּאִישׁ

D. Read aloud and translate the following into English:

1. הָאִישׁ צוֹחֵק בְּקוֹל גָּדוֹל.
2. נָתַן הָאִישׁ אֶת־הַסֵּפֶר לַיֶּלֶד.
3. בָּרָא אֱלֹהִים אִשָּׁה מִן־הַצֵּלָע אֲשֶׁר לָקַח מִן־הָאָדָם.
4. תִּשְׁמַע רָחֵל אֶת־הַתּוֹרָה.
5. הָלְכוּ הַנְּעָרִים אֶל־הָעִיר בָּעֶרֶב.
6. נָתְנָה הָאִשָּׁה אֶת־הַפְּרָחִים לַיֶּלֶד הַקָּטָן.
7. בְּרֵאשִׁית בָּרָא אֱלֹהִים אֵת הַשָּׁמַיִם וְאֵת הָאָרֶץ.
8. לָקַח יוֹסֵף מַיִם מִן־הַנַּחַל אֶל־הַפֶּה.

E. Answer the following questions, based on Exercise D, in complete Hebrew sentences, without vowels.

1. אֵיךְ צָחַק הָאִישׁ?
2. מָה נָתַן הָאִישׁ לַיֶּלֶד?
3. מִי בָּרָא אֶת־הָאִשָּׁה?
4. מִי הָאִשָּׁה אֲשֶׁר תִּשְׁמַע אֶת־הַתּוֹרָה?
5. מָתַי הָלְכוּ הַנְּעָרִים אֶל־הָעִיר?
6. מָה נָתְנָה הָאִשָּׁה לַיֶּלֶד?
7. מָה בָּרָא אֱלֹהִים?
8. מִי לָקַח אֶת־הַמַּיִם מִן־הַנַּחַל?

F. Write the plural of the following:

9. סֵפֶר		5. רֶגֶל		1. יוֹם	
10. שָׂפָה		6. מֶלֶךְ		2. עַיִן	
11. בְּרָכָה		7. מִצְוָה		3. דּוֹדָה	
12. כֶּרֶם		8. לַיְלָה		4. דּוֹד	

15. אִישׁ   14. עַם   13. יָד

G. Give the English names corresponding to the following:

6. סִינַי	1. יַרְדֵּן
7. פָּרַס	2. מִצְרַיִם
8. כַּרְמֶל	3. יְרוּשָׁלַיִם
9. אַשּׁוּר	4. יִשְׂרָאֵל
10. כְּנַעַן	5. בֵּית לֶחֶם

H. Decline in full: חֲלוֹם *dream* and אוֹר *light*.

I. Translate the following into Hebrew:

1. our song
2. your (m. pl.) city
3. her dream
4. your (m. pl.) voice
5. your (m.) horse
6. my light
7. their (f.) hand
8. their (m.) hand
9. your (f.) city
10. his head
11. my song
12. your (m. pl.) head
13. our dream
14. their (m.) dream
15. your (m.) dream
16. her horse
17. our voice
18. your (f.) hand
19. my father
20. their (f.) tree

J. Conjugate the following: זָכַרְתִּי אֶת־שִׁירִי (*I remembered my song, you remembered your song*, etc.).

K. Write the perfect, present, and imperfect of מָכַר *to sell*.

L. Translate the following into English:

11. עָמַדְתְּ	6. תִּסְלְחִי	1. הֵם קוֹרְאִים
12. אֶשְׁמַע	7. נִזְכֹּר	2. מָצְאָה
13. תִּשְׁכַּחְנָה	8. לָקַחְתָּ	3. נָתְנוּ
14. אַתְּ לוֹמֶרֶת	9. תִּכְתֹּב	4. שְׁלַחְתֶּם
15. יָשַׁבְתִּי	10. יִמְלֹךְ	5. הִיא יוֹדַעַת

M. Add any of the following adjectives, קָטָן or שָׁחוֹר, טוֹב, גָּדוֹל, לָבָן, in the appropriate form to each of the following nouns:

6. פָּנִים		1. עֵינַיִם	
7. פָּרָס		2. רֶגֶל	
8. מַיִם		3. מִצְוָה	
9. סְפָרִים		4. סוּסוֹת	
10. חַיִּים		5. יְרוּשָׁלַיִם	

Nazareth Market

N. Write the Hebrew for the following words:

1. eat	26. come	51. son	76. night
2. learn	27. speak	52. sea	77. evening
3. sit	28. be	53. darkness	78. day
4. say	29. you (m. sg.)	54. tent	79. voice
5. write	30. you (f. sg.)	55. big	80. under
6. father	31. we	56. old	81. from
7. man	32. they (m. pl.)	57. beautiful	82. door
8. brother	33. I	58. bad	83. people
9. man, mankind	34. he	59. candlestick, lamp	84. woman
10. house	35. youth	60. good	85. mother
11. give	36. river	61. aunt	86. command
12. finish	37. flower	62. blessing	87. who, which
13. go	38. gate	63. there is, exists	88. flood
14. shut	39. stone	64. young	89. earth
15. stand	40. dog	65. small	90. no
16. book	41. rain	66. tree	91. apple
17. eye	42. garment	67. black	92. heaven, sky
18. ear	43. cow	68. family	93. dream
19. hand	44. beast	69. year	94. create
20. foot	45. king	70. girl	95. build
21. mouth	46. name	71. to	96. take
22. tongue	47. white	72. on	97. see
23. head	48. song	73. without	98. remember
24. nose	49. horse	74. field	99. these
25. back (of body)	50. boy	75. one	100. forget

These above words correspond to the list given in Lesson 24, Exercise A. Check your work with that list.

Note:

If you do 90 per cent of Exercises I, L, M, and N correctly, you may congratulate yourself. With this lesson you have covered more than one half of the work of First Semester Biblical Hebrew.

Lesson Twenty-six
DECLENSION OF MASCULINE NOUNS IN THE PLURAL

GRAMMAR AND NOTES

1. *Regular Masculine Nouns in the Plural*

In Lesson 21 we studied the declension of the regular masculine nouns in the singular, for instance, שִׁירִי *my song,* שִׁירְךָ *your song,* etc. We shall now learn the declension of the regular masculine nouns in the plural: *my songs, your songs,* etc. The pronominal suffixes (see Lesson 21) of nouns in the plural are slightly different from those used with the singular. These suffixes are the same for *all* nouns in the plural, as follows:

Pronominal Suffixes to Plural Nouns

our	ֵינוּ	my	ַי
your (m., pl.)	ֵיכֶם	your (m., sg.)	ֶיךָ
your (f., pl.)	ֵיכֶן	your (f., sg.)	ַיִךְ
their (m., pl.)	ֵיהֶם	his, its (m.)	ָיו
their (f., pl.)	ֵיהֶן	her, its (f.)	ֶיהָ

The declension of שִׁירִים *songs* is therefore as follows:

our songs	שִׁירֵינוּ	my songs	שִׁירַי
your (m., pl.) songs	שִׁירֵיכֶם	your (m., sg.) songs	שִׁירֶיךָ
your (f., pl.) songs	שִׁירֵיכֶן	your (f., sg.) songs	שִׁירַיִךְ
their (m., pl.) songs	שִׁירֵיהֶם	his songs	שִׁירָיו
their (f., pl.) songs	שִׁירֵיהֶן	her songs	שִׁירֶיהָ

143

Notes:

a. The pronominal suffixes to plural nouns always contain the letter י, for example, סוּסֵנוּ *our horse*, but סוּסֵינוּ *our horses*. In texts without vowel points, this is often the only sign for the plural: ספרך *your book*, but ספריך *your books*; בנכם *your son*, but בניכם *your sons*.

b. The suffix ה of the third person feminine singular has no mappiq. (For an explanation of mappiq, see Lesson 21.) This mappiq is used with the declension of singular nouns only.

c. Bear in mind that before adding the suffixes to masculine nouns, the plural ending ים‎ָ is omitted:

songs	שִׁירִים,	*but* my songs	שִׁירַי	(not	שִׁירִימַי)
trees	עֵצִים,	*but* our trees	עֵצֵינוּ	(not	עֵצִימֵינוּ)

For the sake of comparison, we shall now give the full declension of a regular masculine noun, in the singular and in the plural. Let us take the word סוּס *horse*:

my horses	סוּסַי	my horse	סוּסִי
your (m. sg.) horses	סוּסֶיךָ	your (m. sg.) horse	סוּסְךָ
your (f. sg.) horses	סוּסַיִךְ	your (f. sg.) horse	סוּסֵךְ
his horses	סוּסָיו	his horse	סוּסוֹ
her horses	סוּסֶיהָ	her horse	סוּסָה
our horses	סוּסֵינוּ	our horse	סוּסֵנוּ
your (m. pl.) horses	סוּסֵיכֶם	your (m. pl.) horse	סוּסְכֶם
your (f. pl.) horses	סוּסֵיכֶן	your (f. pl.) horse	סוּסְכֶן
their (m.) horses	סוּסֵיהֶם	their (m.) horse	סוּסָם
their (f.) horses	סוּסֵיהֶן	their (f.) horse	סוּסָן

2. *Biblical Word List Twelve* (verbs occurring 200 to 5000 times)

to command	צִוָּה
to lift up, carry	נָשָׂא
to die	מוּת
to put	שִׂים
to remember	זָכַר

STUDY HINTS

1. In Lesson 21 we learned the declension of regular masculine nouns in the singular, such as *my book, your book, our book,* etc. This lesson deals with the declension of the regular masculine nouns in the plural such as *my books, your books, our books,* etc. The pronominal suffixes in the plural are slightly different from those attached to the singular. But these suffixes are *regular and invariable* for all plural nouns so declined. Once you learn these suffixes carefully you can use them with the declension of any plural noun, whether the noun is masculine or feminine. The suffixes do not change, although change may take place in the noun itself.

2. Another important point to remember is that the pronominal suffixes to the plural *always* contain the letter י. In texts without vowel points this י will help you determine the number: ידנו *our hand,* ידינו *our hands;* שירו *his song,* שיריו *his songs,* etc. Exercise A gives you ample opportunity for practice in declining the plural.

3. The mappiq, or the dot in the suffix of the third person feminine singular, is not used with plural nouns.

4. Memorize the complete declension of סוס *horse* as given in this lesson.

5. Try Exercises A, C, and D orally before attempting to write them.

6. The Biblical Word List is very useful; make sure you know and review the other word lists in this series.

EXERCISES

A. Decline the following nouns in the plural, orally and in writing, with vowels: עֵצִים *trees,* דּוֹדִים *uncles,* סוּסִים *horses.*

B. Decline שִׁיר *song* in full, in the singular and in the plural, with vowels.

C. Translate the following into English:

7. דּוֹדֶיךָ	4. סוּסֵיהֶן	1. סוּסֵינוּ
8. יָדֵינוּ	5. שִׁירַיִךְ	2. יָדָיו
9. שִׁירַי	6. שִׁירֵיכֶם	3. דּוֹדֵךְ

14. סוּסֶׂיהָ	12. סוּסַׂיִךְ	10. סוּסָיו
15. סוּסֵיכֶן	13. דּוֹדֵיהֶן	11. יָדַי

D. Translate the following into English:

11. קוֹלוֹ	6. דּוֹדִי	1. אוֹרֵנוּ
12. שִׁירָיו	7. רֹאשְׁכֶם	2. עִירְכֶם
13. רֹאשָׁהּ	8. שִׁירַיִךְ	3. סוּסֵיכֶם
14. עִירֵנוּ	9. שִׁירֵיהֶם	4. סוּסָהּ
15. סוּסֵׂינוּ	10. שִׁירָם	5. סוּסֶׂיהָ

E. The following words, which you have already learned, change their inner vowels when declined. We shall study these changes systematically in due course. Try at this stage to guess their meaning.

11. שְׁמְכֶם	6. בָּנֶיךָ	1. בֵּיתָם
12. עָלֶיךָ	7. בָּנֶיהָ	2. בֵּיתֵנוּ
13. סְפָרֶיהָ	8. סְפָרֵינוּ	3. עִירוֹ
14. יַלְדְכֶם	9. סְפָרֵנוּ	4. דְּבָרָיו
15. יַלְדֵיכֶם	10. עֵינֵיכֶם	5. כַּלְבָּם

F. Translate the following into Hebrew, with vowels:

1. my horse
2. their (m.) horses
3. your (m.) city
4. your (m. pl.) city
5. your (m. sg.) hands
6. your (f. sg.) hands
7. our head
8. her songs
9. his horses
10. his voice
11. her hand
12. my songs
13. their (m.) voice
14. our horses
15. our uncle

G. Translate the following into Hebrew, without vowels (בַּיִת house, כֶּלֶב dog, סֵפֶר book, שַׁעַר gate, עַיִן eye):

1. our gate
2. our gates
3. your (m. sg.) eye
4. your (m. sg.) eyes
5. your (f. sg.) house
6. his dog
7. his dogs
8. your (f. sg.) books
9. my eye
10. my eyes
11. her books
12. her book
13. his eyes
14. their (m.) house
15. their (f.) dogs

Lesson Twenty-seven
THE IMPERATIVE; PREPOSITIONS;
DECLENSION OF FEMININE NOUNS

VOCABULARY

to forgive	סָלַח	to shut	סָגַר
to forget	שָׁכַח	to remember	זָכַר
to send	שָׁלַח	to finish	גָּמַר
there	שָׁם	to rule	מָשַׁל
here	פֹּה, הֵנָּה	where to?	אָן, אָנָה?
how many? how much?	כַּמָּה?	where from?	מֵאַיִן?

GRAMMAR AND NOTES

1. *Imperative of Regular Qal Verbs*

Compare the following:

B. *Imperative*		A. *Imperfect*	
keep! (m. sg.)	שְׁמֹר	you (m. sg.) will keep	תִּשְׁמֹר
keep! (f. sg.)	שִׁמְרִי	you (f. sg.) will keep	תִּשְׁמְרִי
keep! (m. pl.)	שִׁמְרוּ	you (m. pl.) will keep	תִּשְׁמְרוּ
keep! (f. pl.)	שְׁמֹרְנָה	you (f. pl.) will keep	תִּשְׁמֹרְנָה

You have probably recognized the second person (singular and plural) of the imperfect tense. Notice that the imperative is formed from the imperfect by dropping the prefix –תּ. Thus:

שְׁמֹר < (תִּ)שְׁמֹר   (תִּ)שְׁמְרוּ > שִׁמְרוּ

שִׁמְרִי > (תִּ)שְׁמְרִי   (תִּ)שְׁמֹרְנָה > שְׁמֹרְנָה

147

Note: שָׁמְרִ and שָׁמְרוּ become שִׁמְרִי and שִׁמְרוּ because Hebrew words never begin with two shvas. (See Lesson 16.)

Accordingly, the imperative of גָּמַר *to finish* and סָגַר *to shut* is as follows:

finish! גְּמֹר, גִּמְרִי, גִּמְרוּ, גְּמֹרְנָה

shut! סְגֹר, סִגְרִי, סִגְרוּ, סְגֹרְנָה

Verbs having a guttural in their ל׳ הַפֹּעַל or ע׳ הַפֹּעַל (Lesson 23) therefore are as follows:

hear! שְׁמַע, שִׁמְעִי, שִׁמְעוּ, שְׁמַעְנָה

forgive! סְלַח, סִלְחִי, סִלְחוּ, סְלַחְנָה

send! שְׁלַח, שִׁלְחִי, שִׁלְחוּ, שְׁלַחְנָה

We shall now review the full conjugation of the regular Qal verbs such as מָשַׁל *to rule, govern.*

Perfect: I have ruled, I ruled, etc.

מָשַׁלְתִּי, מָשַׁלְתָּ, מָשַׁלְתְּ, מָשַׁל, מָשְׁלָה

מָשַׁלְנוּ, מְשַׁלְתֶּם, מְשַׁלְתֶּן, מָשְׁלוּ

Present: I am ruling, I rule, etc.

אֲנִי, אַתָּה, הוּא – מוֹשֵׁל

אֲנִי, אַתְּ, הִיא – מוֹשֶׁלֶת (מוֹשְׁלָה)

אֲנַחְנוּ, אַתֶּם, הֵם – מוֹשְׁלִים

אֲנַחְנוּ, אַתֶּן, הֵן – מוֹשְׁלוֹת

Imperfect: I shall rule, etc.

אֶמְשֹׁל, תִּמְשֹׁל, תִּמְשְׁלִי, יִמְשֹׁל, תִּמְשֹׁל

נִמְשֹׁל, תִּמְשְׁלוּ, תִּמְשֹׁלְנָה, יִמְשְׁלוּ, תִּמְשֹׁלְנָה

Imperative: Rule!

מְשֹׁל, מִשְׁלִי, מִשְׁלוּ, מְשֹׁלְנָה

2. *The Preposition "From"*

	Group A	Group B
from a book	מִן סֵפֶר *	מִסֵּפֶר
from a house	מִן בַּיִת *	מִבַּיִת

---

*The preposition מִן as a separate word, followed by an indefinite noun, is seldom found in the Hebrew Bible; the form in Group B is used.

from there	מִן שָׁם *	מִשָּׁם
from a city	מִן עִיר *	מֵעִיר
from a father	מִן אָב *	מֵאָב
from the book	מִן־הַסֵּפֶר	מֵהַסֵּפֶר
from the house	מִן־הַבַּיִת	מֵהַבַּיִת
from the city	מִן־הָעִיר	מֵהָעִיר

In Group A מִן *from*, as a separate word, is used. In Group B, the inseparable preposition –מִ or –מֵ is used. מִ is followed by a dagesh to compensate for the loss of the nun in the word מִן. However, before a guttural (which does not admit a dagesh) or before ר, –מֵ with the long vowel (ֵ) is used instead of –מִ. Thus: מִשָּׁם *from there*, מִיּוֹם *from a day*, מִשָּׁנָה *from a year*, but: מֵעִיר *from a town*, מֵהָעִיר *from the city*, מֵהַבַּיִת *from the house*, מֵרַע *from evil*. Notice that the –מֵ does not assimilate the definite article ה as do the other inseparable prepositions. (See Lesson 16.)

3. *Biblical Word List Thirteen* (nouns based on frequently occurring biblical radicals)

face	פָּנִים
man, mankind	אֱנוֹשׁ
life	חַיִּים
holiness	קֹדֶשׁ
living	חַי

(So far, 60 biblical words have been listed. Review all thirteen lists and test your progress to find out how many of these words you know.)

4. *Declension of Feminine Nouns Ending in ה ֶ*

The pronominal suffixes are the same as those used with the masculine nouns. In the singular, the ה is changed into ת before the suffixes are added. In the plural, the suffixes are added to the plural form –וֹת without any changes. As an illustration, the declension of מְנוֹרָה *lamp* is given on the following page.

	Plural מְנוֹרוֹת		*Singular* מְנוֹרָה
מְנוֹרוֹתֵינוּ	מְנוֹרוֹתַי	מְנוֹרָתֵנוּ	מְנוֹרָתִי
מְנוֹרוֹתֵיכֶם	מְנוֹרוֹתֶיךָ	מְנוֹרַתְכֶם*	מְנוֹרָתְךָ
מְנוֹרוֹתֵיכֶן	מְנוֹרוֹתַיִךְ	מְנוֹרַתְכֶן*	מְנוֹרָתֵךְ
מְנוֹרוֹתֵיהֶם	מְנוֹרוֹתָיו	מְנוֹרָתָם	מְנוֹרָתוֹ
מְנוֹרוֹתֵיהֶן	מְנוֹרוֹתֶיהָ	מְנוֹרָתָן	מְנוֹרָתָהּ

STUDY HINTS

1. The vocabulary contains a review of some of the words frequently used in connection with the imperative.

2. Review the imperfect tense (Lesson 23) before learning the imperative. The imperative is formed from the imperfect minus the prefix תּ. (See Grammar and Notes 1 of this lesson.)

3. The Note in Grammar and Notes 1 contains an important rule in Hebrew grammar. *No Hebrew words may begin with two shvas.* (See also Lesson 16.)

4. Now is the time to review the entire Qal conjugation of מָשַׁל as given in this lesson.

5. Carefully note the use of the prepositions מִן and –מ, both meaning *from*. This use is different from the use of the other attached prepositions בְּ, כְּ, and לְ. (See Lesson 16.)

6. In Biblical Word List Thirteen, remember that פָּנִים *face* and חַיִּים *life* are found in the plural form only, although they may be singular in meaning. (See Lesson 22.)

7. For practice, first do Exercises A, B, C, D, and E orally.

EXERCISES

A. Write the imperfect tense of גָּמַר *to finish* and שָׁלַח *to send*.

B. Write the imperative of גָּמַר *to finish,* זָכַר *to remember,* שָׁלַח *to send,* and שָׁמַע *to hear*.

C. Write the perfect, present, imperfect, and imperative of סָגַר *to shut* and סָלַח *to forgive*.

---

*Notice that in the singular declension the qamats under the ר changes to a pataḥ in the second person plural, masculine and feminine.

Jericho seen from old Roman road.

D. Translate the following into English:

1. לַמְּנוֹרָה	6. מִשָּׁמַיִם	11. מֵהָעִיר
2. מִשָּׁם	7. מִפֹּה	12. מֵהָעֵינַיִם
3. מֵהַדֶּלֶת	8. מִלַּיְלָה	13. מִן־הַבַּיִת
4. מֵאֹזֶן	9. מִן־הָעִיר	14. מִנַּחַל
5. כְּאַף	10. בָּעִיר	15. מִן־הַשָּׂדֶה

E. Translate the following into English:

1. מִיּוֹם	6. מִפֹּה לְשָׁם
2. כְּקָטֹן כַּגָּדוֹל	7. מֵהָעֵץ לַפֶּה
3. מֵעִיר, לְעִיר	8. מֵהָאָב לַבֵּן
4. הַבַּיִת	9. מִבַּיִת לְבַיִת
5. מִבֹּקֶר עַד עֶרֶב	10. מֵהָאָב לָאֵם

F. Translate the following into Hebrew (use –מִ or –מֵ *from*):

1. from year to year
2. from the house to the garden
3. from this day
4. from this house
5. from this family

6. from Egypt
7. from Jerusalem
8. from the heaven to the earth
9. from the city
10. from this beautiful city

G. Write the correct form of the verb, as indicated below:

Verb	Imperfect	Perfect	Participle	Personal Pronoun
1. מָשַׁל	1. אֶמְשֹׁל	1. מָשַׁלְתִּי	1. מוֹשֵׁל	1. אֲנִי (m.)
2. זָכַר	2.	2.	2.	2. הוּא
3. שָׁמַר	3.	3.	3.	3. אֲנַחְנוּ (f.)
4. שָׁלַח	4.	4.	4.	4. אַתֶּן
5. צָחַק	5.	5.	5.	5. אַתָּה
6. סָלַח	6.	6.	6.	6. אֲנִי (f.)
7. מָכַר	7.	7.	7.	7. הִיא
8. שָׁמַע	8.	8.	8.	8. אַתֶּם
9. מָלַךְ	9.	9.	9.	9. הֵם
10. כָּתַב	10.	10.	10.	10. אַתְּ

H. Translate the following into Hebrew, without vowels:

1. The man who stood near the door is my brother.
2. The woman who remembered the prophet is my mother.
3. This prophet is writing on the tablet.
4. In the morning I say, "Good morning!"
5. At night my little brother* says, "Good night!" to my father and to my mother.

I. Give the Hebrew for the following:

1. my big brother
2. our small book
3. his beautiful song
4. his beautiful songs
5. her small lamp

6. our holy law
7. your (m. pl.) great commandments
8. your (m. sg.) good star
9. our big city (f.)
10. my good uncle

---

*Translate, "in the night, my brother, the little (one)" בַּלַּיְלָה אָחִי הַקָּטָן

J. Write the following in Hebrew, without vowels (these are all very common biblical words):

1. to go up	11. to give birth	21. land
2. to make	12. to go out	22. man
3. to command	13. to come	23. one
4. to read	14. to speak	24. brother
5. to take	15. to be	25. mother
6. to give	16. father	26. God
7. to carry	17. face	27. city
8. to pass	18. people	28. eye
9. to walk	19. heart	29. I
10. to know	20. mountain	30. voice

K. Give the declension of מְנוֹרָה *lamp* and סוּסָה *mare* in the singular and the plural.

Lesson Twenty-eight
NUMBERS; MORE ABOUT DEFINITE ARTICLE *THE*; MORE ABOUT CONJUNCTION *AND*

VOCABULARY

new	חָדָשׁ (חֲדָשִׁים)	nought (zero*)	אֶפֶס
month	חֹדֶשׁ (חֲדָשִׁים)	yet, still, again	עוֹד
wise	חָכָם (חֲכָמִים)	thousand	אֶלֶף (אֲלָפִים)
moment	רֶגַע	continually	תָּמִיד
suddenly	פִּתְאֹם	very, exceedingly	מְאֹד
hundred	מֵאָה (מֵאוֹת)	until	עַד
bird (f.)	צִפּוֹר (צִפֳּרִים)	hour	שָׁעָה (שָׁעוֹת)
		week	שָׁבוּעַ (שָׁבוּעוֹת)

GRAMMAR AND NOTES

1. *Numbers*

Feminine	Masculine		Feminine	Masculine	
שֵׁשׁ	שִׁשָּׁה	6.	אַחַת	אֶחָד	1.
שֶׁבַע	שִׁבְעָה	7.	שְׁתַּיִם (שְׁתֵּי)	שְׁנַיִם (שְׁנֵי)	2.
שְׁמוֹנֶה	שְׁמוֹנָה	8.	שָׁלֹשׁ	שְׁלֹשָׁה	3.
תֵּשַׁע	תִּשְׁעָה	9.	אַרְבַּע	אַרְבָּעָה	4.
עֶשֶׂר	עֲשָׂרָה	10.	חָמֵשׁ	חֲמִשָּׁה	5.

Zero in Modern Hebrew.

Feminine	Masculine		Feminine	Masculine	
שֵׁשׁ עֶשְׂרֵה	שִׁשָּׁה עָשָׂר	.16	אַחַת עֶשְׂרֵה	אַחַד עָשָׂר	.11
שְׁבַע עֶשְׂרֵה	שִׁבְעָה עָשָׂר	.17	שְׁתֵּים עֶשְׂרֵה	שְׁנֵים עָשָׂר	.12
שְׁמֹנֶה עֶשְׂרֵה	שְׁמֹנָה עָשָׂר	.18	שְׁלֹשׁ עֶשְׂרֵה	שְׁלֹשָׁה עָשָׂר	.13
תְּשַׁע עֶשְׂרֵה	תִּשְׁעָה עָשָׂר	.19	אַרְבַּע עֶשְׂרֵה	אַרְבָּעָה עָשָׂר	.14
עֶשְׂרִים	עֶשְׂרִים	.20	חֲמֵשׁ עֶשְׂרֵה	חֲמִשָּׁה עָשָׂר	.15

We shall first discuss the numbers from 1 through 10. We have already noted that in Hebrew the numbers have two forms: masculine and feminine.

The numbers, 3 through 10, used with the masculine nouns, have the feminine ending הָ. This is one of the peculiarities of the Semitic languages: Numbers with the *feminine* ending הָ are used with the *masculine* nouns.

The nouns usually follow the numbers, as in English, with the exception of אֶחָד (m.) or אַחַת (f.). (See next paragraph.)

Examples:

	three boys	שְׁלֹשָׁה יְלָדִים
	ten books	עֲשָׂרָה סְפָרִים
But:	three women	שְׁלֹשׁ נָשִׁים
	ten blessings	עֶשֶׂר בְּרָכוֹת

Note: In Classical Hebrew the numbers may follow the noun, but this is rare, for example:

three horses	סוּסִים שְׁלֹשָׁה

The number *one*, אֶחָד (m.) and אַחַת (f.), is treated as an adjective, and hence it always follows the noun and agrees with it.

one man	אִישׁ אֶחָד	one woman	אִשָּׁה אַחַת
one book	סֵפֶר אֶחָד	one blessing	בְּרָכָה אַחַת

The number *one*, אֶחָד (m.) or אַחַת (f.), may also stand for the indefinite article *a* or *an*:

	a man or one man	אִישׁ אֶחָד
	a woman or one woman	אִשָּׁה אַחַת
	an apple or one apple	תַּפּוּחַ אֶחָד

אֶחָד *one* (m.) has a plural form אֲחָדִים *a few, not many;* for instance, אֲחָדִים סְפָרִים *few books,* דְּבָרִים אֲחָדִים *few words* or *few things.*

The Hebrew word for *two* שְׁנַיִם (m.) and שְׁתַּיִם (f.) has, naturally, a dual ending (ַיִם–). These forms are used when they follow the noun or when used separately.

Examples:

Two sons (i.e., *sons, a pair*)	בָּנִים שְׁנַיִם

How many books (are there) on the table? Two.

כַּמָּה סְפָרִים עַל־הַשֻּׁלְחָן? שְׁנַיִם

When שְׁנַיִם or שְׁתַּיִם are placed before the noun, they assume the shorter forms שְׁנֵי and שְׁתֵּי, respectively. These forms are known as *construct forms*. (See Lesson 32.)

Examples:

two boys	שְׁנֵי יְלָדִים	*but:*	יְלָדִים שְׁנַיִם
two blessings	שְׁתֵּי בְּרָכוֹת	*but:*	בְּרָכוֹת שְׁתַּיִם

The forms on the right are rarely used. The shorter forms are regularly used.

Study carefully:

	two books	שְׁנֵי סְפָרִים
But:	the two books	שְׁנֵי הַסְּפָרִים
	two girls	שְׁתֵּי יְלָדוֹת
But:	the two girls	שְׁתֵּי הַיְלָדוֹת

Note the following idiomatic inflection of שְׁנַיִם and שְׁתַּיִם:

שְׁתֵּינוּ	both of us	שְׁנֵינוּ
שְׁתֵּיכֶן	both of you	שְׁנֵיכֶם
שְׁתֵּיהֶן	both of them	שְׁנֵיהֶם

Example:

Both of them (m.) went to the mountain.

שְׁנֵיהֶם הָלְכוּ אֶל־הָהָר.

2. *The Numerals 11 Through 19*

These numerals are expressed by placing a number (from *1* through *10*) before either עָשָׂר (m.) or עֶשְׂרֵה (f.), depending on the gender of the objects being counted. Notice that the *number + ten* always agree in gender with each other and with the object they modify.

Example:

fourteen mares (four/ten mares)	אַרְבַּע עֶשְׂרֵה סוּסוֹת
fourteen horses (four/ten horses)	אַרְבָּעָה עָשָׂר סוּסִים

3. *The "Tens" From 20 Through 90*

With the exception of עֶשְׂרִים *twenty*, which is derived from עֲשָׂרָה, the "tens" are expressed by the plural form of their corresponding units:

3	שְׁלֹשָׁה	30	שְׁלֹשִׁים
4	אַרְבָּעָה	40	אַרְבָּעִים
5	חֲמִשָּׁה	50	חֲמִשִּׁים
6	שִׁשָּׁה	60	שִׁשִּׁים
7	שִׁבְעָה	70	שִׁבְעִים
8	שְׁמוֹנָה	80	שְׁמוֹנִים
9	תִּשְׁעָה	90	תִּשְׁעִים

The numerals 20 through 90 are used with both masculine and feminine nouns.

The tens are usually connected with the "units" by the conjunction *and*. For instance, *24* is עֶשְׂרִים וְאַרְבָּעָה, *36 boys* שְׁלֹשִׁים וְשִׁשָּׁה יְלָדִים, *36 girls* שְׁלֹשִׁים וְשֵׁשׁ יְלָדוֹת.

Notes:

a. The units may precede the tens but this order is not frequently used.

b. The following numerals are used with both masculine and feminine nouns.

hundred	מֵאָה – מֵאוֹת
two hundred	מָאתַיִם – שְׁתֵּי מֵאוֹת
thousand	אֶלֶף – אֲלָפִים
ten thousand, myriad	רְבָבָה – רְבָבוֹת

Note: We shall deal more fully with the numerals in future lessons. Memorize the following:

one girl	יַלְדָּה אַחַת	one boy	יֶלֶד אֶחָד
two girls	שְׁתֵּי יְלָדוֹת	two boys	שְׁנֵי יְלָדִים
three girls	שָׁלֹשׁ יְלָדוֹת	three boys	שְׁלֹשָׁה יְלָדִים
four girls	אַרְבַּע יְלָדוֹת	four boys	אַרְבָּעָה יְלָדִים
five girls	חָמֵשׁ יְלָדוֹת	five boys	חֲמִשָּׁה יְלָדִים

4. *More About Definite Article "The"* –הַ

The definite article –הַ is usually pointed with pataḥ, followed by a dagesh: לַיְלָה *night*, הַלַּיְלָה *the night*. (See Lesson 6.)

Before a word beginning with א, ר, and ע (when the latter is not pointed with qamats), the definite article is –הָ. (See Lesson 9.)

evening	עֶרֶב	the evening	הָעֶרֶב
light	אוֹר	the light	הָאוֹר

Before a word beginning with unaccented –חָ, –הָ, and –עָ, the definite article is –הֶ.

strong (one)	חָזָק	the strong (one)	הֶחָזָק
loyal (one)	חָסִיד	the loyal (one)	הֶחָסִיד

Israeli cowboys use the arid Negev desert as a cattle range.

poor (one)	עָנִי	the poor (one)	הֶעָנִי
mountains	הָרִים	the mountains	הֶהָרִים

But הַחָכְמָה *the wisdom* since the qamats under ח is a short vowel, pronounced "o".

5. *More About Conjunction "And" –*וְ

The usual form for *and* is the prefix –וְ.

a man and a woman	אִישׁ וְאִשָּׁה
a day and a night	יוֹם וְלַיְלָה

If the word begins with a shva (ְ) or with any of the letters בומפ (known as *Bumaf*), the conjunction *and* will be וּ (pronounced as the Hebrew אוּ).

	Moses and David	מֹשֶׁה וְדָוִד
But:	David and Moses	דָוִד וּמֹשֶׁה
	one and two	אֶחָד וּשְׁנַיִם
	twenty-three	עֶשְׂרִים וּשְׁלֹשָׁה
	and in the house	וּבַבַּיִת

6. *Biblical Word List Fourteen.* (adjectives with frequently occurring biblical roots; these adjectives are found often in the psalms)

wicked	רָשָׁע
strong, firm	חָזָק
holy	קָדוֹשׁ
righteous, just	צַדִּיק
pious, loyal	חָסִיד

STUDY HINTS

1. You must begin by first memorizing the numerals 1 through 10 in the masculine and then in the feminine. Write these numerals from memory, with vowels. Check your work and correct any mistakes you may have made.

2. The shorter forms שְׁנֵי and שְׁתֵּי are used when they are followed by nouns: שְׁנֵי יְלָדִים *two boys*, שְׁתֵּי מְנוֹרוֹת *two lamps*. One may also write שְׁנַיִם יְלָדִים *two boys*.

3. Note that there is no Hebrew equivalent for *a* and *an*. סֵפֶר means both *book* and *a book*, דוֹד *uncle* or *an uncle*.

4. Carefully note the distinction between שְׁנֵי סְפָרִים and שְׁנֵי הַסְּפָרִים. The former means *two books*, the latter *the two books*.

5. You can easily learn the tens if you know the corresponding units.

6. The numeral *one* as an adjective follows the noun and agrees with it in gender, e.g., אִישׁ אֶחָד *one man*, אִשָּׁה אַחַת *one woman*. The numerals 3 through 10 can either precede or follow the noun. More will be said in following lessons regarding the numerals 1 and 3 through 10 in the construct state.

7. Learn carefully the idiomatic usage of שְׁנַיִם and שְׁתַּיִם; *both of us* (m.), שְׁנֵינוּ *both of you* (f.), שְׁתֵּיכֶן, etc.

8. Study the rules for the definite article before a guttural with the examples given. At this stage it is useful for you to review the simpler rules for the definite article in Lessons 6 and 9.

9. The paragraph on the conjunction *and* is important. All you have to remember is that if a word begins with the sign shva or one of the letters בומפ, the conjunction *and* is וּ (not וְ).

Moses	מֹשֶׁה	and Moses	וּמֹשֶׁה
a law	מִצְוָה	and a law	וּמִצְוָה
eighty	שְׁמוֹנִים	and eighty	וּשְׁמוֹנִים

EXERCISES

A. Write the numbers in Hebrew, from 1 through 10, first in the masculine and then in the feminine, with vowels.

B. Write the numbers in Hebrew, from 11 through 19, first in the masculine and then in the feminine, with vowels.

C. Write the numbers in Hebrew, from 30 through 50, in the masculine only, without vowels.

D. Write the numbers in Hebrew, from 70 through 99, in the masculine only, without vowels.

E. Give the corresponding English numbers of the following (indicate gender):

6. עֶשְׂרִים וּשְׁלֹשָׁה	1. שְׁמוֹנָה
7. שִׁבְעִים וְשִׁבְעָה	2. שְׁבַע־עֶשְׂרֵה
8. שִׁשִּׁים וְחָמֵשׁ	3. שְׁלֹשִׁים וְאַרְבָּעָה
9. שְׁלֹשִׁים וְאֶחָד	4. חֲמִשִּׁים וְתֵשַׁע
10. אֶלֶף מֵאָה וְאַרְבָּעִים	5. תִּשְׁעִים וְתֵשַׁע

11. אַרְבָּעִים וְתִשְׁעָה   16. שִׁשִּׁים וּשְׁלֹשָׁה

12. שְׁמוֹנִים וּשְׁמוֹנָה   17. שְׁלֹשִׁים וּשְׁנַיִם

13. שִׁבְעִים וְאֶחָד   18. שְׁמוֹנִים וְשִׁבְעָה

14. עֶשְׂרִים וְתֵשַׁע   19. תִּשְׁעִים וְאַרְבַּע

15. חֲמִשִּׁים וְחָמֵשׁ   20. מֵאָה עֶשְׂרִים וְשִׁשָּׁה

F. Write the following numbers in Hebrew, first in the masculine and then in the feminine, without vowels: 40, 45, 31, 24, 48, 98, 16, 11, 94, 10, 39, 68, 62, 9, 72, 88, 70, 92, 133, 174, 186, 199, 200, 376, 1000, 1368, 1975.

G. Answer the following questions in Hebrew, without vowels.

1. חֲמִשָּׁה וְאַרְבָּעָה, כַּמָּה הֵם?

2. עֶשְׂרִים וְאֶחָד וְאַרְבָּעִים וּשְׁנַיִם?

3. חֲמִשִּׁים וְחָמֵשׁ וּשְׁלֹשִׁים?

4. עֶשְׂרִים וְאֶחָד וְשִׁבְעִים וּשְׁלֹשָׁה?

5. שְׁלֹשִׁים וְאַרְבָּעָה וְשִׁשִּׁים וְשִׁשָּׁה?

6. מֵאָה וְאֶחָד וְשִׁבְעִים וּשְׁנַיִם?

7. מֵאָה וְשִׁבְעִים וּמֵאָה וְעֶשְׂרִים?

8. שִׁבְעִים וְאַרְבָּעִים?

9. שִׁבְעִים וְאַרְבַּע וַחֲמִשִּׁים?

10. שְׁמוֹנִים וְאֶחָד וְעֶשְׂרִים וְתִשְׁעָה?

H. Answer the following questions in complete Hebrew sentences, without vowels:

1. כַּמָּה שָׁנִים יָשַׁבְתָּ בָּעִיר?   6. כַּמָּה אָזְנַיִם לַסּוּס?

2. כַּמָּה יָמִים בְּשָׁבוּעַ?   7. כַּמָּה עֵינַיִם לְאִישׁ?

3. כַּמָּה יָמִים בְּשָׁנָה?   8. כַּמָּה עֵינַיִם לִשְׁנֵי סוּסִים?

4. כַּמָּה יָדַיִם לְאִישׁ?   9. כַּמָּה רַגְלַיִם לְצִפּוֹר?

5. כַּמָּה רַגְלַיִם לְכֶלֶב?   10. כַּמָּה שָׁעוֹת בַּיּוֹם אַתָּה לוֹמֵד?

Note: The plural of יוֹם *day* is יָמִים, not יוֹמִים. The plural of שָׁנָה *year* is שָׁנִים, not שָׁנוֹת.

I. Write the correct number in Hebrew, without vowels.

סוּסִים	(6)	6.	סְפָרִים	(8)
כְּלָבִים	(6)	7.	יְלָדִים	(3)
שָׁנִים	(5)	8.	יְלָדוֹת	(4)
מִשְׁפָּחוֹת	(4)	9.	שִׁירִים	(2)
מְנוֹרוֹת	(10)	10.	סוּסוֹת	(2)

J. Translate the following into Hebrew, without vowels.

1. God created the heaven and the earth in 7 days.
2. He is reading 6 books and 8 songs.
3. I took 5 boys with me[1] to the city.
4. He gave me[2] 5 lamps and 2 horses.
5. We took 39 books to the city.

עִמִּי [1]   לִי [2]

K. Memorize the following:

אַחַת וְאַחַת, הֵן שְׁתַּיִם.	אַחַת וְאַחַת, הֵן שְׁתַּיִם.	אַחַת וְאַחַת, הֵן שְׁתַּיִם.
יֵשׁ לְאִישׁ שְׁתֵּי יָדַיִם.	יֵשׁ לְאִישׁ שְׁתֵּי אָזְנַיִם.	יֵשׁ לְאִישׁ שְׁתֵּי עֵינַיִם.
שְׁתֵּי יָדַיִם וּפֶה אֶחָד?	שְׁתֵּי אָזְנַיִם וּפֶה אֶחָד?	שְׁתֵּי עֵינַיִם וּפֶה אֶחָד?
עֲבֹד הַרְבֵּה וְדַבֵּר מְעַט!	שְׁמַע הַרְבֵּה וְדַבֵּר מְעַט!	רְאֵה הַרְבֵּה וְדַבֵּר מְעַט!

Notes:

a. יֵשׁ לְאִישׁ *there is to the man*, or *the man has*; יֵשׁ לִי *there is to me*, or *I have*, etc. יֵשׁ *there is, there are.*

b. עַיִן *eye*, אֹזֶן *ear*, and יָד *hand* are feminine. (Why? See Lesson 13.)

c. רְאֵה *see!* Imperative of רָאָה *to see.*

d. הַרְבֵּה *much, many*; מְעַט *little, few.*

e. דַּבֵּר *speak!* Imperative of דִּבֵּר *to speak.*

f. עֲבֹד *work!* Imperative of עָבַד *to work.*

Lesson Twenty-nine

REVIEW OF LESSONS 20–28

IMPORTANT POINTS TO REMEMBER

1. The active participles of verbs with the last letter of the root a guttural, such as יָדַע and סָלַח, are formed as follows (Lesson 20):

   knowing   יוֹדֵעַ, יוֹדַעַת, יוֹדְעִים, יוֹדְעוֹת

   forgiving   סוֹלֵחַ, סוֹלַחַת, סוֹלְחִים, סוֹלְחוֹת

2. Names of countries, cities, and towns are feminine (Lesson 20).

   בָּבֶל, מִצְרַיִם, יִשְׂרָאֵל, בֵּית לֶחֶם, יְרוּשָׁלַיִם, אַשּׁוּר

   (The Hebrew words אֶרֶץ *land* and עִיר *city* are also feminine.) (Lesson 20)

3. Biblical Word List Eight (Lesson 20).

   קוּם, עָלָה, נָתַן, קָרָא, עָשָׂה

4. The negative אֵין *no, not, there is not*, is used with the present tense; לֹא is used with the past and future tenses (Lesson 21).

   I do not remember   אֵין אֲנִי זוֹכֵר

   I did not remember   לֹא זָכַרְתִּי

   I shall not remember   לֹא אֶזְכֹּר

5. Declension of masculine nouns in the singular (Lesson 21).

   שִׁירִי, שִׁירְךָ, שִׁירֵךְ, שִׁירוֹ, שִׁירָהּ

   שִׁירֵנוּ, שִׁירְכֶם, שִׁירְכֶן, שִׁירָם, שִׁירָן

6. The suffix ה of the third person feminine, attached to singular nouns, always has a dot called *mappiq* (Lesson 21).

   her song   שִׁירָהּ   her uncle   דּוֹדָהּ

7. Biblical Word List Nine (Lesson 21).

עַיִן, עִיר, עַם, קוֹל, שָׁנִים, שְׁתַּיִם

8. Double members of the body and things that come in pairs usually have a dual form ending in ‏יִם‎ (Lesson 22).

אָזְנַיִם, שְׂפָתַיִם, שְׁנַיִם, רַגְלַיִם, יָדַיִם

9. ‏מַיִם‎ *water* and ‏שָׁמַיִם‎ *sky* are dual in form but singular in meaning (Lesson 22).

good water   מַיִם טוֹבִים

10. The following nouns are found in the plural only (Lesson 22).

פָּנִים, שָׁמַיִם, מַיִם, אֱלֹהִים, רַחֲמִים, חַיִּים

11. Biblical Word List Ten (Lesson 22).

עָבַר, צִוָּה, שָׁמַע, שׁוּב, אָהַב

12. Imperfect or future of ‏שָׁמַר‎ (Lesson 23):

אֶשְׁמֹר, תִּשְׁמֹר, תִּשְׁמְרִי, יִשְׁמֹר, תִּשְׁמֹר

נִשְׁמֹר, תִּשְׁמְרוּ, תִּשְׁמֹרְנָה, יִשְׁמְרוּ, תִּשְׁמֹרְנָה

13. Imperfect or future of a verb whose second or third root-letter is a guttural (Lesson 23).

אֶשְׁלַח, תִּשְׁלַח, תִּשְׁלְחִי, יִשְׁלַח, תִּשְׁלַח

נִשְׁלַח, תִּשְׁלְחוּ, תִּשְׁלַחְנָה, יִשְׁלְחוּ, תִּשְׁלַחְנָה

14. Biblical Word List Eleven (Lesson 23).

דֶּלֶת, לֵב, קוֹל

15. The declension of regular masculine nouns in the singular and plural (Lesson 26)

   a.   שִׁיר *song, my song, your song,* etc.

שִׁירִי, שִׁירְךָ, שִׁירֵךְ, שִׁירוֹ, שִׁירָהּ

שִׁירֵנוּ, שִׁירְכֶם, שִׁירְכֶן, שִׁירָם, שִׁירָן

   b.   שִׁירִים *songs, my songs, your songs,* etc.

שִׁירַי, שִׁירֶיךָ, שִׁירַיִךְ, שִׁירָיו, שִׁירֶיהָ

שִׁירֵינוּ, שִׁירֵיכֶם, שִׁירֵיכֶן, שִׁירֵיהֶם, שִׁירֵיהֶן

    Note that the plural contains ‏י‎ throughout the declension: ‏יָדֵינוּ‎ *our hand,* ‏יָדֵינוּ‎ *our hands.*

16. Biblical Word List Twelve (Lesson 26).

צִוָּה, נָשָׂא, מוּת, שִׂים, זָכַר

17. The imperatives of ‏כָּתַב‎ and ‏שָׁמַע‎ (Lesson 27):

        Write!   כְּתֹב, כִּתְבִי, כִּתְבוּ, כְּתֹבְנָה

Hear! שְׁמַע, שִׁמְעִי, שִׁמְעוּ, שְׁמַעְנָה

18. For the full conjugation of the regular Qal verbs, see Lesson 27.

19. Preposition מִן *from* or prefix –מ followed by a dagesh to compensate for the loss of נ, or –מ without a dagesh before a word beginning with a guttural (Lesson 27).

from a book	מִן סֵפֶר	*Or*	מִסֵּפֶר
from an evening	מִן עֶרֶב	*Or*	מֵעֶרֶב
from the book	מִן הַסֵּפֶר	*Or*	מֵהַסֵּפֶר
from the town	מִן הָעִיר	*Or*	מֵהָעִיר

20. Biblical Word List Thirteen (Lesson 27).

פָּנִים, אֱנוֹשׁ, חַיִּים, קֹדֶשׁ, חַי

21. Numbers (Lesson 28)

a. With masculine nouns (1 through 10):

אֶחָד, שְׁנַיִם (שְׁנֵי), שְׁלֹשָׁה, אַרְבָּעָה, חֲמִשָּׁה
שִׁשָּׁה, שִׁבְעָה, שְׁמוֹנָה, תִּשְׁעָה, עֲשָׂרָה

b. With feminine nouns (1 through 10):

אַחַת, שְׁתַּיִם (שְׁתֵּי), שָׁלֹשׁ, אַרְבַּע, חָמֵשׁ
שֵׁשׁ, שֶׁבַע, שְׁמוֹנֶה, תֵּשַׁע, עֶשֶׂר

c. With masculine or feminine nouns:

שְׁלֹשִׁים, אַרְבָּעִים, חֲמִשִּׁים, שִׁשִּׁים
שִׁבְעִים, מֵאָה, אֶלֶף

22. The numbers אֶחָד and אַחַת follow the noun, but the numerals 2 through 10 may either follow or precede the noun (Lesson 28). (The numerals אֶחָד and אַחַת may precede the noun only in construct; the construct will be dealt with in Lessons 31 and 32.)

	one man	אִישׁ אֶחָד
	one woman	אִשָּׁה אַחַת
But:	three girls	שָׁלֹשׁ יְלָדוֹת *Or* יְלָדוֹת שָׁלֹשׁ
	twenty-four books	עֶשְׂרִים וְאַרְבָּעָה סְפָרִים

23. Note the following (Lesson 28):

two books	שְׁנֵי סְפָרִים
two pictures	שְׁתֵּי תְמוּנוֹת
the two books	שְׁנֵי הַסְּפָרִים
the two lamps	שְׁתֵּי הַמְּנוֹרוֹת

both of us (m. and f.)	שְׁנֵינוּ, שְׁתֵּינוּ
both of you (m. and f.)	שְׁנֵיכֶם, שְׁתֵּיכֶן
both of them (m. and f.)	שְׁנֵיהֶם, שְׁתֵּיהֶן

24. Before a noun beginning with –עַ, –חָ, or –הָ, the definite article is הֶ (Lesson 28).

הֶעָנִי, הֶהָרִים, הֶחָזָק

25. Before a word beginning with a shva or one of the letters בומף, *and* is – וּ (not –וְ) (Lesson 28).

26. Biblical Word List Fourteen (Lesson 28).

רָשָׁע, חָזָק, קָדוֹשׁ, צַדִּיק, חָסִיד

STUDY HINT

This lesson contains a valuable summary of all the important rules given in Lessons 20-28. It is important that you understand them thoroughly. Do not hesitate to refer to the lessons indicated under each point.

EXERCISES

Translate the following exercises into Hebrew, without vowels:

A. 1. this lamp
   2. this big lamp
   3. This lamp is big.
   4. This is an apple.
   5. These are apples.
   6. These are beautiful apples.
   7. These beautiful apples are on the tree.
   8. These apples are in this house.

B. 1. I remember.
   2. I do not remember.
   3. You (m. sg.) ate.
   4. You (m. sg.) have not eaten.
   5. You (m. sg.) did not eat.
   6. We shall shut the gate.
   7. We shall not shut the gate.
   8. They have shut the gates.

C. 1. We went.
   2. I am eating.
   3. She knows.
   4. He knows.
   5. We do not know.
   6. He shall forgive.
   7. They took.
   8. You (f. sg.) shall finish.
   9. They (f.) will hear.
   10. We have finished.

D. 1. his song
2. our head
3. their (m.) hand
4. her uncle
5. my horse
6. my lamp
7. your (m. sg.) horse
8. their (f.) song
9. your (m. pl.) lamp
10. your (f. sg.) song

E. 1. like a book
2. like the book
3. the dog
4. from a dog
5. from the dog
6. in a house
7. in a small house
8. in the small house
9. in this small house
10. from the king

F. 1. near the river
2. from the mountain
3. under the tree
4. without water
5. until this day
6. between the horses
7. before the flood
8. after the rain

G. 1. his songs
2. our commandments
3. their (m.) hands
4. her horses
5. my law
6. my laws
7. your (m. sg.) horses
8. their (f.) songs
9. your (m. pl.) horses
10. your (f. sg.) songs

H. 1. one book
2. a lamp
3. an apple
4. one city
5. from a garden
6. from the garden
7. from the book
8. from books
9. from evening to evening
10. from the house to the field

I. 1. five books
2. one family
3. two lamps
4. one boy
5. two boys
6. eight ribs
7. three kings
8. nine lamps
9. ten horses
10. ten mares

J. Write the Hebrew of the following numerals, without vowels, in both masculine and feminine.
    1. thirty-two
    2. fifty-one

3. sixty-two

4. twenty-one

5. five

6. two

7. thirty

8. ten

9. ninety-one

10. one hundred

K. Translate the following into Hebrew:

1. the mountains

2. the great mountains

3. the poor man

4. the beautiful woman

5. the strong king

6. and a book, and books, and the books

7. and a prophet, and prophets, and the prophets

8. twenty-four, twenty-three, one hundred and thirty

Lesson Thirty

REVIEW TEST

This one-hour test reviews the material covered in the previous lessons (approximately twelve weeks of work).

PART I: VOCABULARY

A. Translate the following into English:

1. ‏הַמֶּלֶךְ צוֹחֵק בְּקוֹל גָּדוֹל.‏

_____

2. ‏לָקַח הַכֶּלֶב אֶת־הַבֶּגֶד מִן־הַיֶּלֶד.‏

_____

3. ‏הַנְּבִיאָה יוֹדַעַת אֶת־הָרָעָה אֲשֶׁר עָשָׂה הָאִישׁ הַזֶּה.‏

_____

4. ‏לָקַח הַסּוֹפֵר עֶשְׂרִים וְאַרְבָּעָה סְפָרִים מִן־הָאִישׁ הֶחָכָם.‏

_____

5. ‏אַחֲרֵי הַדְּבָרִים הָאֵלֶּה זָכַר הַבֵּן אֶת־הַחֲלוֹם‏
   ‏אֲשֶׁר רָאָה בַּלַּיְלָה.‏

_____

_____

6. ‏סָגְרָה הַבַּת אֶת־הַדֶּלֶת.‏

_____

169

B. Write the Hebrew for the following:

1. dog	_____	11. to read	_____
2. ear	_____	12. tree	_____
3. we	_____	13. land	_____
4. young	_____	14. mouth	_____
5. rib	_____	15. blessing	_____
6. water	_____	16. tongue	_____
7. dream	_____	17. who	_____
8. white	_____	18. name	_____
9. to forgive	_____	19. daughter	_____
10. son	_____	20. here	_____

C. Write the opposite of the following:

_____	6. אֶל	_____	1. לָבָן
_____	7. בֹּקֶר	_____	2. גָּדוֹל
_____	8. לָקַח	_____	3. יָשַׁב
_____	9. בְּלִי	_____	4. לַיְלָה
_____	10. זָכַר	_____	5. זָקֵן

PART II: GRAMMAR

D. Translate the following into Hebrew, without vowels:

1. He went to my garden.

_____ .1

2. The son remembered the dream which he had dreamt in the night.

_____ .2

3. These boys will learn this beautiful song.

_____ .3

4. We took our lamps from the man.

_____ .4

5. The prophetess read the book.

_____ .5

6. She did not eat the bread which she had taken from this old man.

_____ .6

7. We shall hear her songs.

_____ .7

8. These girls are big.

_____ .8

9. You (m. sg.) took this beautiful lamp from the house.

_____ .9

10. God created the woman from the rib which he had taken from the man.

_____ .10

E. Write the perfect tense of כָּתַב *to write,* with vowels:

_____   _____

_____   _____

_____   _____

_____   _____

_____   _____

F. Write the imperfect tense of שָׁמַר *to guard,* with vowels:

_____   _____

_____   _____

_____   _____

_____   _____

_____   _____

G. Decline the singular of קוֹל *voice:*

_____   _____

_____   _____

_____   _____

_____   _____

H. Decline the singular of תּוֹרָה *law:*

_____   _____

_____   _____

_____   _____

_____   _____

A vendor of cold refreshment in the Old City of Jerusalem.

I. Write the Hebrew, without vowels, for the following:

1. to our songs _____ .1

2. like your (m. pl.) voice _____ .2

3. in her city _____ .3

4. for his horse _____ .4

5. under your (sg.) tree _____ .5

6. with my little brother _____ .6

7. from my hand _____ .7

8. with your (m. pl.) head _____ .8

9. to our city _____ .9

10. without their (f.) prayer _____ .10

11. he will reign _____ .11

12. he is reading _____ .12

13. you have sent _____ .13

14. they will learn _____ .14

15. we ate _____ .15

16. I shall remember _____ .16

17. you (m. sg.) took _____ .17

18. he stood _____ .18

19. she ate _____ .19

20. they (f.) will forget _____ .20

PART III: COMPOSITION

J. Translate the following into Hebrew:

1. This man laughed with (–בְּ) a loud (גָּדוֹל) voice.

   _____ .1

2. In the beginning God created the heaven and the earth.

   _____ .2

   _____

3. These good boys gave the white flowers to this old woman.

   _____ .3

   _____

4. The woman went to the city with her sons.

   _____ .4

5. He took the water which she had given to the old man.

   _____ .5

K. Write the following numbers in Hebrew in the masculine form, without vowels:

_____	29	.6	_____ 5	.1
_____	78	.7	_____ 99	.2
_____	63	.8	_____ 39	.3
_____	50	.9	_____ 28	.4
_____	61	.10	_____ 65	.5

Lesson Thirty-one

SINGULAR NOUNS IN THE CONSTRUCT STATE

VOCABULARY

work	עֲבוֹדָה	servant, slave	עֶבֶד
request	שְׁאֵלָה	sea	יָם
prayer	תְּפִלָּה	room	חֶדֶר
joy, rejoicing	שִׂמְחָה	street, broad place	רְחוֹב
queen	מַלְכָּה	table	שֻׁלְחָן
animal, beast	חַיָּה	silver	כֶּסֶף
province	מְדִינָה	judge	שׁוֹפֵט
hero, mighty one	גִּבּוֹר	gold	זָהָב
love	אַהֲבָה	name	שֵׁם
cup (f.)	כּוֹס	garment	בֶּגֶד

GRAMMAR AND NOTES

Study the following carefully:

the servant of Abraham	עֶבֶד אַבְרָהָם
the king of Israel	מֶלֶךְ יִשְׂרָאֵל
the book of the Torah (Law)	סֵפֶר הַתּוֹרָה
the name of the father	שֵׁם הָאָב
the judge of the city	שׁוֹפֵט הָעִיר
the garment of the servant	בֶּגֶד הָעֶבֶד
the book of the kings	סֵפֶר הַמְּלָכִים

174

In each of these Hebrew pairs, two words are closely connected. In English, the preposition *of* (or sometimes *with* or *for*) is used. The first of these two closely connected Hebrew words is said to be in the *construct state*. Thus in the above, שֵׁם, מֶלֶךְ, עֶבֶד, etc. are said to be in the construct state.

In the expression שֵׁם הָאָב, the first word שֵׁם is translated *the name of*, thus שֵׁם already implies the definite article *the*. It is obvious, therefore, that a noun in the construct state *never* takes the definite article.

The name of the city is שֵׁם הָעִיר, not הַשֵּׁם הָעִיר; *the song of songs* is שִׁיר הַשִּׁירִים, not הַשִּׁיר הַשִּׁירִים. Note that שֵׁם עִיר means *a name of a city*, but שֵׁם הָעִיר means *the name of the city*.

The king's book is translated in the same way as *the book of the king* סֵפֶר הַמֶּלֶךְ.

Observe the difference:

a king of a people	מֶלֶךְ עַם
the king of the people	מֶלֶךְ הָעָם

Two words thus connected are considered as one compound word and are therefore not to be separated in the sentence. Thus, if an adjective qualifies the noun in the construct, this adjective is placed after the second noun. *The wise servant of the king* is עֶבֶד הַמֶּלֶךְ הֶחָכָם, not עֶבֶד הֶחָכָם הַמֶּלֶךְ. However, the expression עֶבֶד הַמֶּלֶךְ הֶחָכָם is ambiguous because it may mean (a) the wise *servant* of the king, or (b) the servant of the wise *king*. The exact meaning is usually determined by the context.

Now study the following feminine nouns in the construct state:

the Torah (Law) of Moses	תּוֹרַת מֹשֶׁה
the prayer of the prophet	תְּפִלַת הַנָּבִיא
the joy of the man	שִׂמְחַת הָאִישׁ
the request of the queen	שְׁאֵלַת הַמַּלְכָּה
the lamp of the house	מְנוֹרַת הַבַּיִת

The Hebrew words for *law, mare, lamp,* and *prayer* are תּוֹרָה, סוּסָה, מְנוֹרָה, and תְּפִלָה, respectively. It is clear, therefore, that feminine nouns, when used in the construct state, change their הָ into תַ: שִׂמְחָה *joy*, שִׂמְחַת הָאִישׁ *the joy of the man*.

Two or more words may come together in the construct:

the horses *of* the king *of* Egypt   סוּסֵי מֶלֶךְ מִצְרַיִם

Note that לַיְלָה is masculine (see Lesson 6). The construct is לֵיל:

לֵיל הַמִּשְׁפָּחָה   *the family's night.*

Special Construct Forms

     The following frequently used forms undergo some changes when the construct state is formed. Study the constructs carefully.

בֵּן, בֶּן, בֶּן הַנָּבִיא	son
נָבִיא, נְבִיא, נְבִיא יִשְׂרָאֵל	prophet
דָּבָר, דְּבַר, דְּבַר הַמֶּלֶךְ	word, matter
בַּיִת, בֵּית, בֵּית הָאִשָּׁה	house
עַיִן, עֵין, עֵין הַבַּת	eye, spring (well)
אִשָּׁה, אֵשֶׁת, אֵשֶׁת אַבְרָהָם	woman, wife
חֶדֶר, חֲדַר, חֲדַר הַבֵּן	room, chamber
מִשְׁפָּחָה, מִשְׁפַּחַת, מִשְׁפַּחַת הַמַּלְכָּה	family
שָׂפָה, שְׂפַת, שְׂפַת הָעָם	language, lip, shore

(The above construct forms are used in Exercise E.)

STUDY HINT

Read the examples and comments in this lesson several times. The construct state is a peculiar usage of the Semitic languages. The nearest English equivalents are expressions such as "the man's friend," "the teacher's book," etc. Note, however, that in Hebrew אִישׁ הַסֵּפֶר means *the man of the book,* not *the book of the man*. The latter would be סֵפֶר הָאִישׁ.

EXERCISES

A. Translate the following into English:

6. דּוֹד הַיֶּלֶד	1. שֵׁם, אִישׁ, שֵׁם הָאִישׁ
7. דֶּלֶת הַבַּיִת	2. שֵׁם אִישׁ
8. רֹאשׁ הָעִיר	3. גַּן, עִיר, גַּן עִיר
9. כּוֹס מַיִם	4. גַּן הָעִיר
10. שׁוֹפֵט הָעִיר	5. אֶרֶץ מִצְרַיִם

B. Translate the following into English:

.6 שִׂמְחַת חַיִּים   .1 אַהֲבַת הַיֶּלֶד

.7 חַיַּת הַשָּׂדֶה   .2 תְּפִלַּת הָאֵם

.8 מַלְכַּת הָעִיר   .3 בַּת הַמֶּלֶךְ

.9 מִשְׁפַּחַת הַמֶּלֶךְ   .4 אֵם הַיֶּלֶד

.10 סֵפֶר הַתּוֹרָה   .5 תּוֹרַת מֹשֶׁה

C. Translate the following into Hebrew, using only two words for each phrase:

1. the queen's name
2. a day of rain
3. the Queen's prayer
4. the girl's mother
5. the lamp of the house

6. the book of the people
7. the land of Israel
8. the man's uncle
9. the head of the family
10. the joy of the boys

D. Write two sets of five examples each, with an English translation, of (1) the masculine singular noun and (2) the feminine singular noun in Hebrew, illustrating the use of the construct state, as in the following examples:

(1)	book	סֵפֶר
	songs	שִׁירִים
	a book of songs	סֵפֶר שִׁירִים
(2)	joy	שִׂמְחָה
	mother	אֵם
	the joy of the mother	שִׂמְחַת הָאֵם

E. Translate the following into English; circle the nouns in the construct which undergo change, and memorize them:

.1 לֹא שָׁמְעוּ הָאֲנָשִׁים לִדְבַר אֱלֹהִים.

.2 מָצָא־בֶּן הַמֶּלֶךְ אֶת־הַכֶּלֶב עַל שְׂפַת הַיָּם.

.3 מִשְׁפַּחַת הַמֶּלֶךְ יָשְׁבָה בַּחֶדֶר הַנָּבִיא.

.4 קָרָא נְבִיא הָעִיר מִסֵּפֶר הַתּוֹרָה אֲשֶׁר הָיָה בְּיָדוֹ.

.5 אֵשֶׁת הַמֶּלֶךְ יָצְאָה מִן־הָעִיר הַזֹּאת.

.6 לֹא יָדַעְתִּי אֶת־שְׂפַת הָעָם הַזֶּה.

F. Write the Hebrew equivalents, with vowels, for the following without referring to the exercises above:

1. the lip of the man
2. the wife of the king
3. the family of the prophet
4. The son of the man is in the hand of the king.
5. In the king's house is the prophet's room.

Lesson Thirty-two

PLURAL NOUNS IN THE CONSTRUCT STATE

VOCABULARY

the songs of Solomon	שִׁירֵי שְׁלֹמֹה
the horses of the king	סוּסֵי הַמֶּלֶךְ
the hands of the queen	יְדֵי הַמַּלְכָּה
the life of the people	חַיֵּי הָעָם
the children of Israel	בְּנֵי יִשְׂרָאֵל
the face of the prophet	פְּנֵי הַנָּבִיא
the eyes of Rachel	עֵינֵי רָחֵל
the ears of the lads	אָזְנֵי הַנְּעָרִים
the feet of the horse	רַגְלֵי הַסּוּס

GRAMMAR AND NOTES

The Hebrew words for *songs, horses*, and *sons* are שִׁירִים, סוּסִים, and בָּנִים, respectively. From the above examples, it is clear that plural nouns ending in ־ִים form their construct state by changing ־ִים into ־ֵי: שִׁירִים *songs*, שִׁירֵי *the songs of*, שִׁירֵי שְׁלֹמֹה *the songs of Solomon* or *Solomon's songs*; בָּנִים *sons*, בְּנֵי *the sons of*, בְּנֵי הַמֶּלֶךְ *the sons of the king*.

The Hebrew words for *eyes, ears*, and *feet* are עֵינַיִם, אָזְנַיִם, and רַגְלַיִם, respectively. From the last three examples given in the Vocabulary, it is obvious that nouns with a dual plural also change their ending ־ַיִם into ־ֵי: עֵינַיִם *eyes*, עֵינֵי *the eyes of*, עֵינֵי רָחֵל *the eyes of Rachel*; אָזְנַיִם *ears*, אָזְנֵי *the ears of*, אָזְנֵי הַסּוּס

179

the ears of the horse, etc.

Note: אֱלֹהִים *God*, אֱלֹהֵי אַבְרָהָם *God of Abraham*.

Study the following:

the lamps of the house	מְנוֹרוֹת הַבַּיִת
the works of the boys	עֲבוֹדוֹת הַיְלָדִים
the beasts of the field	חַיּוֹת הַשָּׂדֶה
the prayers of the mother	תְּפִלּוֹת הָאֵם
the requests of the prophet	שְׁאֵלוֹת הַנָּבִיא
the mares of the king	סוּסוֹת הַמֶּלֶךְ

The Hebrew words for *lamps*, *works*, and *prayers* are עֲבוֹדוֹת, מְנוֹרוֹת, and תְּפִלּוֹת, respectively. From the above examples, it is clear that the construct form of nouns ending in וֹת– also ends in וֹת–, with no changes in the suffixes of the nouns: מְנוֹרוֹת *lamps* or *the lamps of*, מְנוֹרוֹת הַבַּיִת *the lamps of the house*; תְּפִלּוֹת *prayers* or *the prayers of*, תְּפִלּוֹת הָאֵם *the prayer of the mother*.

In the expression עֲבוֹדוֹת הַיְלָדִים *the works of the boys*, the word עֲבוֹדוֹת means *the works of*. Therefore, a noun in the construct already contains the definite article הַ. It is thus clear that a noun in the construct never takes the definite article ה. (See Lesson 31.) *The requests of the prophets* is always שְׁאֵלוֹת הַנָּבִיא (never הַשְׁאֵלוֹת הַנָּבִיא).

Some nouns undergo various changes in the vowels when the construct state is formed. We shall learn these in due course. For the present, it is sufficient for you to study the following carefully:

hands	יָדַיִם, יְדֵי, יְדֵי הָאִישׁ
boys	יְלָדִים, יַלְדֵי, יַלְדֵי הָאָרֶץ
words, things	דְּבָרִים, דִּבְרֵי, דִּבְרֵי הַנָּבִיא
face	פָּנִים, פְּנֵי, פְּנֵי מֹשֶׁה
proverbs	מְשָׁלִים, מִשְׁלֵי, מִשְׁלֵי שְׁלֹמֹה
men	אֲנָשִׁים, אַנְשֵׁי, אַנְשֵׁי הָעִיר
women	נָשִׁים, נְשֵׁי, נְשֵׁי הָעִיר
books	סְפָרִים, סִפְרֵי, סִפְרֵי מֹשֶׁה
water	מַיִם, מֵי, מֵי הַיָּם
sons	בָּנִים, בְּנֵי, בְּנֵי אַבְרָהָם
families	מִשְׁפָּחוֹת, מִשְׁפְּחוֹת, מִשְׁפְּחוֹת כֹּהֵן

Note also the following idioms:

סֵפֶר הַסְּפָרִים   the book of books, i.e., the finest book

מֶלֶךְ הַמְּלָכִים   the king of kings, i.e., the supreme king

שִׁיר הַשִּׁירִים   the song of songs, i.e., the first song

STUDY HINTS

1. This lesson and the previous one (Lesson 31) deal with the main rules of the construct state. In future lessons you will learn about some of the changes that occur in the inner structure of the nouns (such as vowels) when the construct is formed following the rules dealt with in these two lessons.

2. You must read the examples given in Lessons 31 and 32 several times before you begin the Exercises in this lesson.

3. There are many examples in the following lessons of the use of the construct in sentences.

EXERCISES

A. Rewrite the following in the construct state: (For example, change סוּס וּמֶלֶךְ to סוּס מֶלֶךְ or change הַסּוּס וְהַמֶּלֶךְ to הַסּוּס הַמֶּלֶךְ.)

1. הַשִּׁירִים וּשְׁלֹמֹה
2. הַסּוּסוֹת וְהָאִישׁ
3. הַסּוּסִים וְהָאִישׁ
4. הַחַיִּים וְאַבְרָהָם
5. הָעָם וְהָעִיר

6. תְּפִלּוֹת וְאָב
7. הָעֲבוֹדוֹת וְהַבַּיִת
8. מְנוֹרוֹת וְאִישׁ
9. הָעֵינַיִם וְהָאִשָּׁה
10. הַיְלָדִים וְהַנָּבִיא

B. Translate the following into English:

1. חַיֵּי הָעָם
2. אָזְנֵי הַסּוּס
3. אֱלֹהֵי יִשְׂרָאֵל
4. מְנוֹרַת שֻׁלְחָן
5. מְנוֹרַת הַבַּיִת

6. מְנוֹרוֹת הַחֶדֶר
7. עֵינֵי הַיַּלְדָּה
8. שִׂמְחַת הָאִשָּׁה
9. שִׂמְחַת אִשָּׁה
10. רַגְלֵי הַצִּפּוֹר

C. Translate the following into English:

6. יְדֵי הָאִשָּׁה		1. בְּנֵי הָאָרֶץ	
7. סוּסוֹת הַמֶּלֶךְ		2. יַלְדֵי יְרוּשָׁלַיִם	
8. עֵינֵי הָאָב		3. מֵי הַיַּרְדֵּן	
9. תְּפִלוֹת הָעָם		4. דִּבְרֵי סֵפֶר	
10. מִשְׁפְּחוֹת הָעִיר		5. סִפְרֵי הַנְּבִיאִים	

D. Write the construct forms of the following words and use them in complete sentences.

Example: בָּנִים, בְּנֵי, הָלְכוּ בְּנֵי יִשְׂרָאֵל אֶל־הָעִיר הַזֹּאת.

11. אֲנָשִׁים	6. יָדַיִם	1. עֵינַיִם			
12. מִשְׁפָּחוֹת	7. שִׁירִים	2. מְנוֹרָה			
13. דָּבָר	8. אָזְנַיִם	3. סְפָרִים			
14. פָּנִים	9. מַיִם	4. דּוֹדִים			
15. תּוֹרָה	10. יְלָדִים	5. סוּסוֹת			

E. Write 10 sentences of four to seven words, each containing one of the following construct forms:

6. מְנוֹרוֹת		1. שִׁירֵי	
7. בְּנֵי		2. יַלְדֵי	
8. יוֹם		3. תְּפִלַּת	
9. שִׂמְחַת		4. פְּנֵי	
10. דִּבְרֵי		5. עֵינֵי	

F. Translate the following sentences into English:

1. מַה שֵׁם הָרְחוֹב הַזֶּה?
2. בְּנֵי יִשְׂרָאֵל יָצְאוּ מֵאֶרֶץ מִצְרַיִם עִם מֹשֶׁה.
3. שֵׁם הָעִיר הַזֹּאת יְרוּשָׁלַיִם.
4. קָרָאתִי אֶת־דִּבְרֵי הַסֵּפֶר הַזֶּה.
5. גָּמְרָה הָאִשָּׁה אֶת־עֲבוֹדוֹת הַבַּיִת.
6. מִי כָּתַב אֶת־הַתּוֹרָה?
7. מֹשֶׁה עוֹנֶה עַל שְׁאֵלוֹת הַנָּשִׁים.
8. שִׂמְחַת הַנָּשִׁים הָיְתָה גְדוֹלָה.
9. בָּאָה בַּת הַמֶּלֶךְ לְאֶרֶץ יִשְׂרָאֵל לִפְנֵי שָׁנָה.
10. לֹא יָדְעוּ אַנְשֵׁי הָעִיר כִּי יָצָא מֶלֶךְ יִשְׂרָאֵל מֵאֶרֶץ יַרְדֵּן.

Lesson Thirty-three

BIBLICAL PASSAGE FROM GENESIS, CHAPTER 3: ADAM, EVE, AND THE SERPENT

VOCABULARY

from it	מִמֶּנּוּ	serpent	נָחָשׁ
die	מוֹת	was (m.)	הָיָה
because	כִּי	cunning, shrewd	עָרוּם
that (conj.)	כִּי	naked	עָרוֹם
in the midst, within	בְּתוֹךְ	animal, beast	חַיָּה
lest	פֶּן	all, every	כֹּל, כָּל־
and she saw	וַתֵּרֶא	garden	גַּן
and she took	וַתִּקַּח	also	גַּם
and she gave	וַתִּתֵּן	food	מַאֲכָל
your eating	אָכָלְכֶם	fruit	פְּרִי

GRAMMAR AND NOTES

1. וְהַנָּחָשׁ הָיָה עָרוּם מִכָּל־חַיַּת הַשָּׂדֶה אֲשֶׁר עָשָׂה יְהוָה אֱלֹהִים

2. וַיֹּאמֶר אֶל־הָאִשָּׁה: אֱלֹהִים אָמַר לֹא תֹאכְלוּ מִכָּל־עֵץ הַגָּן

3. וַתֹּאמֶר הָאִשָּׁה אֶל־הַנָּחָשׁ: מִפְּרִי עֵץ הַגָּן נֹאכֵל, וּמִפְּרִי הָעֵץ אֲשֶׁר בְּתוֹךְ הַגָּן, אָמַר אֱלֹהִים לֹא תֹאכְלוּ מִמֶּנּוּ פֶּן־תְּמֻתוּ.

4. וַיֹּאמֶר הַנָּחָשׁ אֶל־הָאִשָּׁה: לֹא מוֹת תְּמֻתוּן כִּי יֹדֵעַ אֱלֹהִים כִּי בְּיוֹם אֲכָלְכֶם מִמֶּנּוּ וְהְיִיתֶם כֵּאלֹהִים יֹדְעֵי טוֹב וָרָע

5. וַתֵּרֶא הָאִשָּׁה כִּי טוֹב הָעֵץ לְמַאֲכָל וַתִּקַּח מִפִּרְיוֹ וַתֹּאכַל וַתִּתֵּן גַּם לְאִישָׁהּ עִמָּהּ וַיֹּאכַל:

183

Notes: (Numbers refer to lines above.)

1. The plural of נָחָשׁ is נְחָשִׁים and the plural of דָּבָר is דְּבָרִים. כָּל *all* or *every;* the vowel is qamats qaṭan (see Lesson 5), and it is therefore pronounced *o* ("kol" not "kal"); when followed by the definite article (the), it means *all, the whole, the entire;* when followed by a noun in the singular and without the definite article, it means *every.* כָּל־יוֹם *every day,* כָּל־הַיּוֹם *the whole day;* כָּל־אִישׁ *every man;* כָּל־עֵץ *every tree,* כָּל־הָעֵצִים *all the trees.* Note also כֻּלִּי *all of me,* כֻּלָּם *all of them,* etc.

   חַיָּה *beast,* חַיַּת *the beast of;* similarly, מְנוֹרָה *candlestick, lamp,* מְנוֹרַת הַבַּיִת *the lamp of the house.* (See Lesson 32.)

2. וַיֹּאמֶר *and he said,* וַתֹּאכַל *and she ate.* All these forms are imperfect (or future); nevertheless, they are translated in the perfect (or past), whereas וִהְיִיתֶם in Line 4, though perfect in form is translated in the imperfect *and you will be.* Such form is an outstanding feature of Biblical Hebrew.

   When the conjunction וֹ, meaning *and,* is prefixed to the perfect, it changes its meaning into imperfect; similarly, when וֹ is prefixed to the imperfect, it gives the latter a perfect sense. We shall deal with this peculiarity more fully in due course.

   יִזְכֹּר *he will remember,* but וַיִּזְכֹּר *and he remembered.* אֶשְׁלַח *I shall send,* but וָאֶשְׁלַח *and I sent.* Similarly, אָהַבְתָּ *you loved,* but וְאָהַבְתָּ *and you shall love;* רָאִיתָ *you saw,* but וְרָאִיתָ *and you will see.* This waw is called the *Waw conversive* or the *Waw consecutive.*

   עֵץ הַגָּן *the tree of the garden,* פְּרִי הָעֵץ *the fruit of the tree.* When two nouns closely connected are placed one next to the other, the first is said to be in the construct state. In English, the preposition *of* is generally used. A word in the *construct* state *never* takes the definite article ─הַ *the.* (See Lesson 32.)

3. וַתֹּאמֶר *and she said.* (See Note on וַיֹּאמֶר, Line 2.)

   פְּרִי הָעֵץ *the fruit of the tree.* (See Note on עֵץ הַגָּן, Line 2.)

   בְּתוֹךְ *in the midst of (within).* In Hebrew, prepositions may be inflected, hence בְּתוֹכִי *in my midst* or *within me,* בְּתוֹכֵנוּ *in our midst* or *within us,* etc.

   מִמֶּנּוּ *from it* or *from him* (מִן *from*). The declension of the preposition מִן

is slightly irregular, as follows:

מִמֶּנִּי, מִמְּךָ, מִמֵּךְ, מִמֶּנּוּ, מִמֶּנָּה

מִמֶּנּוּ, מִכֶּם, מִכֶּן, מֵהֶם, מֵהֶן

4. זָכֹר תִּזְכֹּר ,מוֹת תָּמוּת, literally, *dying you will die* or *you shall surely die.* *you shall indeed remember.* This is a special construction used for the sake of emphasis. זָכֹר is an infinitive known as the *Infinitive absolute.*

אֲכָלְכֶם *your eating.* This form is the infinitive construct. It is treated as a noun. This is a common usage in Biblical Hebrew.

וִהְיִיתֶם *and you will be* from, הָיָה *to be.* (See Note on *Waw conversive,* Line 2.)

Snake and bird cult object from the Philistine Southern Beth-shan Temple ("Temple of Dagon").

5. וַתֵּרֶא *and she saw* is the imperfect (future) of רָאָה *to see* with the waw consecutive.

וַתִּקַּח *and she took* is the imperfect of לָקַח *to take* with the waw consecutive. This is the only verb in Hebrew where the פ״ל (first letter of the root is ל) is omitted and a dagesh is inserted in the following letter "for compensation."

וַתִּתֵּן *and she gave* is the imperfect of נָתַן *to give,* with the waw consecutive. *Peh-nun* verbs, or verbs beginning with the root-letter נ, usually drop the נ in the imperfect and imperative. A similar example is נָפַל *to fall,* יִפֹּל (for יִנְפֹּל) *he shall fall.*

עִמָּה *with her* has a more regular declension than מִן. Its pattern is as follows:

עִמִּי, עִמְּךָ, עִמָּךְ, עִמּוֹ, עִמָּה
עִמָּנוּ, עִמָּכֶם, עִמָּכֶן, עִמָּהֶם, עִמָּהֶן

Notice that עִם always takes a dagesh when adding a suffix. Similarly, לְ *to, for* is declined like עִם: לִי, לְךָ, לָךְ, לוֹ, לָהּ / לָנוּ, לָכֶם, לָכֶן, לָהֶם, לָהֶן.

Study the following very carefully. They occur frequently in biblical texts. They are, indeed, irregular forms, but they are regularly used:

Past		Future		Future with Waw Conversive	
אָכַל	he ate	יֹאכַל	he will eat	וַיֹּאכַל	and he ate
אָכְלָה	she ate	תֹּאכַל	she will eat	וַתֹּאכַל	and she ate
אָמַר	he said	יֹאמַר	he will say	וַיֹּאמֶר	and he said
אָמְרָה	she said	תֹּאמַר	she will say	וַתֹּאמֶר	and she said
לָקַח	he took	יִקַּח	he will take	וַיִּקַּח	and he took
לָקְחָה	she took	תִּקַּח	she will take	וַתִּקַּח	and she took
נָתַן	he gave	יִתֵּן	he will give	וַיִּתֵּן	and he gave
נָתְנָה	she gave	תִּתֵּן	she will give	וַתִּתֵּן	and she gave
רָאָה	he saw	יִרְאֶה	he will see	וַיַּרְא	and he saw
רָאֲתָה	she saw	תִּרְאֶה	she will see	וַתֵּרֶא	and she saw

STUDY HINTS

1. Note that כָּל is pronounced *kol* with qamats qaṭan. (See Lesson 5 on the vowels.) כָּל followed by a noun with the definite article means *all, the whole of*; otherwise it means *every*.

כָּל־יוֹם   every day

כָּל־הַיּוֹם   the whole day

2. Carefully learn the use of the waw conversive, or waw consecutive as it is sometimes called. It is an unusual peculiarity confined to Biblical Hebrew. It may sound strange to you in the beginning, but you will get used to it once you read the Bible regularly. Read Notes 2 and 5 carefully. They are very important.

3. Another peculiarity of Biblical Hebrew is touched on in Note 4. מוֹת תָּמוּת *you shall surely die* literally means *dying you shall die*. This construction in Hebrew is known as the *Infinitive absolute*.

4. Note the inflection of the prepositions מִן *from*, בְּתוֹךְ *in the midst of*, לְ *to, for*, and עִם *with*.

5. The list of verbs with the waw consecutive given in Note 5 is most important for Biblical Hebrew. Learn these verbs well.

6. Read the biblical passage several times.

EXERCISES

A. What is the root and meaning of the following verbs?

6. וִהְיִיתֶם   1. תֹּאכְלוּ

7. וַתִּתֵּן   2. וַתֹּאמֶר

8. יוֹדֵעַ   3. נֹאכַל

9. וַתֵּרֶא   4. תְּמוּתוּ

10. אֲכָלְכֶם   5. וַתִּקַּח

B. The verb אָכַל belongs to the פ״א group. To what groups do the following verbs belong? מוּת, יָדַע, רָאָה, נָפַל, קָרָא

C. Translate the following into Hebrew, without vowels:

1. every evening
2. the entire evening
3. the beast of the field
4. from her, from them (m.)
5. the day of the year
6. all the snakes, every snake
7. for her, with us, to him, with me
8. the tree of the garden
9. with thee (m.); with him
10. the love of the law

D. Translate the following into Hebrew, without vowels; begin with the verb:

1. You may eat from all the fruit of the trees which are in the garden.
2. And the woman took (see Note, Line 5) from the fruit of the tree and she gave (see Note, Line 5) to her husband and he ate.
3. And the woman saw (see Note, Line 5) that the fruit [was] good for eating, and she ate from it (m.).
4. The snake was near the tree which [was] in the midst of the garden.
5. The man knew that (כִּי) every tree of the garden [was] good for eating.

E. Memorize the declension of מִן *from*. (See Note, Line 3.)

F. Decline the prepositions בְּתוֹךְ *within* and עִם *with*.

G. Decline the prepositions לְ *to, for* and מִן *from*.

H. Test on Biblical Word Lists

Give the Hebrew for the following:

1. to take
2. to know
3. to read
4. head
5. seven
6. to go out
7. way
8. mountain
9. to pass
10. to send
11. to find
12. to love
13. to hear
14. to call
15. voice
16. life
17. mother
18. God
19. to put
20. to remember
21. brother
22. eye
23. to create
24. heart
25. to die
26. to return

27. to command   29. to go up

28. to carry   30. face

Grades

27-30 words correct............A

24-27 words correct............B

20-23 words correct............C

18-19 words correct............D

0-17 words correct............F

If you missed more than six words in the above list, review all the vocabulary lists and all the biblical word lists in previous lessons.

Lesson Thirty-four

THE SEVEN VERB PATTERNS שִׁבְעַת הַבִּנְיָנִים

GRAMMAR AND NOTES

In Hebrew, there are seven Verb Patterns (sometimes called "Conjugations").

1. *Qal* קַל

The most frequently used verb pattern is the Qal קַל, also known as the פָּעַל.
It expresses the *simple* or *casual* action of the root in the active voice.
Examples: יָשַׁב *he sat*; אָכַל *he ate*; הָלַךְ *he went*; אָמַר *he said*; קָם *he rose*; קָנָה
he bought, etc.

2. *Niphal* נִפְעַל

   a. This verb pattern expresses the *passive* of the Qal.

Qal		Niphal	
רָאָה	he saw	נִרְאָה	he was seen, he appeared
רָאָה אֶת־הַמַּלְאָךְ	he saw the angel	נִרְאָה הַמַּלְאָךְ	the angel was seen
שָׁלַח	he sent	נִשְׁלַח	he was sent
		אֶל אַבְרָהָם	to Abraham
שָׁלַח יַעֲקֹב אֶת־יוֹסֵף	Jacob sent Joseph	נִשְׁלַח הַמֶּלֶךְ	the king was sent
אֶל־אֶחָיו	to his brothers	אֶל־הַנָּבִיא	to the prophet
בָּרָא	he created	נִבְרָא	it was created
בָּרָא אֱלֹהִים	God created	נִבְרָא אָדָם	Adam was created
אֶת־הָאָרֶץ	the earth	בַּיּוֹם הַשִּׁשִּׁי	on the sixth day

   b. The Niphal sometimes expresses a *reflexive* action.

שָׁמַר	he guarded	נִשְׁמַר	he was guarded, *also,* he guarded himself

c. Several verbs in Hebrew are used in the Niphal, although they express simple action and are active in English. Some commonly used verbs of this type are:

נִלְחַם	he fought	נִשְׁבַּע	he swore
נִשְׁאַר	he remained	נִכְנַס	he entered

3. *Piel* פִּעֵל, also known as כָּבֵד *heavy*

a. It usually expresses an *intensive* or *intentional* action.

Qal		*Piel*	
שָׁבַר	he broke	שִׁבֵּר	he broke to pieces, he smashed
שָׁבַר הָאִישׁ אֶת־רַגְלוֹ	The man broke his leg	שִׁבֵּר מֹשֶׁה אֶת־הַלֻּוחוֹת	Moses smashed the tablets
שָׁלַח	he sent	שִׁלַּח	he sent away, he expelled
שָׁלַח אַבְרָהָם אֶת־הָעֶבֶד	Abraham sent the servant	שִׁלַּח אֶת־הָעֶבֶד	he sent away the servant

b. Sometimes the Piel is used to introduce a new meaning to the Qal form.

סָפַר	he counted	סִפֵּר	he recounted, he told
שָׁלַם	he completed	שִׁלֵּם	he paid, he compensated
לָמַד	he learned	לִמֵּד	he taught

c. It may also express a *repeated* or *extended* action.

קָפַץ	he jumped	קִפֵּץ	he skipped, hopped

d. Some intransitive verbs in Qal become transitive in Piel.

Qal		*Piel*	
חָזַק	to be strong	חִזֵּק	to strengthen, fortify
גָּדַל	to become great	גִּדֵּל	to make great

e. Some verbs, although Piel in form, possess a Qal or "simple" meaning. Verbs of this type often lack a Qal form:

דִּבֵּר	he spoke	בֵּרֵךְ	he blessed
צִוָּה	he commanded		

4. *Pual* פֻּעַל—The Pual expresses the *passive* of the Piel.

Piel		*Pual*	
שִׁבֵּר	he smashed	שֻׁבַּר	it was smashed
שִׁבֵּר אֶת הַלּוּחַ	he smashed the tablet	הַלּוּחַ שֻׁבַּר	the tablet was smashed

סִפֵּר	he told	סֻפַּר	it was told
סִפֵּר אֶת הַחֲלוֹם	he told the dream	סֻפַּר הַחֲלוֹם	the dream was told
		לַמֶּלֶךְ	to the king

5.   הִפְעִיל *Hiphil*

    a.   This form is sometimes called "Causative" in English, because it usually expresses the *causative* action of the Qal.

Qal		*Hiphil*	
אָכַל	he ate	הֶאֱכִיל	he caused to eat, he fed
אָכַל אֶת־הַלֶּחֶם	he ate the bread	הֶאֱכִיל אֶת־בְּנוֹ	he fed his son
בָּא	he came	הֵבִיא	he caused to come, he brought
בָּא הַנָּבִיא אֶל־הָעִיר	the prophet came to the city	הֵבִיא הָאִישׁ אֶת־הַלֶּחֶם	the man brought the bread
קָם	he got up, he rose	הֵקִים	he raised, he lifted up
קָם הַיֶּלֶד מִן־הַכִּסֵּא	the child rose from the chair	הֵקִים הָאִישׁ אֶת־יָדוֹ	the man raised his hand
מָלַךְ	he reigned	הִמְלִיךְ	he made king, he crowned
מָלַךְ דָּוִד עַל־יְרוּשָׁלַיִם	David reigned over Jerusalem	הִמְלִיךְ שְׁמוּאֵל אֶת־שָׁאוּל	Samuel crowned Saul

    b.   The Hiphil is often used to form verbs from nouns or adjectives.

Noun or Adjective		*Hiphil*	
אֹזֶן	ear	הֶאֱזִין	to listen (lend an ear)
רָחוֹק	far	הִרְחִיק	to remove oneself, put far away

    c.   Some "simple" verbs are found in Hiphil.

הִשְׁמִיד	to destroy	הִשְׁלִיךְ	to cast
הִשְׁכִּים	to get up early	הִגִּיד	to tell, explain

6.   הָפְעַל *Hophal*

    The Hophal expresses the *passive* of the Hiphil.

הִגִּיד	he told	הֻגַּד	it was told

הִשְׁלִיךְ he threw   הָשְׁלַךְ he was thrown

N.B. The Pual and Hophal are rarely used.

7.   *Hithpael* הִתְפָּעֵל

     a.   This verb pattern primarily expresses a *reflexive* action of Qal or Piel.

Qal		*Hithpael*	
לָבֵשׁ	he wore	הִתְלַבֵּשׁ	he dressed himself
רָחַץ	he washed	הִתְרַחֵץ	he washed himself, he bathed
נָפַל	he fell	הִתְנַפֵּל	he flung himself, he fell upon, he attacked
מָכַר	he sold	הִתְמַכֵּר	he sold himself, he devoted himself

     b.   It also expresses a reciprocal action.

Qal		*Hithpael*	
רָאוּ	they saw	הִתְרָאוּ	they looked upon one another
לָחֲשׁוּ	they whispered	הִתְלַחֲשׁוּ	they whispered to one another

     c.   Some verbs in Hithpael are translated as a simple action. The reflexive action is understood.

          הִתְפַּלֵּל   he prayed (he himself did this action)

          הִתְאַבֵּל   he mourned   הִתְרַגֵּז   he became angry

This is only a brief introduction to the Hebrew verb patterns. *Biblical Hebrew Step by Step II* covers these patterns again in some detail.

STUDY HINT

This is an important lesson. Although at this point in your study you cannot expect to understand the seven verb patterns fully, this lesson does give you some idea of this important feature of Hebrew grammar. You will study the verb patterns in future Hebrew courses.

For the complete conjugation of the seven verb patterns of the regular verb, see the Supplement at the end of Lesson Forty.

EXERCISES

A. Give the verb pattern and the meaning of the following verbs. The Qal of each verb is given. (*Example*: רָאָה *he saw*, נִרְאָה Niphal, *he was seen*)

1.	אָכַל	he ate	נֶאֱכַל
2.	שָׁבַר	he broke	שִׁבֵּר
3.	זָכַר	he remembered	הִזְכִּיר
4.	חָבָא	he hid	הִתְחַבֵּא
5.	מָלַךְ	he reigned	הִמְלִיךְ
6.	גָּנַב	he stole	נִגְנַב
7	מָלַךְ	he reigned	הָמְלַךְ
8.	אָכַלְנוּ	we ate	נֶאֱכַלְנוּ
9.	שָׁבְרוּ	they broke	שִׁבְּרוּ
10.	אָכְלָה	she ate	הֶאֱכִילָה

B. Derive the meaning of the verbs from the given noun or adjective. (*Example*: קָטָן *small*, הִקְטִין *to make small, to reduce*)

1.	אוֹר	light	הֵאִיר
2.	טוֹב	good	הֵטִיב
3.	חֹשֶׁךְ	darkness	הֶחֱשִׁיךְ
4.	לָבָן	white	הִלְבִּין
5.	קָרוֹשׁ	holy	קִדֵּשׁ
6.	חָזָק	strong	הִתְחַזֵּק
7.	גָּדוֹל	big, great	הִגְדִּיל
8.	מֶלֶךְ	king	הִמְלִיךְ
9.	גָּדוֹל	big, great	גִּדֵּל
10.	אֹזֶן	ear	הֶאֱזִין

C. Describe the seven verb patterns and write a Hebrew sentence to illustrate each.

D. Attempt your own translation of the following:

1. נָפַל הַיֶּלֶד וְשָׁבַר אֶת־רַגְלוֹ.

2. יָרַד[1] מֹשֶׁה מִן־הָהָר וְשִׁבֵּר אֶת־הַלּוּחוֹת אֲשֶׁר הָיוּ בְּיָדוֹ.

3. גָּנְבוּ הָאֲנָשִׁים אֶת־הַזָּהָב מִן־הַהֵיכָל.[2]

4. כַּאֲשֶׁר[3] בָּאוּ הַכֹּהֲנִים[4] אֶל־הַהֵיכָל קָרְאוּ בְּקוֹל: נִגְנְבוּ הַכֶּסֶף וְהַזָּהָב.

5. שָׁלַח מֹשֶׁה אֲנָשִׁים אֶל יְרִיחוֹ[5] הָעִיר הַגְּדוֹלָה.

6. שִׁלְּחוּ הַמִּצְרִים אֶת־בְּנֵי יִשְׂרָאֵל מִמִּצְרַיִם.

7. הִתְנַבֵּא הַנָּבִיא עַל יְרוּשָׁלַיִם.

8. הֶאֱכִילָה הָאֵם אֶת־בְּנָהּ הַקָּטֹן.

9. הֶעֱבִידוּ[6] הַמִּצְרִים אֶת־בְּנֵי יִשְׂרָאֵל בַּעֲבוֹדָה קָשָׁה.[7]

10. הִתְחַבְּאוּ הָאָדָם וְאִשְׁתּוֹ כִּי יָדְעוּ כִּי הֵם עֲרֻמִּים.[8]

[1]he went down	[4]priests	[7]hard, difficult
[2]temple, palace	[5]Jericho	[8]naked
[3]when	[6]they caused to work, i.e., enslaved.	

Lesson Thirty-five
BIBLICAL PASSAGE FROM GENESIS, CHAPTER 1: THE CREATION

VOCABULARY

that	כִּי	in the beginning	בְּרֵאשִׁית	
and he called	וַיִּקְרָא	day	יוֹם (יָמִים)	
night (m.)	לַיְלָה (לֵילוֹת)	seven	שִׁבְעָה	
fourth	רְבִיעִי	was	הָיָה, הָיְתָה	
sun	שֶׁמֶשׁ	darkness	חֹשֶׁךְ	
moon	יָרֵחַ	face (m. sg.)	פָּנִים	
sixth	שִׁשִּׁי	wind, spirit (f.)	רוּחַ	
image	צֶלֶם	let it be	יְהִי	
and he saw	וַיַּרְא	light (m.)	אוֹר (אוֹרוֹת)	
land (f.)	אֶרֶץ (אֲרָצוֹת)	saw	רָאָה	
		star	כּוֹכָב	

GRAMMAR AND NOTES

בְּרֵאשִׁית

1. בְּרֵאשִׁית בָּרָא אֱלֹהִים אֵת הַשָּׁמַיִם וְאֵת הָאָרֶץ בְּשִׁבְעָה יָמִים

2. בְּרֵאשִׁית הָיָה חֹשֶׁךְ עַל־פְּנֵי הָאָרֶץ

3. וְרוּחַ אֱלֹהִים הָיְתָה עַל־פְּנֵי הַמָּיִם

4. וַיֹּאמֶר אֱלֹהִים: יְהִי אוֹר בַּשָּׁמַיִם. וַיַּרְא אֱלֹהִים אֶת־הָאוֹר כִּי־טוֹב

5. וַיִּקְרָא אֱלֹהִים לָאוֹר יוֹם וְלַחֹשֶׁךְ קָרָא לַיְלָה.

196

6. בַּיּוֹם הָרְבִיעִי בָּרָא אֱלֹהִים אֶת־הַשֶּׁמֶשׁ וְאֶת־הַיָּרֵחַ וְאֶת־הַכּוֹכָבִים.

7. בַּיּוֹם הַשִּׁשִּׁי בָּרָא אֱלֹהִים אֶת־הָאָדָם בְּצַלְמוֹ. וַיַּרְא אֱלֹהִים כִּי־טוֹב.

Notes: (Numbers refer to the lines above.)

1. בְּרֵאשִׁית *in the beginning*. Compare with רֹאשׁ *head*.

שָׁמַיִם *heavens, sky*. Note that שָׁמַיִם occurs only in the dual form and is singular or plural in meaning. (See Lesson 22.)

אֶרֶץ *land*, but הָאָרֶץ *the land*.

2. פָּנִים *face, surface*, פְּנֵי *the face of*. פָּנִים *face* occurs in the plural form though it is singular in meaning. (See Lesson 22.)

3. רוּחַ *spirit* or *wind*. Here it means *Spirit*. The plural is רוּחוֹת. Observe that רוּחַ is feminine.

הָיְתָה *she (it, i.e., the Spirit) was*. Notice הָיָה *he was* and הָיְתָה *she (or it f.) was*.

מַיִם *water* is another plural form with a singular meaning. (See Lesson 22.)

4. וַיֹּאמֶר *and he said*, from אָמַר *to say*. For this biblical usage, see Lesson 33, Line 2. It is the Qal imperfect of אָמַר with the waw consecutive.

יְהִי *let it be*, from הָיָה *be*. יְהִי is a shortened form of יִהְיֶה *it will be*.

וַיַּרְא *and He saw*, from רָאָה. This is the Qal imperfect with the waw consecutive. (See Lesson 33, Note 5.)

כִּי טוֹב *that it is* (or *was*) *good*. Under the wide category of a relative conjunction, כִּי can also be translated *because, so that, since*, etc.

5. וַיִּקְרָא *and he called*, from קָרָא *to call*; here the Qal imperfect of קָרָא with the waw consecutive.

לַיְלָה *night*. Remember that לַיְלָה is masculine. (See Lesson 6.)

6. בַּיּוֹם הָרְבִיעִי *on the fourth day*. In English we say *on the day* but in Hebrew *in the day*. Similarly, בַּיּוֹם הַשִּׁשִּׁי *in the sixth day*. (See Note 7, below.)

רְבִיעִי *fourth* is from אַרְבָּעָה *four*, and likewise, שִׁשִּׁי *sixth* is from שִׁשָּׁה *six*. Observe that אֶת is repeated before each defined direct object.

7. בַּיּוֹם הַשִּׁשִּׁי *on the sixth day*. (See Note 6, above.)

בְּצַלְמוֹ *in his image*, צֶלֶם *image*.

וַיַּרְא (See Note 4, above.)

Writing tables and bench from the Qumran scriptorium.

STUDY HINTS

1. It should be exciting for you to be able to read the Hebrew Bible in the original tongue. If you have really mastered the vocabulary and the elements of Hebrew grammar in this course, you should encounter no difficulty in reading easy passages from the Bible.
2. Read the biblical passage several times and make sure you understand it thoroughly.
3. It is important that you review Lesson 33 well before doing this lesson.
4. Make a special effort to memorize the Vocabulary in this lesson.

EXERCISES

A. Give the plural of the following:

2. אִישׁ   1. רוּחַ

7. עֵץ

8. אֶרֶץ

9. אִשָּׁה

10. צֶלֶם

3. יוֹם

4. כּוֹכָב

5. אוֹר

6. לַיְלָה

B. Give the meaning and the root of the following words:

6. וַתִּתֵּן*

7. וַיַּרְא

8. תֹּאכְלוּ*

9. תָּמוּתוּ*

10. וִהְיִיתֶם*

1. וַיִּקְרָא

2. הָיְתָה

3. בְּרֵאשִׁית

4. וַיֹּאמֶר

5. וַתִּקַּח*

C. Translate the following into English:

1. בְּרֵאשִׁית הָיָה חֹשֶׁךְ עַל־פְּנֵי הָאָרֶץ וְעַל־פְּנֵי הַמָּיִם.

2. בָּרָא אֱלֹהִים אֶת־הָאוֹר וַיִּקְרָא לוֹ° יוֹם וְלַחֹשֶׁךְ קָרָא לַיְלָה.

3. נִבְרָא† הָאָדָם בְּצֶלֶם אֱלֹהִים בַּיוֹם הַשִּׁשִּׁי.

4. וַיַּרְא אֱלֹהִים אֶת־הָאוֹר כִּי הָיָה טוֹב.

5. נִבְרְאוּ† הַשֶּׁמֶשׁ וְהַיָּרֵחַ וְהַכּוֹכָבִים בַּיוֹם הָרְבִיעִי.

D. Give the Hebrew for the following:

1. And God saw that it was good.
2. The man was like the image of God.
3. And He called the light "day" (*literally,* "and He called to the light day").
4. Joseph saw in his dream the sun, the moon, and the stars.
5. In the beginning the Spirit of God was upon the face of the water.

E. Write the full declension of צֶלֶם *image* in the singular. (צַלְמִי, etc.)

---

*See Lesson 33.

°See Lesson 39, note 14.

†*Niphal of* בָּרָא *he created.* (See Lesson 34 on the verb patterns.)

Lesson Thirty-six

BIBLICAL PASSAGE FROM GENESIS, CHAPTER 22: ABRAHAM AND ISAAC

VOCABULARY

donkey	חֲמוֹר	Isaac	יִצְחָק
lad, youth	נַעַר	after	אַחֲרֵי
and they went	וַיֵּלְכוּ	he tested, tried	נִסָּה
all of them	כֻּלָּם	thing, word	דָּבָר
place (m.)	מָקוֹם	to him	אֵלָיו
fire	אֵשׁ	here I am	הִנֵּנִי
where?	אַיֵּה	take! (imperative)	קַח
lamb	שֶׂה	and go	וְלֵךְ
burnt offering	עוֹלָה	with him	עִמּוֹ
and he lifted	וַיִּשָּׂא	one	אֶחָד
ram	אַיִל	I shall say	אֹמַר
from afar	מֵרָחוֹק	and he rose up early	וַיַּשְׁכֵּם
and it was	וַיְהִי	and he took	וַיִּקַּח
Abraham	אַבְרָהָם		

GRAMMAR AND NOTES

1. אַחַר הַדְּבָרִים הָאֵלֶּה נִסָּה אֱלֹהִים אֶת־אַבְרָהָם וַיֹּאמֶר אֵלָיו: אַבְרָהָם. וַיֹּאמֶר: הִנֵּנִי

2. וַיֹּאמֶר: קַח אֶת־בִּנְךָ יִצְחָק אֲשֶׁר אָהַבְתָּ וְלֵךְ עִמּוֹ אֶל־אַחַד הֶהָרִים אֲשֶׁר אֹמַר אֵלֶיךָ.

3. וַיַּשְׁכֵּם אַבְרָהָם בַּבֹּקֶר וַיַּחֲבשׁ אֶת־חֲמֹרוֹ וַיִּקַּח אֶת־שְׁנֵי נְעָרָיו אִתּוֹ וְאֵת יִצְחָק בְּנוֹ וְאֶת־שְׁנֵי נְעָרָיו.

4. וַיֵּלְכוּ כֻּלָּם אֶל־הַמָּקוֹם אֲשֶׁר אָמַר לוֹ הָאֱלֹהִים.

5. וַיֹּאמֶר יִצְחָק אֶל־אַבְרָהָם: הִנֵּה הָאֵשׁ וְהָעֵצִים וְאַיֵּה הַשֶּׂה לְעֹלָה?

6. וַיִּשָּׂא אַבְרָהָם אֶת־עֵינָיו וַיַּרְא אֶת־הָאַיִל מֵרָחוֹק.

Notes: (Numbers refer to the lines above.)

1. וַיְהִי *and it was*, usually translated *and it came to pass*. It is shortened from יִהְיֶה, which is the imperfect of הָיָה with the Waw consecutive. (See Lesson 33, Note 2.) Thus וַיִּהְיֶה becomes וַיְהִי. The imperfect of almost all ל״ה and ע״ו verbs are shortened when used with the Waw consecutive; for example, יִבְנֶה (*he will build*, an imperfect from בָּנָה) is shortened to וַיִּבֶן in the Waw consecutive. See also וַיַּרְא (from וַיִּרְאֶה) in Note 6, below.

   אַחַר *after*, also אַחֲרֵי.

   נִסָּה *he tried, he tested*. This verb pattern is known as Piel. (See Lesson 34, Grammar and Notes 3.)

   אֱלֹהִים *God*, but ה׳ (for יְהֹוָה) *Lord* (pronounced אֲדֹנָי). See the Note under Biblical Word List Four in Lesson 14.

   וַיֹּאמֶר *and he said*, imperfect of אָמַר *say* with the Waw consecutive. (See Lesson 33, Line 2.)

   אֵלָיו *unto him, to him*. Prepositions in Hebrew can be declined like nouns. Some are declined like singular nouns, such as the declension of עִם (see Lesson 33, Note 5), or like plural nouns such as אֶל here. Be familiar with the following forms:

   אֵלַי אֵלֶיךָ אֵלַיִךְ אֵלָיו אֵלֶיהָ
   אֵלֵינוּ אֲלֵיכֶם אֲלֵיכֶן אֲלֵיהֶם אֲלֵיהֶן

   הִנְנִי *here I am*. הִנְנִי is from הִנֵּה + אֲנִי *behold, (here) I am*.

2. קַח *take*, imperative of לָקַח *to take*. This is the only פ״ל verb in Hebrew that omits the initial ל in the imperfect and imperative. (See וַיִּקַּח in Note 3, below.) The forms of the imperative of לקח are as follows: קַח, קְחִי, קְחוּ, קַחְנָה.

   בִּנְךָ *thy son*, בֵּן *son*.

   יִצְחָק *Isaac*. The word is derived from the verb צָחַק *to laugh*.

   וְלֶךְ *and go*, from הָלַךְ *to go, walk*. Verbs containing י, ו, ה, א in their roots are "weak" and therefore have irregular forms. In future lessons, you will learn these verbs systematically. The forms for the imperative of הָלַךְ are as follows: לֵךְ, לְכִי, לְכוּ, לֵכְנָה.

עִמּוֹ *with him,* עִם *with.* See the notes on the declension of the prepositions in Hebrew. (See Lesson 33, Note 5 and Note 1, above.)

אַחַד הֶהָרִים *one of the mountains.* אַחַד *one of,* is a construct form of אֶחָד. הָרִים is the plural of הַר *mountain.*

אֹמַר (for אאמר) *I shall say;* this is the imperfect, first person singular of אָמַר *to say.*

אֵלֶיךָ *unto thee, unto you.* (See Note 1, above.)

3. וַיַּשְׁכֵּם *and he rose up early.* This is a Hiphil verb pattern, but it lacks a causative meaning. (See Lesson 34, Grammar and Notes 5c.)

וַיִּקַּח (for וַיִּלְקַח) *and he took,* imperfect of לָקַח *to take.* The dagesh in the ק is for the missing ל. (See Note 2, above.)

שְׁנֵי *two* from שְׁנַיִם *two.* When followed by a noun, שְׁנֵי is used.

נְעָרָיו *his lads, his boys.* נַעַר *lad, boy, youth,* plural, נְעָרִים.

4. וַיֵּלְכוּ *and they went,* imperfect of הָלַךְ *to go, walk* with the Waw consecutive. (See Note 2, above.)

כֻּלָּם *all of them,* from כָּל־,כֹּל *all.* Observe, however, כָּל־יוֹם *every day,* but כָּל־הַיּוֹם *the whole day.*

מָקוֹם *place.* This is a masculine noun with a feminine plural form מְקוֹמוֹת.

הָאֱלֹהִים *God* (literally, *the God*). אֱלֹהִים is used with the definite article. Compare with ה' הוּא הָאֱלֹהִים *The Lord, He is the God* (I Kings 18:39).

5. עֵצִים *trees,* also *wood.*

אַיֵּה *where.* Another word is אֵיפֹה.

לְעוֹלָה *for a burnt offering.* עוֹלָה is from עָלָה *to go up.* A possible explanation for the relationship of these two words may lie in the nature of the burnt offering whose smoke ascends toward heaven.

6. וַיִּשָּׂא *and he lifted up.* This is the imperfect of נָשָׂא *to carry, lift up* with the Waw consecutive. It is a פ״ן and ל״א verb, and hence its conjugation is irregular.

עֵינָיו *his eyes.* עַיִן *eye.* עֵינַיִם *eyes;* hence, עֵינָיו *his eyes.*

וַיַּרְא *and he saw,* imperfect of רָאָה *to see* with the Waw consecutive. See also

וַתֵּרֶא *and she saw*. (See Lesson 33, Note 5 and also Note 1, above.)

מֵרָחוֹק *from afar*. This is from מִן *from* and רָחוֹק *far*.

STUDY HINTS

1. You should find that it is not excessively difficult for you to translate the passages in this lesson, even though you have been introduced to a number of irregular verb forms. You will be given a more detailed discussion of these forms in future lessons, but for now the material in this lesson should at least enable you to translate the passages and to have *some* idea for the reasons behind the various forms of the weak verb. The verb forms used here are all very common to the Old Testament and to every dialect of Hebrew.

A figure of a goat eating leaves, from Ur, ca. 2500 B.C. The figure has been likened to the "ram caught in the thicket" (Gen. 22:13) but is at least five hundred years earlier than the time of Abraham.

2. Make sure that you review the material in previous lessons as indicated in the Notes. If you do not have a thorough mastery of the material in previous lessons, you will have an ever-increasing inability to deal with future lessons.

3. Memorize the Vocabulary in this lesson and be able especially to recall the meaning of the basic forms of the irregular verbs. For example, the basic form of וַיִּשָּׂא (see Note 6 of this lesson) is נָשָׂא *to lift up* (i.e., the third person masculine singular).

EXERCISES

A. Give the exact meaning, root, and pattern of the following verbs:
(*Example*: וַתִּקַּח *and she took*, לָקַח, פ״ל)

6. וַיִּרָא	1. וַיֵּלֶךְ
7. לֵךְ	2. וַיֹּאמֶר
8. וַיֵּלְכוּ	3. וַיִּקַּח
9. וַיִּשָּׂא	4. וַיְהִי
10. קַח	5. אֹמַר

B. Give the plural forms of the following:

6. עַיִן	1. דָּבָר
7. עוֹלָה	2. בֵּן
8. חָזֶה	3. חֲמוֹר
9. עֵץ	4. נַעַר
10. הַר	5. מָקוֹם

C. Write an explanatory note on each of the following:

4. עֵצִים	1. וַיְהִי
5. עוֹלָה	2. הָאֱלֹהִים
6. אַחַד הֶהָרִים	3. עִמּוֹ, אֵלָיו

D. Translate the following into English:

1. לָקַח אַבְרָהָם אֶת־בְּנוֹ אֶל־אַחַד הֶהָרִים.

2. וַיִּקַּח אַבְרָהָם אֶת־חֲמוֹרוֹ וְאֶת־שְׁנֵי נְעָרָיו וַיֵּלְכוּ

אֶל־הַמָּקוֹם אֲשֶׁר הָיָה עַל־הָהָר.

3. וַיַּרְא יִצְחָק אֶת־הָאֵשׁ וְאֶת־הָעֵצִים וַיֹּאמַר: אָבִי,
אַיֵּה הַשֶּׂה לְעוֹלָה?

4. וַיְהִי כַּאֲשֶׁר נָשָׂא אַבְרָהָם אֶת־עֵינָיו וַיַּרְא אֶת־הָאַיִל
מֵרָחוֹק בֵּין הָעֵצִים.

E. Translate the following into Hebrew, with vowels:

1. God tried Abraham and He said unto him, "Take thy son to the mountains."

2. And Abraham took his son and his two lads and went to the place which he saw from afar.

3. And Isaac lifted up his eyes and saw the donkeys in the field.

4. And it came to pass after these things [that] Abraham and Isaac took the ram and went to the house.

F. Summarize the story given in this lesson in your own words in Hebrew, with vowels.

Lesson Thirty-seven
BIBLICAL PASSAGE FROM GENESIS, CHAPTER 37: JOSEPH'S DREAM

VOCABULARY

night	לַיְלָה (לֵילוֹת)		dream	חֲלוֹם (חֲלוֹמוֹת)
sun	שֶׁמֶשׁ		Joseph	יוֹסֵף
moon	יָרֵחַ		when	כַּאֲשֶׁר
eleven	אַחַד עָשָׂר		seventeen	שְׁבַע-עֶשְׂרֵה
star	כּוֹכָב (כּוֹכָבִים)		year	שָׁנָה (שָׁנִים)
standing (part.)	עוֹמֵד		shepherding, pasturing	רוֹעֶה
before me	לְפָנַי		flock (m. sg.)	צֹאן
what?	מָה?		Jacob	יַעֲקֹב
(interrogative prefix: see Note 5)	הֲ-		he loved greatly	אָהַב מְאֹד
come	בּוֹא		because	כִּי
thy mother	אִמֶּךָ		a son of old age, a late-born son	בֶּן-זְקוּנִים
to stand	לַעֲמֹד		he dreamed	חָלַם
before thee	לְפָנֶיךָ		hear! (imperative)	שִׁמְעוּ

GRAMMAR AND NOTES

חֲלוֹם יוֹסֵף

1. כַּאֲשֶׁר הָיָה יוֹסֵף בֶּן-שְׁבַע-עֶשְׂרֵה שָׁנָה הָיָה רוֹעֶה אֶת-הַצֹּאן עִם אֶחָיו.

2. יַעֲקֹב אָהַב מְאֹד אֶת-יוֹסֵף כִּי הוּא הָיָה בֶּן-זְקוּנִים לוֹ.

3. וַיַּחֲלֹם יוֹסֵף חֲלוֹם. הָלַךְ יוֹסֵף אֶל-אֶחָיו וַיֹּאמֶר אֲלֵיהֶם: שִׁמְעוּ

206

אֶת־הַחֲלוֹם אֲשֶׁר חָלַמְתִּי הַלָּיְלָה.

4. בַּחֲלוֹמִי וְהִנֵּה הַשֶּׁמֶשׁ, וְהַיָּרֵחַ וְאַחַד עָשָׂר כּוֹכָבִים עוֹמְדִים לְפָנָי.

5. וַיֹּאמֶר יַעֲקֹב אֶל יוֹסֵף: מָה הַחֲלוֹם הַזֶּה אֲשֶׁר חָלָמְתָּ? הֲבוֹא נָבוֹא אֲנִי וְאִמְּךָ וְאַחֶיךָ לְעֲמֹד לְפָנֶיךָ?

Notes: (Numbers refer to the lines above.)

1. כַּאֲשֶׁר *when*, but *when?* is מָתַי. *Examples*: מָתַי הָלַךְ הָאִישׁ? *when did the man go?* כַּאֲשֶׁר שָׁמַע אֶת־הַחֲלוֹם *when he heard the dream.*

בֶּן־שְׁבַע־עֶשְׂרֵה שָׁנָה *seventeen years old* (literally, *a son of seventeen year*). Some nouns denoting time, such as יוֹם or שָׁנָה, can be used in the singular form with numerals. You will learn more about this peculiarity in future lessons.

רוֹעֶה *shepherding*, a Qal present participle from רָעָה *to pasture.*

רוֹעֶה is also used as a noun *shepherd.*

צֹאן *flock*, a collective noun used in the singular.

אֶחָיו *his brothers*. Observe: אָח *brother*, אַחִים *brothers.*

2. בֶּן־זְקוּנִים *late-born son* (literally, *son of old age*). It usually means *the youngest son.* Compare with זָקֵן *old.*

3. וַיַּחֲלֹם *and he dreamed*, imperfect of חָלַם *to dream* with the Waw consecutive.

אֲלֵיהֶם *to them.* (See Lesson 36, Note 1 on the declension of the preposition אֶל.)

שִׁמְעוּ *hear!* Imperative of שָׁמַע *to hear.* (See Lesson 27 on the imperative.)

הַלָּיְלָה *this night, tonight.* (Literally, *the night.*) Similarly, הַיּוֹם *the day*, but also *this day, today.* Observe that לַיְלָה is masculine (see Lesson 6); לֵילוֹת *nights.*

4. שֶׁמֶשׁ *sun.* It occurs in the Bible as both masculine and feminine.

יָרֵחַ *moon* (m.). Also לְבָנָה, occurring in Isaiah and Song of Songs only.

עוֹמְדִים לְפָנָי *standing before me.* The Hebrew text has מִשְׁתַּחֲוִים לִי *are bowing down to me.* This is a difficult form to explain at this stage.

לְפָנָי *before me.* The prepositions לִפְנֵי *before* and אַחֲרֵי *after* use the plural pronominal suffixes when declined. (See Lesson 36, Note 1.) The declension of לִפְנֵי and אַחֲרֵי are as follows:

before:

לְפָנַי, לְפָנֶיךָ, לְפָנַיִךְ, לְפָנָיו, לְפָנֶיהָ

לְפָנֵינוּ, לִפְנֵיכֶם, לִפְנֵיכֶן, לִפְנֵיהֶם, לִפְנֵיהֶן

after:

אַחֲרַי, אַחֲרֶיךָ, אַחֲרַיִךְ, אַחֲרָיו, אַחֲרֶיהָ

אַחֲרֵינוּ, אַחֲרֵיכֶם, אַחֲרֵיכֶן, אַחֲרֵיהֶם, אַחֲרֵיהֶן

5. הֲבוֹא נָבוֹא *Shall we indeed come?* (literally, *Is it coming we shall come?*) הֲבוֹא is בּוֹא + הֲ. בּוֹא *coming*. The prefix הֲ is used to introduce an interrogative sentence; for example: הֲיָדַעְתָּ אֶת־הַדָּבָר הַזֶּה? *Have you known this thing?* בּוֹא נָבוֹא *We shall indeed come* (literally, *Coming we shall come*). This is a peculiar construction in Classical Hebrew. See the expression מוֹת־תָּמוּת *You shall surely die*, in Lesson 33, Note 4. Such words as *indeed, surely, certainly* are used to express the emphasis in this idiom. Here מוֹת is used as infinitive absolute and is invariable.

אִמְּךָ *thy mother.* אֵם *mother.*

STUDY HINTS

1. This lesson should give you no great difficulty since the vocabulary and sentence structure are familiar to you from previous lessons. Of course, at this stage you cannot expect to understand everything about the verb forms, but make an effort to master the information presented here and in previous lessons; e.g., the peculiarity of the infinitive absolute in Biblical Hebrew. (See Lesson 33, Note 4, and Note 5, above.)

2. Be able to decline prepositions such as אַחֲרֵי, לִפְנֵי, and אֶל, which take the plural endings, as well as prepositions such as עִם and לְ, which take the singular endings.

3. Make sure to master all the Vocabulary given in these lessons adapted from biblical texts. These words and phrases occur repeatedly throughout the Old Testament and are basic to a fundamental grasp of its language.

EXERCISES

(Some of the words used here have been used in previous lessons.)

A. Give the plural of the following:

2. מָקוֹם   אֲנִי .1

7. בֵּן

8. לְפָנֶיךָ

9. אָח

10. שָׁנָה

3. כּוֹכָב

4. לַיְלָה

5. רוֹעֶה

6. חֲלוֹם

B. Write the exact meaning and an explanatory note on the following:

6. בּוֹא נָבוֹא

7. מָתַי? כַּאֲשֶׁר

8. אֲלֵיהֶם

9. בֶּן־שֶׁבַע־עֶשְׂרֵה שָׁנָה

10. שָׁנָה

1. הַלַּיְלָה

2. בֶּן־זְקוּנִים

3. רוֹעֶה

4. צֹאן

5. הֲיָדַעְתָּ?

C. Use each item in Exercise B, above, in complete sentences of your own composition. (*Example*: הַלַּיְלָה / הָלַךְ הַנָּבִיא אֶל־הָעִיר הַלַּיְלָה)

D. Give the Hebrew for the following:

1. Jacob was fifty years old.

2. Shall we indeed remember this dream?

3. And he saw in his dream, and behold, the moon and the sun were standing before him.

4. Shall you certainly remember this great song?

5. What is this word which you have said unto me?

E. Translate the following into English:

1. יָשַׁב יַעֲקֹב בְּאֶרֶץ כְּנַעַן אַרְבָּעִים שָׁנָה.

2. אָהַב הָאָב אֶת־כָּל־בָּנָיו. הוּא אָהַב אֶת־יוֹסֵף מִכֻּלָּם כִּי הָיָה בֶן־זְקוּנִים לוֹ.

3. חָלַם הַנַּעַר חֲלוֹם: וְהִנֵּה סוּסִים עוֹמְדִים לִפְנֵי הַשֶּׁמֶשׁ וְלִפְנֵי הַיָּרֵחַ וְצוֹחֲקִים בְּקוֹל גָּרוֹל.

4. זָכַר הָאִישׁ אֶת־דִּבְרֵי הַנָּבִיא וַיֵּלֶךְ אֶל־הָעִיר הַגְּדוֹלָה הַזֹּאת.

SAMPLE OF MEDIEVAL HEBREW POETRY BY ABRAHAM IBN EZRA

VOCABULARY

to lie down	שָׁכַב	I go, rise early	אַשְׁכִּים
place for sleeping, bed	מִשְׁכָּב	prince, officer, minister	שַׂר
chariot, carriage	מֶרְכָּב	to ride	רָכַב
or	אוֹ	time	עֵת
either . . . or	אוֹ . . . אוֹ	towards evening	לְעֵת עֶרֶב
woe!	אוֹיָה, אוֹי	poor	עָנִי
star	כּוֹכָב	to be born	נוֹלַד
he shall go up	יַעֲלֶה	already	כְּבָר

GRAMMAR AND NOTES

The following poem by Abraham Ibn Ezra* is a good example of the usage of biblical vocabulary in medieval texts.

אַשְׁכִּים לְבֵית הַשַּׂר

1. אַשְׁכִּים לְבֵית הַשַּׂר   5. אוֹ יַעֲלֶה מֶרְכָּב

2. אוֹמְרִים כְּבָר רָכַב   6. אוֹ יַעֲלֶה מִשְׁכָּב

3. אָבוֹא לְעֵת עֶרֶב   7. אוֹיָה לְאִישׁ עָנִי

4. אוֹמְרִים כְּבָר שָׁכַב   8. נוֹלַד בְּלִי כּוֹכָב

---

*See the biographical note about the author following the Translations.

Notes: (Numbers refer to the lines above.)

1. אַשְׁכִּים *I shall rise early* (root שכם *to go* or *to rise early*); הִשְׁכַּמְתִּי *I rose early*, etc.; בַּבֹּקֶר הַשְׁכֵּם *very early in the morning*. This is a Hiphil verb pattern. (See Lesson 34.)

   בַּיִת *house,* בֵּית *the house of,* בֵּית הַשָּׂר *the house of the prince.*

   שָׂר *prince, officer,* רֹאשׁ הַשָּׂרִים *head of the ministers, prime minister.*

2. אוֹמְרִים *they say* or *people say*. When the personal pronoun is omitted, it is the same as in the French expression "on dit," *one says* or *people say*.

5. מֶרְכָּב *chariot, carriage* from רָכַב *to ride*. In the Bible, מֶרְכָּבָה is usually found. The –מ before the root often denotes "the place of the action"; similarly, מִשְׁכָּב (in Line 6) *place of sleeping, bed* from שָׁכַב *to lie down*.

   אוֹ *or,* BUT אוֹ . . . אוֹ *either . . . or,* אוֹ אַתָּה אוֹ אֲנִי *either you or I.*

8. נוֹלַד *was born* (root יָלַד *to give birth*). When נ is prefixed to the root, it conveys the passive: אָכַל *he ate,* נֶאֱכַל *it was eaten*. This is the Niphal verb pattern. (See Lesson 34.)

   כּוֹכָב *star,* בְּלִי כּוֹכָב *without luck*. The famous Hebrew expression מַזָּל טוֹב for *good luck* really means *good star*.

Translations:

The following translations of the above poem were prepared by two students at the University of Wisconsin.

The Prince's house, I go to at dawn	I come to the prince at break of day;
But the man has already gone.	They told me he had ridden away.
If at evening, I come once more	I came again at eventide.
I'm just in time to hear him snore.	"He's gone to bed," his servants cried.
Either off he rides	Either he is out to roam,
Or else in bed hides	Or he's sleeping in his home.
Woe to the plucky	Alas, unhappy man am I!
Just born unlucky.	No lucky star for me on high!
(Beverly Oberfeld, Milwaukee)	*(Orlando R. Overn, Madison)*

A note on the poet Abraham Ibn Ezra:

Abraham Ibn Ezra was born in 1098 and died in 1164. He established his reputation not only as a poet, but as a biblical commentator, a grammarian, and an astronomer as well. Abraham Ibn Ezra's poetic writings touch almost every subject imaginable. He wrote with a fine sense of humor, as evidenced by the above poem. He was also fond of playing with words and rhymes.

STUDY HINTS

1. Although the poem in this lesson is by the famous medieval poet Abraham Ibn Ezra, it is easy to follow—and even more so if you first go over the Vocabulary carefully.

2. In the Vocabulary, note that אַשְׁכִּים has a verb pattern known as the Hiphil. (See Lesson 34.)

The Thanksgiving Scroll from the Qumran caves.

3. Note the difference between עָנִי *poor* and אֲנִי *I*, and also between עֵת *time* and אֶת the Hebrew particle. (See Lesson 17.)

4. נוֹלַד *he was born* is from יָלַד *to give birth*. The נ as a prefix is often the sign of the passive. כָּתַב *he wrote*, נִכְתַּב *it was written*. This verb pattern is known as Niphal. (See Lesson 34.)

5. אָבוֹא in Line 3 of the poem is from the root בּוֹא *to come*. Learn the common expression בַּבֹּקֶר הַשְׁכֵּם *very early in the morning*.

6. It is useful to learn the origin of מַזָּל טוֹב given in Note 8. Read the biographical note on Abraham Ibn Ezra. If you wish to know more about this poet, read the article on him in one of the standard encyclopedias.

7. Try your own free translation of the poem. See the translations prepared by the two students.

8. Memorize the poem. It should be fun to memorize a Hebrew poem, and a medieval one at that!

EXERCISES

A. Answer the following questions in complete Hebrew sentences, without vowels:

1. מַה־שֵּׁם הָאִישׁ אֲשֶׁר כָּתַב אֶת־הַשִּׁיר הַזֶּה?

2. מַה־שֵּׁם הַשִּׁיר אֲשֶׁר קָרָאתָ?

3. אָנָה הָלַךְ הָאִישׁ? מָתַי?

4. מַדּוּעַ לֹא רָאָה הָאִישׁ אֶת־הַשָּׂר?

5. מָה אָמְרוּ לוֹ בָּעֶרֶב?

6. מָה אָמַר אִבְּן עֶזְרָא?

B. Translate the following into Hebrew, without vowels:
1. Ibn Ezra went to see the prince very early in the morning.
2. He did not find the prince because (כִּי) he had already gone out of the house.
3. Woe to the poor man who was born without a star.

C. Paraphrase the poem in your own words in Biblical Hebrew.

D. Use the following in complete sentences:

1. בְּלִי

.2 כְּבָר

3. לְעֵת עֶרֶב

4. אִישׁ עָנִי

5. אוֹ . . . אוֹ . . .

E. Try your own free translation of the poem.

Lesson Thirty-nine

REVIEW OF LESSONS 31–38

IMPORTANT POINTS TO REMEMBER

1. סֵפֶר הַנָּבִיא *the book of the prophet*, סֵפֶר נָבִיא *a book of a prophet*. (See the form of the construct state in Lesson 31.) Note how the Hebrew indicates whether the translation should read *the book of the prophet* or *a book of the prophet*. Note also that the noun in the construct state is *never* written with the article. (Lesson 31)

2. עֶבֶד הַמֶּלֶךְ הֶחָכָם is translated either *the servant of the wise king* or *the wise servant of the king*. (Lesson 31)

3. Feminine nouns ending in הָ change their הָ into תַ when in the construct state. (Lesson 31)

prayer	תְּפִלָּה
the prayer of the man	תְּפִלַּת הָאִישׁ

4. Two or more nouns may come together in the construct. (Lesson 31)

the horses of the king of Egypt	סוּסֵי מֶלֶךְ מִצְרַיִם

5. Some nouns undergo changes in their vowels when the construct state is formed. (Lesson 31)

hand	יָד	the hand of the prophet	יַד הַנָּבִיא
house	בַּיִת	a house of a prophet	בֵּית נָבִיא

6. Plural nouns ending in יִם form their construct state by changing יִם into יֵ. (Lesson 32)

songs	שִׁירִים, שִׁירֵי דָוִד
heroes	גִּבּוֹרִים, גִּבּוֹרֵי הַיּוֹם

215

7. Nouns with a dual plural also change the ending ־ַיִם into ־ֵי. (Lesson 32)

feet	רַגְלַיִם, רַגְלֵי הָאִישׁ
eyes	עֵינַיִם, עֵינֵי רָחֵל

8. Construct forms of nouns ending in ־וֹת also end in ־וֹת; no change occurs in the suffix. (Lesson 32)

prayers	תְּפִלּוֹת, תְּפִלּוֹת הַנָּבִיא
mares	סוּסוֹת, סוּסוֹת הַמֶּלֶךְ

9. Plural of נָחָשׁ is נְחָשִׁים; plural of דָּבָר is דְּבָרִים. Nouns of this pattern form their plurals accordingly. (Lesson 33)

10. כָּל all, entire, whole, every (Lesson 33)

every day	כָּל־יוֹם	the entire day	כָּל־הַיּוֹם
every house	כָּל־בַּיִת	the whole house	כָּל־הַבַּיִת
all the children	כָּל־הַיְלָדִים	all the book	כָּל־הַסֵּפֶר

11. יֹאכַל he shall eat, but וַיֹּאכַל and he ate; this is the imperfect with the Waw consecutive. Similarly, אָכַלְתָּ you ate, וְאָכַלְתָּ and you will eat. This is a peculiarity of Biblical Hebrew. (Lesson 33)

12. מוֹת תָּמוּת dying you will die. This is the infinitive absolute מוֹת (from מוּת) plus the second person masculine singular Qal imperfect of the same verb. This construction is often used in the Bible to give emphasis and is usually translated with an adverb such as certainly or surely, e.g., you will surely die. (Lesson 33)

13. Declension of prepositions: (Lesson 33)

a. בְּתוֹךְ in the midst, within

בְּתוֹכִי, בְּתוֹכְךָ, בְּתוֹכֵךְ, בְּתוֹכוֹ, בְּתוֹכָהּ

בְּתוֹכֵנוּ, בְּתוֹכְכֶם, בְּתוֹכְכֶן, בְּתוֹכָם, בְּתוֹכָן

b. מִן from

מִמֶּנִּי, מִמְּךָ, מִמֵּךְ, מִמֶּנּוּ, מִמֶּנָּה

מִמֶּנּוּ, מִכֶּם, מִכֶּן, מֵהֶם, מֵהֶן

c. אֵת direct object particle: me, thee, him, etc.

אוֹתִי, אוֹתְךָ, אוֹתָךְ, אוֹתוֹ, אוֹתָהּ

אוֹתָנוּ, אֶתְכֶם, אֶתְכֶן, אוֹתָם, אוֹתָן

14. Note the more regular declension of עִם and לְ. (Lesson 33)

עִמִּי, עִמְּךָ, עִמָּךְ, עִמּוֹ, עִמָּהּ

עִמָּנוּ, עִמָּכֶם, עִמָּכֶן, עִמָּהֶם/עִמָּם, עִמָּהֶן/עִמָּן

לִי, לְךָ, לָךְ, לוֹ, לָהּ, לָנוּ, לָכֶם, לָכֶן, לָהֶם, לָהֶן

15. Note the following verbs with the Waw consecutive (in addition to those in Lesson 33, Note 5):

and he ate	וַיֹּאכַל	(*from*	אכל to eat)
and he saw	וַיַּרְא	(*from*	ראה to see)
and she saw	וַתֵּרֶא	(*from*	ראה to see)

16. The simple action of the verb is expressed by the Qal verb pattern. (Lesson 34) יָשַׁב *he sat* הָלַךְ *he went.*

One of the jars containing scrolls from the Qumran caves.

17. The passive of a verb is expressed by the Niphal. (Although with certain verbs, this pattern may be reflexive or even active in meaning; as you progress in Hebrew, you will become acquainted with these exceptions.) (Lesson 34)

נִשְׁלַח (from שָׁלַח) *he was sent*

נִלְחַם (from לחם) Although this is the Niphal, it is always translated actively, *he fought.*

נִשְׁמַר (from שׁמר) This particular verb is usually translated *he was guarded,* but in certain contexts it may also have a reflexive meaning, *he guarded himself.*

18. The Piel basically indicates an intensification of an action: (Lesson 34)

he broke	שָׁבַר	he smashed	שִׁבֵּר

The Piel may also alter the meaning somewhat:

he counted	סָפַר	he recounted	סִפֵּר

The Piel may indicate repeated action:

he jumped	קָפַץ	he skipped	קִפֵּץ

The Piel may make a verb transitive:

he was strong	חָזַק	he strengthened	חִזֵּק

Some verbs are common only in the Piel and have no special intensive meaning:

he blessed	בֵּרֵךְ

19. The Pual is the passive of the Piel. (Lesson 34)

he smashed	שִׁבֵּר	it was smashed	שֻׁבַּר

20. The Hiphil usually expresses a causative action. (Lesson 34)

he reigned	מָלַךְ	he made king	הִמְלִיךְ

21. The Hophal is the passive of the Hiphil. (Lesson 34)

he made king	הִמְלִיךְ	he was made king	הָמְלַךְ

22. The Hithpael usually expresses a reflexive action. (Lesson 34)

he washed	רָחַץ	he washed himself	הִתְרַחֵץ

23. Some words are plural but can have a singular meaning (Lesson 35). For example, שָׁמַיִם *heavens, sky* can be either singular or plural in meaning; פָּנִים *face* and מַיִם *water* are both singular in meaning.

24. Note that the form of *he was* is הָיָה, but *she was* is הָיְתָה (Lesson 35). Also

let it be is יְהִי shortened from יְהְיֶה (the Qal imperfect of הָיָה).

25. Note that כִּי is used basically as a relative conjunction, for example, "He saw *that* it was good," and אֲשֶׁר tends to be used as a relative pronoun, for example, "He saw the earth *that* he had made." This is the basic difference between these two words, although אֲשֶׁר is also used quite often as a relative conjunction in certain constructions. (Lessons 35 and 17)

26. Although בַּיּוֹם הַשִּׁשִּׁי is translated *on the sixth day* in English, the literal translation of this idiom is <u>*in the sixth day*</u>. (Lesson 35)

27. The ל״ה verbs are shortened when they are used with the Waw consecutive. For example, יִבְנֶה (*he will build* from בָּנָה) is shortened to יִבֶן in the Waw consecutive וַיִּבֶן. (Lesson 36)

28. The name for *Lord* (יהוה) is pointed from the vowels of אֲדֹנָי (יְהֹוָה). (Lesson 36)

29. The preposition אֶל takes the plural ending, e.g., אֵלֶיהָ *to her*. (Lesson 36)

30. לָקַח is the only פ״ל verb in Hebrew to drop its ל in the imperfect and imperative forms, but it is a very common word in the Old Testament. (Lesson 36)

   (imperative) *take!*   קַח   (imperfect) *he will take*   יִקַּח

31. הָלַךְ is an example of a very common weak verb with irregular forms. In this case the initial ה is weak and drops out. (Lesson 36)

   (imperative) *go!*   לֵךְ   (imperfect) *he will go*   יֵלֵךְ

32. אָמַר is a very common verb with irregular forms because of its initial א. Thus, יֹאמַר *he will say* and אֹמַר *I will say*. (Lesson 36)

33. When שְׁנַיִם *two* is followed by a noun, it becomes שְׁנֵי. Thus, שְׁנֵי נְעָרִים *two boys*. (Lesson 36)

34. כֹּל may take suffixes. Thus, כֻּלָּם *all of them*. (Lesson 36)

35. נָשָׂא is a weak verb, especially in regard to the נ (the א is also weak). Thus, the nun drops in certain forms. (Lesson 36)

   (imperative) *lift up!*   שָׂא   (imperfect) *he will lift up*   יִשָּׂא

36. כַּאֲשֶׁר *when, as* has no interrogative meaning, unlike מָתַי *when?* which introduces a question. (Lesson 37)

37. An example of the Hebrew idiom for describing a person's age is the following: בֶּן־שְׁבַע־עֶשְׂרֵה שָׁנָה (literally, *a son of seventeen years*). Note that

some nouns such as שָׁנָה *year* and יוֹם *day* can be used in the singular even though they have a plural meaning. (Lesson 37)

38. הַלַּיְלָה and הַיּוֹם mean, respectively, *this night* (or *tonight*) and *this day* (or *today*), even though literally they would seem to say only *the day* or *the night*. (Lesson 37)

39. Note that plural suffixes are attached to אַחֲרֵי, לִפְנֵי (Lesson 37), and אֶל (Lesson 36) in contrast to עִם and לְ (Lesson 33), which take the singular suffixes.

40. When an action is emphasized in Hebrew, an infinitive absolute of the verb in question is often placed just before it; thus, יִזְכֹּר *he shall remember* (imperfect of זָכַר), but זָכֹר יִזְכֹּר *he shall surely remember*. (Lesson 37)

41. Note the idiom for *very early in the morning* בַּבֹּקֶר הַשְׁכֵּם (literally, *in the morning rising early*). (Lesson 38)

42. אוֹמְרִים is idiomatic for *one says*, or *people say* (literally, *they are saying*); cf., the French "on dit." (Lesson 38)

43. אוֹ means *or*, but when used twice in a clause . . . אוֹ . . . אוֹ it is translated *either . . . or . . .*, e.g., אוֹ אַתָּה אוֹ אֲנִי *either you or I*. (Lesson 38)

44. בְּלִי כּוֹכָב is an idiom meaning *without luck* (literally, *without a star*). Note the famous Hebrew phrase מַזָּל טוֹב *good luck* (literally, *good star*).

EXERCISES

Translate Exercises A through F into Hebrew:

A. one book, two books, five books, thirty books, forty-five books, one lamp, two lamps, five lamps, thirty lamps, sixty-five lamps.

B. the man's prayer, the king's horses, the book of the prophet, the prayers of David (דָּוִד), The Song of Songs, the eyes of the girl, the house of this woman, the heroes of the king of Israel.

C. from the house, for one night, until the morning, on the earth, from day to day, without the father, to the city.

D. to him, from me, with us, within me, for you (m. pl.), to us, in our midst, from him, with her, for him.

E. every night, all the night, each day, all the day, all of us, every year, all the books, throughout the year.

F. he will eat, and he ate, he ate, and he will eat, he took, and he took, she saw, and she saw, he saw, and he saw, he broke, he smashed, he ate, he fed, he sent, he was sent, he washed, he washed the hands, he washed himself (i.e., bathed) in the sea.

G. Write two verbs in each of the following groups:

1. ל״א verbs   3. ל״ה verbs   5. regular verbs

2. פ״י verbs   4. ע״ו verbs

H. Write the infinitive forms of the following verbs, with prefix לְ. (For this exercise, you may refer to the Hebrew-English Vocabulary at the back of this book.)

to see, to forgive, to take, to guard, to hear, to eat, to sit, to get up, to go, to do

Lesson Forty

SAMPLE FINAL EXAMINATION

The following two-hour test is a final review of the material normally covered in one semester of work.

PART I: BIBLICAL HEBREW PASSAGES

A. Translate the following passages into English:

1. וַתֹּאמֶר הָאִשָּׁה אֶל־הַנָּחָשׁ: מִפְּרִי עֵץ הַגָּן נֹאכֵל, וּמִפְּרִי הָעֵץ אֲשֶׁר בְּתוֹךְ הַגָּן, אָמַר אֱלֹהִים לֹא תֹאכְלוּ מִמֶּנּוּ פֶּן תְּמֻתוּ.

_____

_____

2. וַיֹּאמֶר הַנָּחָשׁ אֶל־הָאִשָּׁה: לֹא מוֹת תְּמֻתוּן כִּי יֹדֵעַ אֱלֹהִים כִּי בְּיוֹם אֲכָלְכֶם מִמֶּנּוּ וִהְיִיתֶם כֵּאלֹהִים יֹדְעֵי טוֹב וָרָע.

_____

_____

3. וַיֹּאמֶר אֱלֹהִים: יְהִי אוֹר בַּשָּׁמַיִם. וַיַּרְא אֱלֹהִים אֶת־הָאוֹר כִּי טוֹב.

_____

4. וַיִּקְרָא אֱלֹהִים לָאוֹר יוֹם וְלַחֹשֶׁךְ קָרָא לַיְלָה.

_____

5. בְּיוֹם הַשִּׁשִּׁי בָּרָא אֱלֹהִים אֶת־הָאָדָם בְּצַלְמוֹ.

_____

6. וַיֹּאמֶר: קַח אֶת־בִּנְךָ יִצְחָק אֲשֶׁר אָהַבְתָּ וְלֵךְ עִמּוֹ אֶל אַחַד הֶהָרִים אֲשֶׁר אֹמַר אֵלֶיךָ.

_____

_____

222

7. וַיֹּאמֶר יִצְחָק אֶל־אַבְרָהָם: הִנֵּה הָאֵשׁ וְהָעֵצִים וְאַיֵּה הַשֶּׂה לְעוֹלָה?[1]

_____

8. כַּאֲשֶׁר הָיָה יוֹסֵף בֶּן־שְׁבַע־עֶשְׂרֵה שָׁנָה הָיָה רוֹעֶה[2] אֶת־הַצֹּאן עִם אֶחָיו.

_____

9. וַיַּחֲלֹם יוֹסֵף חֲלוֹם. הָלַךְ יוֹסֵף אֶל־אֶחָיו וַיֹּאמֶר אֲלֵיהֶם: שִׁמְעוּ אֶת־הַחֲלוֹם אֲשֶׁר חָלַמְתִּי הַלַּיְלָה.

_____

_____

10. וַיֹּאמֶר יַעֲקֹב אֶל־יוֹסֵף: מָה הַחֲלוֹם הַזֶּה אֲשֶׁר חָלַמְתָּ? הֲבוֹא נָבוֹא אֲנִי וְאִמְּךָ וְאַחֶיךָ לַעֲמֹד לְפָנֶיךָ?

_____

B. Answer the following questions in complete Hebrew sentences based on the text above.

1. מָה אָמַר הַנָּחָשׁ אֶל־הָאִשָּׁה?

_____

2. מַה קָרָא אֱלֹהִים לַחֹשֶׁךְ?

_____

3. מָתַי וְאֵיךְ בָּרָא אֱלֹהִים אֶת־הָאָדָם?

_____

4. מָה אָמַר אֱלֹהִים אֶל־אַבְרָהָם?

_____

5. בֶּן־כַּמָּה שָׁנָה הָיָה יוֹסֵף כַּאֲשֶׁר הָיָה רוֹעֶה?

_____

C. Translate the following passages into English:

וַיִּשְׁמְעוּ אֶת־קוֹל אֱלֹהִים בַּגָּן וַיִּתְחַבְּאוּ[3] הָאָדָם וְאִשְׁתּוֹ

_____

בְּתוֹךְ עֵץ הַגָּן. וַיִּקְרָא אֱלֹהִים אֶל־הָאָדָם וַיֹּאמֶר לוֹ:

_____

_____

[1]for a burnt offering
[2]shepherd
[3]they hid themselves

אַיֶּכָּה?⁴ וַיֹּאמֶר הָאָדָם: שָׁמַעְתִּי אֶת־קוֹלְךָ בַּגָּן

נָאִירָא⁵ כִּי עֵרוֹם אָנֹכִי וָאֵחָבֵא.⁶ וַיֹּאמֶר אֱלֹהִים:

מִי אָמַר לְךָ כִּי עֵרוֹם אַתָּה? הֲאָכַלְתָּ מִן־הָעֵץ

אֲשֶׁר בְּתוֹךְ הַגָּן? וַיֹּאמֶר הָאָדָם: הָאִשָּׁה הַזֹּאת נָתְנָה

לִי מִן־הָעֵץ וָאֹכַל. וַתֹּאמֶר הָאִשָּׁה: הַנָּחָשׁ נָתַן לִי מִפְּרִי

עֵץ הַגָּן וָאֶתֵּן לְאִישִׁי וַיֹּאכַל גַּם הוּא עִמִּי.

D. Translate the following into Hebrew:

1. You (m. sg.) have eaten from the fruit of the tree in the garden.

   _____

2. The man saw that the tree in the midst of the garden was good to the eyes.

   _____

   _____

3. God called the light "day," and He saw that [it was] good.

   _____

4. And Joseph said to Jacob: "In my dream, behold, [I saw] the sun, the moon and the stars."

   _____

   _____

5. Isaac lifted up his eyes and he saw the ram which God had given to him. (ram אַיִל)

   _____

   _____

---

⁴where art thou?
⁵and I was afraid
⁶and I hid myself

6. Jacob was fifty years old and he said to his servants: "I indeed remember[7] the words which God spoke to me in a dream."

_____

_____

PART II: GRAMMAR

E. Translate the following into Hebrew:

1. the book, this book, this big book, this book is big, these books _____

   _____

   _____

2. these beautiful mares, this mare is beautiful, this night, these nights and these days _____

   _____

   _____

3. I remember, I do not remember, we ate, we did not eat, she saw, they (f. pl.) will remember, we are standing, and he gave, and she saw _____

   _____

   _____

4. his lamp, his lamps, our hand, our hands, her horse, her horses, their (f.) songs, their (m.) star, your (f. pl.) mares, your (m. pl.) mare _____

   _____

   _____

5. like the house, from the house, upon the house, in the house, before the house, under the house, with the man _____

   _____

   _____

6. without life, before the evil day, until this night, between the trees,

---

[7]Use the infinitive absolute.

between the house and the tree _____

_____

_____

7. 2 books, 2 girls, one house, one mare, 35 books, 100 images _____

_____

F. Write the plural of the following:

_____	עַיִן .6	_____	אִישׁ .1
_____	בַּיִת .7	_____	אִשָּׁה .2
_____	סֵפֶר .8	_____	מִשְׁפָּחָה .3
_____	יוֹם .9	_____	דָּבָר .4
_____	יֶלֶד .10	_____	יַלְדָּה .5

G. Write the following in Hebrew, with vowels:

1. The perfect, imperfect, and imperative of כָּתַב.

_____

_____

2. The full declension of חֲלוֹם *dream* in the singular (*my dream*, etc.).

_____

_____

3. The full declension of תּוֹרוֹת *laws* in the plural (*my laws*, etc.).

_____

_____

H. Choose 8 of the following 10 words. Use each of the 8 words in a separate
    sentence.

לֹא .6		שָׁמַיִם .1	
אֵין .7		מָתַי .2	
תּוֹרַת .8		כַּאֲשֶׁר .3	
אֵת .9		בְּנֵי .4	
יְרוּשָׁלַיִם .10		יָד .5	

_____ .1

_____ .2

_____ .3

_____ .4

_____ .5

_____ .6

_____ .7

_____ .8

I. Give the English of *25* of the following 30 words:

_____	מָכַר .21	_____	לִפְנֵי .11	_____	לָמָה .1
_____	דֶּרֶךְ .22	_____	רַק .12	_____	אִם .2
_____	הַר .23	_____	בָּרָא .13	_____	אֵלֶה .3
_____	רוּחַ .24	_____	כָּתַב .14	_____	בֹּקֶר .4
_____	עִיר .25	_____	כָּנָף .15	_____	מֶלֶךְ .5
_____	עַיִן .26	_____	כִּי .16	_____	כֶּסֶף .6
_____	תְּפִלָּה .27	_____	כַּמָה .17	_____	זָהָב .7
_____	שָׁם .28	_____	דֶּלֶת .18	_____	חַיִּים .8
_____	זָכַר .29	_____	עֵר .19	_____	פָּנִים .9
_____	יָרַד .30	_____	מָתַי .20	_____	מַיִם .10

J Write the Hebrew of *25* of the following 30 words, without vowels:

1. to go up _____	11. to speak _____	21. heart _____
2. to make, do _____	12. to read _____	22. hand _____
3. to command _____	13. to send _____	23. city _____
4. tongue _____	14. to find _____	24. brother _____
5. to give _____	15. to reign _____	25. lip _____
6. to take _____	16. river _____	26. head _____
7. to walk _____	17. chair _____	27. land _____
8. to give birth _____	18. eye _____	28. to hear _____
9. to go out _____	19. father _____	29. to know _____
10. to come _____	20. people _____	30. face _____

SUPPLEMENT

Conjugations of the Seven Patterns
of the Regular (Strong) Verbs
(See Lesson Thirty-Four)

There are seven verb patterns in Hebrew. The first six are conjugated in *pairs*, since each *pair* expresses a specific meaning of the root in the active and in the passive; the seventh verb pattern expresses the reflexive.

It is important to remember that:

a. *Rarely* are all seven patterns used in the same verb.

b. The meaning of a verb pattern often differs from the regular significance. (See Lesson Thirty-Four for further details.)

Most grammar textbooks use the verb קָטַל *to kill* as a model for the conjugations, since it contains three regular (*strong*) consonants (i.e., it does not contain a guttural or a weak letter). For further details, see Lesson Fourteen. For the meanings of each verb pattern, see Lesson Thirty-Four.

CONJUGATIONS OF THE QAL AND THE NIPHAL

1. QAL קָטַל *to kill*

Qal expresses the simple form of the verb.

Perfect (Past): קָטַלְתִּי *I killed*, etc.

קָטַלְתִּי, קָטַלְתָּ , קָטַלְתְּ, קָטַל, קָטְלָה

קָטַלְנוּ, קָטַלְתֶּם, קָטַלְתֶן, קָטְלוּ, קָטְלוּ

Imperfect (Future): אֶקְטֹל *I shall kill*, etc.

אֶקְטֹל, תִּקְטֹל, תִּקְטְלִי, יִקְטֹל, תִּקְטֹל

נִקְטֹל, תִּקְטְלוּ, תִּקְטֹלְנָה, יִקְטְלוּ, תִּקְטֹלְנָה

Imperative: קְטֹל *kill!*

קְטֹל, קִטְלִי, קִטְלוּ, קְטֹלְנָה

Participle: Active—*killing*; Passive—*being killed*

Active קֹטֵל, קֹטֶלֶת, קֹטְלִים, קֹטְלוֹת

Passive קָטוּל, קְטוּלָה, קְטוּלִים, קְטוּלוֹת

Infinitive Absolute: קָטוֹל *to kill*

Infinitive Construct: קְטֹל *to kill*

2. NIPHAL נִקְטַל *to be killed*

Niphal expresses the passive of the Qal.

Perfect (Past): נִקְטַלְתִּי *I was killed*, etc.

נִקְטַלְתִּי, נִקְטַלְתָּ, נִקְטַלְתְּ, נִקְטַל, נִקְטְלָה

נִקְטַלְנוּ, נִקְטַלְתֶּם, נִקְטַלְתֶּן, נִקְטְלוּ, נִקְטְלוּ

Imperfect (Future): אֶקָּטֵל *I shall be killed*, etc.

אֶקָּטֵל, תִּקָּטֵל, תִּקָּטְלִי, יִקָּטֵל, תִּקָּטֵל

נִקָּטֵל, תִּקָּטְלוּ, תִּקָּטַלְנָה, יִקָּטְלוּ, תִּקָּטַלְנָה

Imperative: הִקָּטֵל *be killed!*

הִקָּטֵל, הִקָּטְלִי, הִקָּטְלוּ, הִקָּטַלְנָה

Participle: נִקְטָל *being killed*

נִקְטָל, נִקְטָלָה (נִקְטֶלֶת), נִקְטָלִים, נִקְטָלוֹת

Infinitive Absolute: נִקְטֹל *to be killed*

Infinitive Construct: הִקָּטֵל *to be killed*

CONJUGATIONS OF THE PIEL AND THE PUAL

3. PIEL קִטֵּל *to kill violently* or *to slay*

Piel usually expresses the *intensive* form of the Qal in the active voice (see Lesson Thirty-Four).

Perfect (Past): קִטַּלְתִּי *I slew*, etc.

קִטַּלְתִּי, קִטַּלְתָּ, קִטַּלְתְּ, קִטֵּל, קִטְּלָה

קִטַּלְנוּ, קִטַּלְתֶּם, קִטַּלְתֶּן, קִטְּלוּ, קִטְּלוּ

Imperfect (Future): אֲקַטֵּל *I shall slay*, etc.

אֲקַטֵּל, תְּקַטֵּל, תְּקַטְּלִי, יְקַטֵּל, תְּקַטֵּל

נְקַטֵּל, תְּקַטְּלוּ, תְּקַטֵּלְנָה, יְקַטְּלוּ, תְּקַטֵּלְנָה

Imperative: קַטֵּל *slay!*

קַטֵּל, קַטְּלִי, קַטְּלוּ, קַטֵּלְנָה

Participle: מְקַטֵּל *slaying*

מְקַטֵּל, מְקַטֶּלֶת (מְקַטְּלָה), מְקַטְּלִים, מְקַטְּלוֹת

Infinitive Absolute: קַטֹּל *to slay*

Infinitive Construct: קַטֵּל *to slay*

4. PUAL קֻטַּל *to be slain*

        Pual is normally the passive of the Piel.

Perfect (Past): קֻטַּלְתִּי *I was slain*, etc.

קֻטַּלְתִּי, קֻטַּלְתָּ, קֻטַּלְתְּ, קֻטַּל, קֻטְּלָה

קֻטַּלְנוּ, קֻטַּלְתֶּם, קֻטַּלְתֶּן, קֻטְּלוּ, קֻטְּלוּ

Imperfect (Future): אֲקֻטַּל *I shall be slain*, etc.

אֲקֻטַּל, תְּקֻטַּל, תְּקֻטְּלִי, יְקֻטַּל, תְּקֻטַּל

נְקֻטַּל, תְּקֻטְּלוּ, תְּקֻטַּלְנָה, יְקֻטְּלוּ, תְּקֻטַּלְנָה

Participle: מְקֻטָּל *being slain*

Imperative: Not used.

Infinitive Absolute: קֻטֹּל *to be slain*

Infinitive Construct: Not used.

CONJUGATIONS OF THE HIPHIL AND THE HOPHAL
(See Lesson Thirty-Four)

5. HIPHIL הִקְטִיל *to cause to kill*, i.e., *to murder*

        Hiphil is usually the *causative* form of the Qal. (Qal קָטַל *to kill*, Piel קִטֵּל *to slay*, but הִקְטִיל *to cause to kill*, i.e., *to murder*)

Perfect (Past): הִקְטַלְתִּי *I murdered*, etc.

הִקְטַלְתִּי, הִקְטַלְתָּ, הִקְטַלְתְּ, הִקְטִיל, הִקְטִילָה

הִקְטַלְנוּ, הִקְטַלְתֶּם, הִקְטַלְתֶּן, הִקְטִילוּ, הִקְטִילוּ

Imperfect (Future): אַקְטִיל *I shall murder*, etc.

אַקְטִיל, תַּקְטִיל, תַּקְטִילִי, יַקְטִיל, תַּקְטִיל

נַקְטִיל, תַּקְטִילוּ, תַּקְטֵלְנָה, יַקְטִילוּ, תַּקְטֵלְנָה

Imperative: הַקְטֵל *murder!*

הַקְטֵל, הַקְטִילִי, הַקְטִילוּ, הַקְטֵלְנָה

Participle: מַקְטִיל *murdering*

מַקְטִיל, מַקְטִילָה, מַקְטִילִים, מַקְטִילוֹת

Infinitive Absolute: הַקְטֵל *to murder*

Infinitive Construct: הַקְטִיל *to murder*

6. HOPHAL   הָקְטַל *to cause to be killed*, i.e., *to be murdered*
             Hophal is the passive of the Hiphil.

Perfect (Past): הָקְטַלְתִּי *I was murdered*, etc.

הָקְטַלְתִּי, הָקְטַלְתָּ, הָקְטַלְתְּ, הָקְטַל, הָקְטְלָה

הָקְטַלְנוּ, הָקְטַלְתֶּם, הָקְטַלְתֶּן, הָקְטְלוּ, הָקְטְלוּ

Imperfect (Future): אָקְטַל *I shall be murdered*, etc.

אָקְטַל, תָּקְטַל, תָּקְטְלִי, יָקְטַל, תָּקְטַל

נָקְטַל, תָּקְטְלוּ, תָּקְטַלְנָה, יָקְטְלוּ, תָּקְטַלְנָה

Participle: מָקְטָל *being murdered*

מָקְטָל, מָקְטֶלֶת (מָקְטָלָה), מָקְטָלִים, מָקְטָלוֹת

Imperative: Not used.

Infinitive Absolute: הָקְטֵל *to cause to murder*

Infinitive Construct: Not used.

CONJUGATION OF THE HITHPAEL

7. HITHPAEL   הִתְקַטֵּל *to kill oneself*
              Hithpael usually signifies the reflexive.

Perfect (Past): הִתְקַטַּלְתִּי *I killed myself*, etc.

הִתְקַטַּלְתִּי, הִתְקַטַּלְתָּ, הִתְקַטַּלְתְּ, הִתְקַטֵּל, הִתְקַטְּלָה

הִתְקַטַּלְנוּ, הִתְקַטַּלְתֶּם, הִתְקַטַּלְתֶּן, הִתְקַטְּלוּ

Imperfect (Future): אֶתְקַטֵּל *I shall kill myself*, etc.

אֶתְקַטֵּל, תִּתְקַטֵּל, תִּתְקַטְּלִי, יִתְקַטֵּל, תִּתְקַטֵּל

נִתְקַטֵּל, תִּתְקַטְּלוּ, תִּתְקַטֵּלְנָה, יִתְקַטְּלוּ, תִּתְקַטֵּלְנָה

Imperative: הִתְקַטֵּל *kill yourself!*

הִתְקַטֵּל, הִתְקַטְּלִי, הִתְקַטְּלוּ, הִתְקַטֵּלְנָה

Participle: מִתְקַטֵּל *killing oneself*

מִתְקַטֵּל, מִתְקַטֶּלֶת (מִתְקַטְּלָה) , מִתְקַטְּלִים, מִתְקַטְּלוֹת

Infinitive Absolute: הִתְקַטֵּל *to kill oneself*

Infinitive Construct: הִתְקַטֵּל *to kill oneself*

HEBREW-ENGLISH VOCABULARY

Most plurals of nouns and infinitive constructs of verbs are given in parentheses.

א

		how?	אֵיךְ?
father	אָב (אָבוֹת)	ram	אַיִל (אֵילִים)
stone (f.)	אֶבֶן (אֲבָנִים)	not, there is (or are) not	אֵין
Abraham	אַבְרָהָם	where?	אֵיפֹה?
the Lord	אֲדוֹנָי	man	אִישׁ (אֲנָשִׁים)
man, mankind	אָדָם	to eat	אָכַל (לֶאֱכֹל)
earth, ground	אֲדָמָה (אֲדָמוֹת)	God, god	אֵל (אֵלִים)
to love, desire	אָהַב (לֶאֱהֹב)	to, toward, against	אֶל-
love	אַהֲבָה	to him	אֵלָיו
tent	אֹהֶל (אֹהָלִים, אֱהָלִים)	these	אֵלֶּה
or	אוֹ	God, gods	אֱלֹהִים
either . . . or	אוֹ . . . אוֹ	thousand	אֶלֶף (אֲלָפִים)
woe!	אוֹי, אוֹיָה	if	אִם
light (m.)	אוֹר (אוֹרוֹת)	mother	אֵם (אִמּוֹת)
ear	אֹזֶן (אָזְנַיִם)	your (m. sg.) mother	אִמְּךָ
brother	אָח (אַחִים)	to say	אָמַר (לֵאמֹר)
one (m.)	אֶחָד	and he said	וַיֹּאמֶר
eleven (m.)	אַחַד עָשָׂר	I shall say	אֹמַר
one (f.)	אַחַת	where to? whither?	אָן? אָנָה?
other, another	אַחֵר (אֲחֵרִים, אֲחֵרוֹת)	man, men	אֱנוֹשׁ
after	אַחֲרֵי	we	אֲנַחְנוּ
where?	אַיֵּה?	I	אֲנִי

232

I	אָנֹכִי
also, even	אַף
end, nothing	אֶפֶס (אֲפָסִים)
finger (f.)	אֶצְבַּע (אֶצְבָּעוֹת)
near, beside	אֵצֶל
four (f.)	אַרְבַּע
four (m.)	אַרְבָּעָה
forty	אַרְבָּעִים
fourth	רְבִיעִי
Aram	אֲרָם
land, earth (f.)	אֶרֶץ (אֲרָצוֹת)
Ashdod	אַשְׁדּוֹד
woman	אִשָּׁה (נָשִׁים)
Assyria	אַשּׁוּר
which, who, that	אֲשֶׁר
(sign of direct object)	אֶת־
you (f. sg.)	אַתְּ
you (m. sg.)	אַתָּה
you (m. pl.)	אַתֶּם
you (f. pl.)	אַתֵּן

ב

in, with	בְּ־
Babylon	בָּבֶל
garment, clothing	בֶּגֶד (בְּגָדִים)
beast, cattle	בְּהֵמָה (בְּהֵמוֹת)
to come	בּוֹא (לָבוֹא)
to choose	בָּחַר (לִבְחֹר)
belly (f.)	בֶּטֶן
between	בֵּין
house (m.)	בַּיִת (בָּתִּים)
Bethel	בֵּית־אֵל

Bethlehem	בֵּית לֶחֶם
without	בְּלִי
son	בֵּן (בָּנִים)
a son of old age, youngest son	בֶּן־זְקוּנִים
to build	בָּנָה (לִבְנוֹת)
morning	בֹּקֶר (בְּקָרִים)
to create	בָּרָא (לִבְרֹא)
blessed (pass. part.)	בָּרוּךְ
to bless	בֵּרַךְ (לְבָרֵךְ)
blessing	בְּרָכָה (בְּרָכוֹת)
daughter	בַּת (בָּנוֹת)
in the midst (of)	בְּתוֹךְ

ג

back	גַּב
hero, mighty one	גִּבּוֹר (גִּבּוֹרִים)
a man (of strength)	גֶּבֶר (גְּבָרִים)
great	גָּדוֹל (גְּדוֹלִים)
to become great	גָּדַל (לִגְדֹּל)
to make great	גִּדֵּל (לְגַדֵּל)
people, nation	גּוֹי (גּוֹיִם)
Gezer	גֶּזֶר
also	גַּם
to finish	גָּמַר (לִגְמֹר)
garden	גַּן (גַּנִּים)
to steal	גָּנַב (לִגְנֹב)
rain	גֶּשֶׁם (גְּשָׁמִים)

ד

word, thing	דָּבָר (דְּבָרִים)

to speak	דִּבֵּר (לְדַבֵּר)
uncle, beloved one	דּוֹד (דּוֹדִים)
aunt	דּוֹדָה (דּוֹדוֹת)
door (f.)	דֶּלֶת (דְּלָתוֹת)
way, path (f.)	דֶּרֶךְ (דְּרָכִים)

ה

the	הַ-
(interrogative prefix)	הַ-
to listen	הֶאֱזִין (אזן)
to feed	הֶאֱכִיל (אכל)
to bring	הֵבִיא (בוא)
to be told	הֻגַּד (נגד)
to tell, report, announce	הִגִּיד (נגד)
he	הוּא
she	הִיא
to be	הָיָה (לִהְיוֹת)
let it (*or* there) be	יְהִי
and it was	וַיְהִי
she (*or* it [f.]) was	הָיְתָה
temple, palace (m.)	הֵיכָל
to go, walk	הָלַךְ (לָלֶכֶת)
go! (imperative)	לֵךְ
and they went	וַיֵּלְכוּ
they (m.)	הֵם
to crown	הִמְלִיךְ (מלך)
they (f.)	הֵן
they (f.)	הֵנָּה
behold	הִנֵּה
here I am (literally, "behold me")	הִנְנִי
to raise	הֵקִים (קום)

mountain	הַר (הָרִים)
much, many	הַרְבֵּה (רבה)
to remove	הִרְחִיק (רחק)
to rise early	הִשְׁכִּים (שכם)
to cast	הִשְׁלִיךְ
to be thrown	הֻשְׁלַךְ (שלך)
to hide oneself	הִתְחַבֵּא (חבא)
to dress oneself	הִתְלַבֵּשׁ (לבש)
to pray	הִתְפַּלֵּל (פלל)
to wash oneself	הִתְרַחֵץ (רחץ)

ו

and	וְ-
and he said	וַיֹּאמֶר (אמר)
and he (or it [m.]) was	וַיְהִי (היה)
and they went	וַיֵּלְכוּ (הלך)
and he took	וַיִּקַּח (לקח)
and he called	וַיִּקְרָא (קרא)
and he saw	וַיַּרְא (ראה)
and he lifted up	וַיִּשָּׂא (נשא)
and he rose early	וַיַּשְׁכֵּם (שכם)
and she (or you, m. sg.) took	וַתִּקַּח (לקח)
and she (or you, m. sg.) saw	וַתֵּרֶא (ראה)
and she (or you, m. sg.) gave	וַתִּתֵּן (נתן)

ז

this (f.)	זֹאת
sacrifice	זֶבַח (זְבָחִים)

this (m.)	זֶה
gold	זָהָב
to remember	זָכַר (לִזְכֹּר)
old (of people)	זָקֵן (זְקֵנִים)

ח

friend, companion	חָבֵר (חֲבֵרִים)
Tigris river	חִדֶּקֶל
chamber, room	חֶדֶר (חֲדָרִים)
holy	קֹדֶשׁ
strong	חָזָק (חֲזָקִים)
to be strong	חָזַק (לַחֲזֹק)
he strengthened	חִזֵּק (לְחַזֵּק)
living, life	חַי
to live	חָיָה (לִחְיוֹת)
animal, beast	חַיָּה (חַיּוֹת)
life	חַיִּים
dream (m.)	חֲלוֹם (חֲלוֹמוֹת)
to dream	חָלַם (לַחֲלֹם)
ass, donkey	חֲמוֹר (חֲמוֹרִים)
five (f.)	חָמֵשׁ
five (m.)	חֲמִשָּׁה
fifty	חֲמִשִּׁים
faithful, devout	חָסִיד (חֲסִידִים)
sword (f.)	חֶרֶב (חֲרָבוֹת)
darkness	חֹשֶׁךְ

ט

good	טוֹב (טוֹבִים)
pure, clean	טָהוֹר

י

hand	יָד (יָדַיִם)(יָדוֹת)
to know	יָדַע (לָדַעַת)
let it (or there) be	יְהִי
day	יוֹם (יָמִים)
Joseph	יוֹסֵף
to give birth	יָלַד (לָלֶדֶת)
to be born	נוֹלַד
boy	יֶלֶד (יְלָדִים)
girl	יַלְדָּה (יְלָדוֹת)
sea	יָם (יַמִּים)
Jacob	יַעֲקֹב
beautiful, fair	יָפֶה (יָפִים)
to go out	יָצָא (לָצֵאת)
Isaac	יִצְחָק
precious, rare	יָקָר
to go down	יָרַד (לָרֶדֶת)
Jordan	יַרְדֵּן
Jerusalem	יְרוּשָׁלַיִם
moon (m.)	יָרֵחַ
Jericho	יְרִיחוֹ
there is, there are	יֵשׁ
to sit, dwell	יָשַׁב (לָשֶׁבֶת)
Israel	יִשְׂרָאֵל

כ

as, like	כְּ-
when, as	כַּאֲשֶׁר
glory, honor	כָּבוֹד
already	כְּבָר

priest	כֹּהֵן (כֹּהֲנִים)
star	כּוֹכָב (כּוֹכָבִים)
cup (f.)	כּוֹס (כּוֹסוֹת)
because, that	כִּי
all, every	כֹּל, כָּל־
all of them	כֻּלָם
dog	כֶּלֶב (כְּלָבִים)
how many? how great? how often?	כַּמָּה
like, as, such as	כְּמוֹ
Canaan	כְּנַעַן
wing (f.)	כָּנָף (כְּנָפַיִם)
silver	כֶּסֶף
vineyard	כֶּרֶם (כְּרָמִים)
Mt. Carmel	כַּרְמֶל
to write	כָּתַב (לִכְתֹּב)

ל

to, for	לְ־
no, not	לֹא
heart (m.)	לֵב (לִבּוֹת)
white	לָבָן
Lebanon	לְבָנוֹן
to wear, put on	לָבַשׁ (לִלְבֹּשׁ)
tablet	לוּחַ (לוּחוֹת)
bread	לֶחֶם
night (m.)	לַיְלָה, לַיִל (לֵילוֹת)
go! (imperative)	לֵךְ (הלך)
to learn	לָמַד (לִלְמֹד)
to teach	לִמֵּד (לְלַמֵּד)
why?	לָמָּה?
to whom	לְמִי

towards evening	לְעֵת עֶרֶב
before	לִפְנֵי
before me	לְפָנַי
before you (m. sg.)	לְפָנֶיךָ
to take	לָקַח (לָקַחַת)
and he took	וַיִּקַּח
and she (or you, m. sg.) took	וַתִּקַּח
take! (imperative)	קַח
tongue (f.)	לָשׁוֹן (לְשׁוֹנוֹת)

מ

from (pref. forms of מִן)	מִ־, מֵ־
very	מְאֹד
hundred	מֵאָה (מָאתַיִם)(מֵאוֹת)
whence? from where?	מֵאַיִן?
flood	מַבּוּל
desert	מִדְבָּר
why?	מַדּוּעַ?
province, country	מְדִינָה
what?	מַה? מֶה? מָה?
opposite, in front of	מוּל
to die	מוּת (לָמוּת)
I shall die	אָמוּת
I shall kill	אָמִית
who?	מִי?
water (m. pl.)	מַיִם
to sell	מָכַר (לִמְכֹּר)
messenger	מַלְאָךְ (מַלְאָכִים)
work, business	מְלָאכָה
to rule	מָלַךְ (לִמְלֹךְ)
to crown	הִמְלִיךְ

king	מֶלֶךְ (מְלָכִים)	to lift up	נָשָׂא (לָשֵׂאת)
queen	מַלְכָּה (מְלָכוֹת)	and he lifted	וַיִּשָׂא
from	מִן־	sent	נִשְׁלַח (שלח)
lampstand, lamp	מְנוֹרָה (מְנוֹרוֹת)	guarded	נִשְׁמַר (שמר)
gift	מִנְחָה	to give	נָתַן (לָתֵת)
a little	מְעַט	and she gave	וַתִּתֵּן
to find	מָצָא (לִמְצֹא)		
commandment	מִצְוָה (מִצְוֹת)		
Egypt	מִצְרַיִם	ס	
place (m.)	מָקוֹם (מְקוֹמוֹת)	to shut	סָגַר (לִסְגֹּר)
chariot	מֶרְכָּב	horse	סוּס (סוּסִים)
bed, couch	מִשְׁכָּב (מִשְׁכָּבִים)	mare	סוּסָה (סוּסוֹת)
Moses	מֹשֶׁה	scribe	סוֹפֵר
to rule	מָשַׁל (לִמְשֹׁל)	Sinai	סִינַי
parable	מָשָׁל (מְשָׁלִים)	to forgive	סָלַח (לִסְלֹחַ)
family	מִשְׁפָּחָה (מִשְׁפָּחוֹת)	book writing, scroll	סֵפֶר (סְפָרִים)
when?	מָתַי?	to count	סָפַר (לִסְפֹּר)
		to tell, proclaim	סִפֵּר (לְסַפֵּר)
		to be told, reported	סֻפַּר

נ		ע	
Nebo, Mt.	נְבוֹ		
prophet	נָבִיא (נְבִיאִים)		
prophetess	נְבִיאָה (נְבִיאוֹת)	slave, servant	עֶבֶד (עֲבָדִים)
to be born	נוֹלַד (ילד)	work	עֲבוֹדָה (עֲבוֹדוֹת)
wadi, stream	נַחַל (נְחָלִים)	to pass over, transgress	עָבַר
serpent	נָחָשׁ (נְחָשִׁים)	toward, until, as far as	עַד
to test	נִסָּה	forever	עַד
shoe, sandal (f.)	נַעַל (נַעֲלַיִם)	yet, still	עוֹד
lad, youth	נַעַר (נְעָרִים)	burnt offering	עוֹלָה (עוֹלוֹת)
to fall	נָפַל (לִנְפֹּל)	forever	עוֹלָם (עוֹלָמִים)
soul, breath, life (f.)	נֶפֶשׁ (נְפָשׁוֹת)	standing (part.)	עוֹמֵד
to be seen,	נִרְאָה (ראה)	stylus	עֵט
appear		eye (f.)	עַיִן (עֵינַיִם)

city (f.)	עִיר (עָרִים)	bud, blossom	פֶּרַח (פְּרָחִים)
upon, over, against	עַל	Persia	פָּרַס
to go up	עָלָה (לַעֲלוֹת)	Euphrates river	פְּרָת
he shall go up	יַעֲלֶה	suddenly	פִּתְאֹם
with	עִם		
with him	עִמּוֹ		
nation, people	עַם (עַמִּים)		צ
to stand	עָמַד (לַעֲמֹד)		
to answer, reply	עָנָה	sheep	צֹאן
poor, afflicted	עָנִי (עֲנִיִּים)	righteous	צַדִּיק (צַדִּיקִים)
tree(s), wood	עֵץ (עֵצִים)	to command	צִוָּה (לְצַוּוֹת)
bone (f.)	עֶצֶם (עֲצָמוֹת)	to laugh	צָחַק (לִצְחֹק)
evening	עֶרֶב (עֲרָבִים)	image	צֶלֶם (צְלָמִים)
cunning, shrewd	עָרוּם	rib (f.)	צֵלָע (צְלָעוֹת)
naked	עָרֹם (עֲרֻמִּים)	young, small, little	צָעִיר (צְעִירִים)
to do, make	עָשָׂה (לַעֲשׂוֹת)	to cry out	צָעַק (לִצְעֹק)
ten (f.)	עֶשֶׂר	bird	צִפּוֹר (צִפֳּרִים)
tens	עֶשְׂרוֹת		
ten (m.)	עֲשָׂרָה		
twenty	עֶשְׂרִים		ק
time	עֵת (עִתִּים)	holy	קָדוֹשׁ (קְדוֹשִׁים)
toward evening	לְעֵת עֶרֶב	holiness	קֹדֶשׁ (קֳדָשִׁים)
now	עַתָּה	voice (m.)	קוֹל (קוֹלוֹת)
		to arise	קוּם
	פ	take! (imperative)	קַח! (לְקַח)
		small, little	קָטָן (קְטַנִּים)
mouth (m.)	פֶּה (פִּיוֹת)	to jump	קָפַץ (לִקְפֹּץ)
here, in this place	פֹּה	to skip, leap	קִפֵּץ (לְקַפֵּץ)
lest	פֶּן	to be short	קָצַר
face (m. or f. pl.)	פָּנִים	to call, read	קָרָא (לִקְרֹא)
to visit, appoint	פָּקַד (לִפְקֹד)	horn	קֶרֶן (קְרָנַיִם)
cow	פָּרָה (פָּרוֹת)	hard	קָשֶׁה

ר

to see	רָאָה (לִרְאוֹת)
and she saw	וַתֵּרֶא
and he saw	וַיַּרְא
he (*or* it) was seen	נִרְאָה
head	רֹאשׁ (רָאשִׁים)
myriad, ten thousand	רְבָבָה (רְבָבוֹת)
fourth	רְבִיעִי
foot (f.)	רֶגֶל (רַגְלַיִם)
moment	רֶגַע (רְגָעִים)
spirit, wind (f.)	רוּחַ (רוּחוֹת)
shepherding, pasturing (part.)	רוֹעֶה
open place (of a town) (m.)	רְחוֹב (רְחוֹבוֹת)
far, distant	רָחוֹק
from afar	מֵרָחוֹק
Rachel	רָחֵל
mercy (m. pl.)	רַחֲמִים
to wash	רָחַץ (לִרְחֹץ)
to ride	רָכַב (לִרְכֹּב)
evil, bad	רַע (רָעִים)
only	רַק
wicked	רָשָׁע (רְשָׁעִים)

שׂ

field (m.)	שָׂדֶה (שָׂדוֹת)
a sheep, lamb	שֶׂה
to put, place	שִׂים
joy, gladness	שִׂמְחָה
lip (f.), language	שָׂפָה (שְׂפָתַיִם)
prince, leader	שַׂר (שָׂרִים)

שׁ

to ask	שָׁאַל (לִשְׁאֹל)
request, question	שְׁאֵלָה
week (m.)	שָׁבוּעַ (שָׁבוּעוֹת)
seven (f.)	שֶׁבַע
seventeen	שְׁבַע עֶשְׂרֵה
seven (m.)	שִׁבְעָה
seventy	שִׁבְעִים
to break	שָׁבַר (לִשְׁבֹּר)
to smash	שִׁבֵּר (לְשַׁבֵּר)
to be smashed	שֻׁבַּר
breast	שַׁד (שָׁדַיִם)
to return	שׁוּב (לָשׁוּב)
judge	שׁוֹפֵט (שׁוֹפְטִים)
black	שָׁחוֹר (שְׁחוֹרִים)
song	שִׁיר (שִׁירִים)
to lie down	שָׁכַב (לִשְׁכַּב)
to forget	שָׁכַח (לִשְׁכֹּחַ)
to rise early (Hiphil)	שכם, הִשְׁכִּים
and he rose up early	וַיַּשְׁכֵּם
I go or rise early	אַשְׁכִּים
peace, wholeness	שָׁלוֹם
to send	שָׁלַח (לִשְׁלֹחַ)
to be sent (Niphal)	נִשְׁלַח
to send away, expel (Piel)	שִׁלַּח
table (m.)	שֻׁלְחָן (שֻׁלְחָנוֹת)
to be complete, finished	שָׁלֵם

to pay, recompense	שָׁלֵם (לְשַׁלֵם)	six (f.)	שֵׁשׁ
three (f.)	שָׁלֹשׁ	six (m.)	שִׁשָּׁה
three (m.)	שְׁלֹשָׁה	sixty	שִׁשִּׁים
thirty	שְׁלֹשִׁים	sixth	שִׁשִּׁי
name (m.)	שֵׁם (שֵׁמוֹת)	to drink	שָׁתָה (לִשְׁתּוֹת)
there	שָׁם	two (f.)	שְׁתַּיִם
eight (f.)	שְׁמוֹנֶה		
eight (m.)	שְׁמוֹנָה		
eighty	שְׁמוֹנִים		ת
heavens	שָׁמַיִם	ark	תֵּבָה (תֵּבוֹת)
to hear	שָׁמַע (לִשְׁמֹעַ)	Mt. Tabor	תָּבוֹר
to guard	שָׁמַר (לִשְׁמֹר)	law	תּוֹרָה (תּוֹרוֹת)
to be guarded	נִשְׁמַר	under, beneath, instead of	תַּחַת
sun	שֶׁמֶשׁ	likeness	תְּמוּנָה
tooth	שֵׁן (שִׁנַּיִם)	continually	תָּמִיד
year	שָׁנָה (שָׁנִים)	apple	תַּפּוּחַ (תַּפּוּחִים)
two (m.)	שְׁנַיִם	prayer	תְּפִלָּה (תְּפִלּוֹת)
gate	שַׁעַר (שְׁעָרִים)	nine (f.)	תֵּשַׁע
to judge	שָׁפַט (לִשְׁפֹּט)	nine (m.)	תִּשְׁעָה
judge	שׁוֹפֵט	ninety	תִּשְׁעִים

ENGLISH-HEBREW VOCABULARY

A

Abraham	אַבְרָהָם
Adam	אָדָם
after	אַחֲרֵי
all, every	כֹּל, (כָּל־)
already	כְּבָר
also	גַּם
also, even	אַף
and	וְ־
animals	חַיָּה (חַיּוֹת)
another	אַחֵר (אֲחֵרִים)
to answer	עָנָה
to appear	נִרְאָה (רְאָה)
apple	תַּפּוּחַ (תַּפּוּחִים)
to appoint	פָּקַד (לִפְקֹד)
Aram (place-name)	אֲרָם
to arise	קוּם
ark	תֵּבָה (תֵּבוֹת)
as, like	כְּ־
as, like, such as	כְּמוֹ
as, when	כַּאֲשֶׁר
Ashdod	אַשְׁדּוֹד

to ask, request	שָׁאַל (לִשְׁאֹל)
Assyria	אַשּׁוּר
aunt	דּוֹדָה (דּוֹדוֹת)

B

Babylon	בָּבֶל
back	גַּב
bad	רַע (רָעִים)
to be	הָיָה (לִהְיוֹת)
let it be	יְהִי (הָיָה)
beasts, cattle	בְּהֵמָה (בְּהֵמוֹת)
beasts, animals	חַיָּה (חַיּוֹת)
beautiful	יָפֶה (יָפִים)
because, for, that	כִּי
bed, couch	מִשְׁכָּב (מִשְׁכָּבִים)
before	מוּל
before	לְפָנֵי
behold	הִנֵּה
belly	בֶּטֶן
beside, near	אֵצֶל
Bethel	בֵּית־אֵל

Bethlehem	בֵּית־לֶחֶם	commandment	מִצְוָה (מִצְוֹת)
between	בֵּין	to be complete	שָׁלֵם
black	שָׁחוֹר (שְׁחוֹרִים)	continually	תָּמִיד
to bless	בֵּרֵךְ	to count	סָפַר (לִסְפֹּר)
blessed	בָּרוּךְ	country, province	מְדִינָה
blessing	בְּרָכָה (בְּרָכוֹת)	cow	פָּרָה (פָּרוֹת)
blossom	פֶּרַח	to create	בָּרָא
bone (f.)	עֶצֶם (עֲצָמוֹת)	to crown	הִמְלִיךְ (מָלַךְ)
book, writing, scroll	סֵפֶר (סְפָרִים)	to cry out	צָעַק (לִצְעֹק)
to be born	נוֹלַד (יָלַד)	cunning, shrewd	עָרוּם
boy	יֶלֶד (יְלָדִים)	cup (f.)	כּוֹס (כּוֹסוֹת)
bread	לֶחֶם		
to break	שָׁבַר (לִשְׁבֹּר)		
breast (m.)	שַׁד (שָׁדִים)	**D**	
to bring	הֵבִיא	darkness	חֹשֶׁךְ
brother	אָח (אַחִים)	daughter	בַּת (בָּנוֹת)
bud	פֶּרַח (פְּרָחִים)	day	יוֹם (יָמִים)
to build	בָּנָה (לִבְנוֹת)	decades, tens	עֲשָׂרוֹת
burnt offering	עוֹלָה (עוֹלוֹת)	desert	מִדְבָּר
		to die	מוּת (לָמוּת)
C		to do	עָשָׂה (לַעֲשׂוֹת)
		dog	כֶּלֶב (כְּלָבִים)
to call	קָרָא (לִקְרֹא)	donkey	חֲמוֹר (חֲמוֹרִים)
Canaan	כְּנַעַן	door (f.)	דֶּלֶת (דְּלָתוֹת)
Carmel, Mt.	כַּרְמֶל	dream (m.)	חֲלוֹם (חֲלוֹמוֹת)
to cast	הִשְׁלִיךְ (שׁלךְ)	to dream	חָלַם
chamber	חֶדֶר (חֲדָרִים)	to dress oneself	הִתְלַבֵּשׁ
chariot	מֶרְכָּב	to drink	שָׁתָה (לִשְׁתּוֹת)
to choose	בָּחַר	to dwell, sit	יָשַׁב (לָשֶׁבֶת)
city (f.)	עִיר (עָרִים)		
clean (adj.)	טָהוֹר		
to come	בּוֹא (לָבוֹא)	**E**	
to command	צִוָּה	ear	אֹזֶן (אָזְנַיִם)

earth, ground	אֲדָמָה (אֲדָמוֹת)	foot (f.)	רֶגֶל (רַגְלַיִם)
earth, land (f.)	אֶרֶץ (אֲרָצוֹת)	for, to	לְ-
to eat	אָכַל (לֶאֱכֹל)	forever	עַד
Egypt	מִצְרַיִם	forever	עוֹלָם (עוֹלָמִים)
eight (f.)	שְׁמוֹנֶה	to forget	שָׁכַח (לִשְׁכֹּחַ)
eight (m.)	שְׁמוֹנָה	to forgive	סָלַח (לִסְלֹחַ)
eighty	שְׁמוֹנִים	forty	אַרְבָּעִים
either . . . or	אוֹ . . . אוֹ	four (f.)	אַרְבַּע
eleven	אַחַד עָשָׂר	four (m.)	אַרְבָּעָה
end, nothing	אֶפֶס (אֲפָסִים)	fourth	רְבִיעִי
Euphrates river	פְּרָת	friend	חָבֵר (חֲבֵרִים)
evening	עֶרֶב (עֲרָבִים)	from	מִן
every, all	כֹּל, כָּל-	from (prefixed	מִ-, מֵ-
evil	רַע (רָעִים)	forms of מִן)	
eye (f.)	עַיִן (עֵינַיִם)	fruit	פְּרִי

F

G

face (m. or f. pl.)	פָּנִים	garden	גַּן (גַּנִּים)
faithful	חָסִיד (חֲסִידִים)	garment	בֶּגֶד (בְּגָדִים)
to fall	נָפַל (לִנְפֹּל)	gate	שַׁעַר (שְׁעָרִים)
family	מִשְׁפָּחָה (מִשְׁפָּחוֹת)	Gezer	גֶּזֶר
far, distant	רָחוֹק	gift	מִנְחָה
father	אָב (אָבוֹת)	girl	יַלְדָּה (יְלָדוֹת)
to feed	הֶאֱכִיל	to give	נָתַן (לָתֵת)
field (m.)	שָׂדֶה (שָׂדוֹת)	to give birth	יָלַד (לָלֶדֶת)
fifty	חֲמִשִּׁים	gladness	שִׂמְחָה
to find	מָצָא (לִמְצֹא)	glory, honor	כָּבוֹד
finger (f.)	אֶצְבַּע (אֶצְבָּעוֹת)	to go, walk	הָלַךְ
to finish	גָּמַר	to go down	יָרַד (לָרֶדֶת)
five (f.)	חָמֵשׁ	to go out	יָצָא (לָצֵאת)
five (m.)	חֲמִשָּׁה	to go up	עָלָה (לַעֲלוֹת)
flood	מַבּוּל	God, god	אֵל (אֵלִים)

God, gods	אֱלֹהִים		**I**	
gold	זָהָב	I	אֲנִי, אָנֹכִי
good	טוֹב (טוֹבִים)	if	אִם
great	גָּדוֹל (גְּדוֹלִים)	image	צֶלֶם (צְלָמִים)
to become great	גָּדַל	in, with	בְּ־
to guard	שָׁמַר (לִשְׁמֹר)	Isaac	יִצְחָק
to be guarded	נִשְׁמַר (שָׁמַר)	Israel	יִשְׂרָאֵל

J

Jacob	יַעֲקֹב
Jericho	יְרִיחוֹ
Jerusalem	יְרוּשָׁלַיִם
Jordan	יַרְדֵּן
Joseph	יוֹסֵף
joy	שִׂמְחָה
to judge	שָׁפַט (לִשְׁפֹּט)
judge	שׁוֹפֵט
to jump	קָפַץ (לִקְפֹּץ)

H

hand	יָד (יָדַיִם)
hard	קָשֶׁה
he	הוּא
head	רֹאשׁ (רָאשִׁים)
to hear	שָׁמַע (לִשְׁמֹעַ)
heart, mind (m.)	לֵב (לִבּוֹת)
heavens	שָׁמַיִם
here	פֹּה
hero	גִּבּוֹר (גִּבּוֹרִים)
to hide oneself	הִתְחַבֵּא
holiness	קֹדֶשׁ (קָדָשִׁים)
holy	קָדוֹשׁ (קְדוֹשִׁים)
honor, glory	כָּבוֹד
horn	קֶרֶן (קַרְנַיִם)
horse	סוּס (סוּסִים)
house (m.)	בַּיִת (בָּתִּים)
how?	אֵיךְ?
how long?	עַד מָתַי?
how many?	כַּמָּה?
how much?	כַּמָּה?
hundred	מֵאָה (מָאתַיִם, מֵאוֹת)

K

king	מֶלֶךְ (מְלָכִים)
to know	יָדַע (לָדַעַת)

L

lad, youth	נַעַר (נְעָרִים)
lamb	שֶׂה
lamp	מְנוֹרָה (מְנוֹרוֹת)
land (f.)	אֶרֶץ (אֲרָצוֹת)
language	שָׂפָה (שָׂפוֹת)

to laugh	צָחַק (לִצְחֹק)		midst (in the)	בְּתוֹךְ
law, instruction	תּוֹרָה (תּוֹרוֹת)		mighty one	גִּבּוֹר (גִּבּוֹרִים)
leader, official	שַׂר (שָׂרִים)		moment	רֶגַע (רְגָעִים)
to learn	לָמַד (לִלְמֹד)		month	חֹדֶשׁ (חֳדָשִׁים)
Lebanon	לְבָנוֹן		moon (m.)	יָרֵחַ
lest	פֶּן		morning	בֹּקֶר (בְּקָרִים)
to lie down	שָׁכַב (לִשְׁכַּב)		Moses	מֹשֶׁה
life	חַיִּים		mother	אֵם (אִמּוֹת)
to lift up, raise	נָשָׂא (לָשֵׂאת)		mountain	הַר (הָרִים)
light (n.)	אוֹר (אוֹרוֹת)		mouth (m.)	פֶּה (פִּיּוֹת)
like, as	כְּמוֹ, כְּ-		much, many	הַרְבֵּה (רַבָּה)
lip (f.)	שָׂפָה (שְׂפָתַיִם)		myriad, ten thousand	רְבָבָה (רְבָבוֹת)
to listen	הֶאֱזִין			
little, few	מְעַט			
little, small, young	צָעִיר		**N**	
to live	חָיָה			
living, life	חַי		naked	עָרוֹם (עֲרֻמִּים)
Lord (used only of God)	אֲדוֹנָי		name	שֵׁם (שֵׁמוֹת)
			nation, people	גּוֹי (גּוֹיִם)
to love	אָהַב (לֶאֱהֹב)		near, beside	אֵצֶל
love (n.)	אַהֲבָה		Nebo	נְבוֹ
			night (m.)	לַיְלָה (לֵיל, לֵילוֹת)
			nine (f.)	תֵּשַׁע
M			nine (m.)	תִּשְׁעָה
			ninety	תִּשְׁעִים
to make, do	עָשָׂה (לַעֲשׂוֹת)		no, not	לֹא
man, mankind	אָדָם		there is (or are) not	אֵין
man	אִישׁ (אֲנָשִׁים)		now	עַתָּה
man	אֱנוֹשׁ			
man (of strength)	גֶּבֶר (גְּבָרִים)			
mare	סוּסָה (סוּסוֹת)		**O**	
matter, thing, word	דָּבָר (דְּבָרִים)			
mercy (m. pl.)	רַחֲמִים		old (of people)	זָקֵן (זְקֵנִים)
messenger	מַלְאָךְ (מַלְאָכִים)		old (of things)	יָשָׁן (יְשָׁנִים)

one (m.), one (f.)	אֶחָד, אַחַת
only	רַק
open place (of a town)	רְחוֹב
or	אוֹ
other	אַחֵר (אֲחֵרִים)

P

parable	מָשָׁל (מְשָׁלִים)
to pass over	עָבַר
pasturing	רוֹעֶה
to pay, recompense	שִׁלֵּם (לְשַׁלֵּם)
peace	שָׁלוֹם
people, nation	עַם (עַמִּים)
Persia	פָּרַס
place (m.)	מָקוֹם (מְקוֹמוֹת)
to place, put	שִׂים
poor	עָנִי (עֲנִיִּים)
to pray	הִתְפַּלֵּל
prayer	תְּפִלָּה (תְּפִלּוֹת)
precious, rare	יָקָר
priest	כֹּהֵן (כֹּהֲנִים)
prince, official	שַׂר (שָׂרִים)
prophet	נָבִיא (נְבִיאִים)
prophetess	נְבִיאָה (נְבִיאוֹת)
province	מְדִינָה
pure, clean	טָהוֹר
to put, place	שִׂים

Q

queen	מַלְכָּה (מְלָכוֹת)

question, request (n.)	שְׁאֵלָה

R

Rachel	רָחֵל
rain	גֶּשֶׁם (גְּשָׁמִים)
to raise	הֵקִים (קוּם)
ram	אַיִל (אֵילִים)
to read	קָרָא (לִקְרֹא)
to reign	מָלַךְ (לִמְלֹךְ)
to remember	זָכַר
to remove, move far away	הִרְחִיק (רָחַק)
reply	עָנָה
request (n.)	שְׁאֵלָה
to return	שׁוּב (לָשׁוּב)
rib (f.)	צֵלָע (צְלָעוֹת)
to ride	רָכַב (לִרְכֹּב)
righteous	צַדִּיק (צַדִּיקִים)
to rise early (Hiphil)	הִשְׁכִּים
river, wadi	נָהָר, נַחַל
to rule	מָשַׁל (לִמְשֹׁל)

S

sacrifice	זֶבַח (זְבָחִים)
sandal (f.)	נַעַל (נְעָלִים)
to say	אָמַר (לֵאמֹר)
scribe	סוֹפֵר
sea	יָם (יַמִּים)
to see	רָאָה (לִרְאוֹת)
to be seen	נִרְאָה (רָאָה)

to sell	מָכַר (לִמְכֹּר)	to speak	דִּבֶּר (לְדַבֵּר)
to send	שָׁלַח (לִשְׁלֹחַ)	spirit, wind	רוּחַ (רוּחוֹת)
to send away	שִׁלַּח (לְשַׁלַּח)	stand	עָמַד (לַעֲמֹד)
to be sent	נִשְׁלַח (שָׁלַח)	standing (part.)	עוֹמֵד (עָמַד)
serpent	נָחָשׁ (נְחָשִׁים)	star	כּוֹכָב (כּוֹכָבִים)
seven (f.)	שֶׁבַע	to steal	גָּנַב (לִגְנֹב)
seven (m.)	שִׁבְעָה	still, yet	עוֹד
seventeen (f.)	שְׁבַע עֶשְׂרֵה	stone (f.)	אֶבֶן (אֲבָנִים)
seventy	שִׁבְעִים	stream, wadi	נַחַל (נְחָלִים)
she	הִיא	to strengthen	חִזֵּק
sheep, flock	צֹאן	strong	חָזָק (חֲזָקִים)
(collective noun)		to be strong	חָזַק
sheep, lamb	שֶׂה	stylus	עֵט
shepherding	רוֹעֶה	such as, like	כְּמוֹ
shoe (f.)	נַעַל (נְעָלַיִם)	suddenly	פִּתְאֹם
to shut	סָגַר (לִסְגֹּר)	sun	שֶׁמֶשׁ
silver	כֶּסֶף	sword (f.)	חֶרֶב (חֲרָבוֹת)
Sinai	סִינַי		
to sit, dwell	יָשַׁב (לָשֶׁבֶת)		
six (f.)	שֵׁשׁ	**T**	
six (m.)	שִׁשָּׁה	table (m.)	שֻׁלְחָן (שֻׁלְחָנוֹת)
sixth	שִׁשִּׁי	tablet (m.)	לוּחַ (לוּחוֹת)
sixty	שִׁשִּׁים	Mt. Tabor	תָּבוֹר
to skip, leap	קָפֵץ (לִקְפֵּץ)	to take	לָקַח (לָקַחַת)
slave, servant	עֶבֶד (עֲבָדִים)	to teach	לִמֵּד (לְלַמֵּד)
small	קָטָן (קְטַנִּים)	to tell	סִפֵּר (לְסַפֵּר)
to smash	שִׁבֵּר (לְשַׁבֵּר)	to tell, report,	
son	בֵּן (בָּנִים)	announce	הִגִּיד (לְהַגִּיד)
son of old age,		to be told	הֻגַּד, סֻפַּר
youngest son	בֶּן זְקוּנִים	temple, palace	הֵיכָל
song	שִׁיר (שִׁירִים)	ten (m.)	עֲשָׂרָה
soul (f.)	נֶפֶשׁ (נְפָשׁוֹת)	ten (f.)	עֶשֶׂר

ten thousand, myriad	רְבָבָה (רְבָבוֹת)	toward, to	אֶל
tens	עֲשָׂרוֹת	toward evening	לְעֵת עֶרֶב
tent	אֹהֶל (אֹהָלִים)	to transgress, pass over	עָבַר
to test	נִסָּה	trees, wood	עֵץ (עֵצִים)
that (conj.)	כִּי	to test	נִסָּה
that (rel. pron.)	אֲשֶׁר	twenty	עֶשְׂרִים
the (def. art.)	הַ-	two	שְׁנַיִם
there	שָׁם	two (f.)	שְׁתַּיִם
there is, there are	יֵשׁ		
there is (or are) not	אֵין		
these	אֵלֶּה	**U**	
they (f.)	הֵנָּה	uncle, beloved	דּוֹד (דּוֹדִים)
they (m.)	הֵם	under, beneath, instead of	תַּחַת
they (f.)	הֵן	upon, against, over	עַל
thing	דָּבָר (דְּבָרִים)		
thirty	שְׁלֹשִׁים		
this (f.)	זֹאת	**V**	
this	זֶה	very	מְאֹד
those	הֵם	vineyard	כֶּרֶם (כְּרָמִים)
those (f.)	הֵן	to visit, attend to	פָּקַד (לִפְקֹד)
thousand	אֶלֶף (אֲלָפִים)	voice (m.)	קוֹל (קוֹלוֹת)
three (f.)	שָׁלֹשׁ		
three (m.)	שְׁלֹשָׁה		
to be thrown	הָשְׁלַךְ	**W**	
Tigris river	חִדֶּקֶל	wadi, stream	נַחַל (נְחָלִים)
time	עֵת (עִתִּים)	to walk, go	הָלַךְ (לָלֶכֶת)
to, for	לְ-	to be	הָיָה (לִהְיוֹת)
to, unto	אֶל	to wash	רָחַץ (לִרְחֹץ)
to whom?	לְמִי?	to wash oneself	הִתְרַחֵץ
tongue (f.)	לָשׁוֹן (לְשׁוֹנוֹת)	water (m. pl.)	מַיִם
tooth	שֵׁן (שִׁנַּיִם)	way, path (f.)	דֶּרֶךְ (דְּרָכִים)
toward, until, as far as	עַד	we	אֲנַחְנוּ
		week	שָׁבוּעַ (שָׁבוּעוֹת)

wind, spirit (f.)	רוּחַ (רוּחוֹת)	woe!	אוֹי, אוֹיָה
with	עִם	woman	אִשָּׁה (נָשִׁים)
what?	מָה? מֶה? מַה?	wood, tree(s)	עֵץ (עֵצִים)
when, as	כַּאֲשֶׁר	word, thing	דָּבָר (דְּבָרִים)
when?	מָתַי?	to wear	לָבַשׁ (לִלְבֹּשׁ)
whence? from where?	מֵאַיִן?	work, business	מְלָאכָה
where?	אַיֵּה?	work, labor	עֲבוֹדָה (עֲבוֹדוֹת)
where?	אֵיפֹה?	to write	כָּתַב (לִכְתֹּב)
where to?	אָן, אָנָה?		
which	אֲשֶׁר		
white	לָבָן (לְבָנִים)		Y
whither? where to?	אָן? אָנָה?	year	שָׁנָה (שָׁנִים, שָׁנוֹת)
who?	מִי?	yet	עוֹד
who, which, that	אֲשֶׁר	you (f. sg.)	אַתְּ
why?	מַדּוּעַ? לָמָה?	you (m. sg.)	אַתָּה
wicked	רָשָׁע (רְשָׁעִים)	you (m. pl.)	אַתֶּם
wing (f.)	כָּנָף (כְּנָפַיִם)	you (f. pl.)	אַתֵּן
with, in	בְּ-	young, small,	
without	בְּלִי	little (m.)	צָעִיר (צְעִירִים)

Index   (to Biblical Hebrew, volumes 1 and 2)